MUDDIED OAFS

THE LAST DAYS OF RUGGER

RICHARD BEARD

Yellow Jersey Press
London

Published by Yellow Jersey Press 2003

4 6 8 10 9 7 5 3

First published in Great Britain in 2003 by
Yellow Jersey Press
Random House, 20 Vauxhall Bridge Road,
London SW1V 2SA

Random House Australia (Pty) Limited
20 Alfred Street, Milsons Points, Sydney,
New South Wales 2061, Australia

Random House New Zealand Limited
18 Poland Road, Glenfield
Auckland 10, New Zealand

Random House (Pty) Limited
Endulini, 5A Jubilee Road, Parktown 2193
South Africa

The Random House Group Limited Reg. No. 954009
www.randomhouse.co.uk

A CIP catalogue record for this book is available from the British Library

ISBN 0-224-06393-6

Lines from 'The Welchman's Hose' by Robert Graves, from *Complete Poems*
(Carcanet), reproduced by kind permission of Carcanet Press Ltd

Lines from 'The Retirement of Bill Beaumont' and 'On the Ambivalence of
Male Contact Sports' by Gavin Ewart, from *Collected Poems 1980–1990*
(Hutchinson), reproduced by kind permission of Margo Ewart

Endpapers: '*Équipe 1ʳᵉ du Sporting-Club Universitaire de France, Champion de
Paris (Saison 1910–11)*'. Reproduced by kind permission of Jean Hospital

Papers used by Random House are natural, recyclable products made from
wood grown in sustainable forests. The manufacturing processes conform to the
environmental regulations of the country of origin

Typeset by SX Composing DTP, Rayleigh, Essex
Printed and bound in Great Britain by
Clays Ltd, St Ives PLC

To Dr Tim Beard

Acknowledgements

For their kind and generous assistance, often unconnected to rugby, I would like to thank, in Scotland, Colin and Sarah at Lunga; in Paris Bruno Martin-Neuville, Mr and Mrs Nicolas Nagy, and Jean Hospital; the boys and staff at Radley College, Abingdon, and in particular Hamish Aird, Richard Greed, Angus MacPhail, Tony Money and Jock Mullard; in Cambridge Alex and Sarah Brown, James Campbell, Professor Howard Erskine-Hill, James Stevenson and Dick Tilley; in Norwich Roy Bishop, Lynne Bryan, Andrew Cowan, and Rose; and in Geneva John Evans, Olivier Cavadini, Florence Marguerat and Guillaume Arlaud. Also Andrew Preston, and in Wells Alison Cholmondeley, for my invaluable garret.

With special thanks to Rachel Cugnoni and Zoe Waldie, for seeing and believing. But most of all to Laurence, for never telling me to act my age.

MUDDIED OAFS

Mid-Argyll Rugby Football Club, Lochgilphead, 1991/2

'I believe that Rugby football . . . is the best instrument which we possess for the development of manly character.'
H.H. Almond, *Rugby Football in Scottish Schools*, 1892

Saturday afternoon in the Western Highlands, early autumn 1991, and not unusually I find myself lying in a corner of the Mushroom Field, seeped in the damp of the nearby Oban to Crinan canal. My cheek and eye are crushed into grass and mud, several half-naked strangers are piled at angles beside and on top of me and softly, from the sea-grey sky, it starts to rain. Which is when I think, I seriously think: God, I love this game.

Only three years earlier, I'd given up rugby for ever. In search of experience of a less boyish kind, I'd set out on life's great adventure with the romantic idea that it was necessary, in pursuit of a dream to write important novels, to reach the end of the road. Steadfastly, I'd followed the dream. It had just as steadfastly avoided me, and before long I reached the edge of the nation on the west coast of Scotland, where in the turrets of Lunga Tower I found work as secretary and ghost-writer to Mathilda, Dowager Duchess of Argyll.

As a duchess, Mathilda was demanding and vain, and bullied her cooks endlessly on the issue of garnish. As a human being, she sent a monthly cheque to the ageing poet Peter Russell, friend and populariser of Ezra Pound. She also owned a convertible five-litre Ford Mustang, which played 'The Star-Spangled Banner' when placed in reverse.

My ghost-writing was complicated by Mathilda's reluctance to make public any intimate information from her long and fascinating life. This presented a daunting obstacle, in an autobiography, and as the writing stalled I was primarily employed to provide conversation, and to eat. The duchess hated eating alone, and after eight months of lunch and confessions in confidence, I stumbled home to my grace-and-favour house in the village, and flopped fat and frustrated in front of England v. New Zealand at Twickenham. It was mid-afternoon, 3 October 1991, and the inaugural game of only the second ever Rugby World Cup.

England's predictable loss, to a failure of nerve, was watched from my three-seater sofa by a quarter of the population of the village of Craobh Haven. There was me, Rhys Kelly from New Zealand, and an alcoholic Welsh electrician who shared the house as another beneficiary of the duchess's whimsical sense of charity.

Craobh Haven was at the dead end of a peninsula, a double-line of brand-new fake fishing-cottages either side of a fresh black road. Intended as the first phase in a major resort development, it was an eighties boom idea which by 1991 was failing with real conviction. Construction had simply stopped, leaving behind a single pristine street in which only four houses were occupied, each with a view of the mooching Atlantic on one side, and on the other scrubland where the ambitious ice-rink and cinema remained unbuilt. There was the one lonely street, and at the end of the road an enormous and empty pub, the Lord of the Isles.

The village was like America. It had no history, and everybody and nobody belonged, but unlike America, a quarter of Craobh Haven's population was slouched on the sofa for the rugby. Rhys was about my age and did odd carpentry jobs, but so discreetly he could have been a spy, for whichever side was not on the side of the Inland Revenue. I was flunkey and manservant to a duchess, and so far, although I was supposed to be writing and becoming a man, I was not writing, and this is what I'd learnt: how to eat expensive, seemingly inedible foodstuffs, many of which came from the sea and were visibly still alive.

It occurred to me that I might grow old like this, trapped in paradise. In the many gilded mirrors of the Tower, I started to notice that the slack and puckered skin which covered my knuckles was advancing along my fingers. I was also, and this was a sure sign of ageing, suffering from a nasty bout of hypochondria, which most recently had me sick with worry for my Adam's apple – it didn't seem to be centred. I was twenty-four years old and wasting away on politesse at the table, and luxury foods with less nutritional value than a pinch of Golden Virginia. I wanted meat and potatoes, and I wanted to run.

That Thursday night, after England's tame submission to New Zealand, I excused myself with some difficulty from the dinner table. I negotiated a loan of the Mustang, then drove myself and Rhys the fifteen miles south to Lochgilphead Sports and Leisure Centre, home to Mid-Argyll Rugby Union Football Club.

In the men's changing rooms, I let Rhys do the talking. He had a New Zealand accent, with the same thin but gritty vowel-sounds made by All Blacks. I sounded more like Will Carling, so I kept my mouth shut. And then, twenty minutes later out on the floodlit training-ground, a gravel pitch marked out for soccer, someone threw me a rugby ball and the miracle happened. From the moment it slapped into my hands, I knew everything was going to be fine, because running and passing and a devastating left-right side-step were a knowledge I had in my body. I remembered I was actually quite good at this, though with no idea how good, because I'd never really tested myself.

I said I'd played a bit, in the backs. They put me on the wing. I caught the ball and scored. I was immediately enjoying myself, and so was Rhys, who turned out to be a mad-eyed flanker of the kind found under every stone in the North Island. We were both picked in the team for Saturday. From nowhere, Mid-Argyll had an instant imported strike-force, and the club which usually struggled in what was then the Glasgow and District First Division didn't lose a game until Christmas.

Twelve years later, I still have a burnished memory of that first game in Mid-Argyll's black and gold: a break inside, a tackle saving a certain try, a kick balanced delicately into the corner. It was eighty minutes of life more sharply etched than at any other time, not counting falling in love or extreme unpleasantness. Unpleasantness I tried to avoid, and falling in love once every weekend at 2.30 on Saturday seemed unlikely, even at twenty-four.

I was playing men's rugby, and never looked back.

At least not until the summer of 2002, aged thirty-five, when I had to engage with an uncomfortable reality. In the coming season, for the first time, I'd be facing opponents half my age. My playing days were numbered, and I felt increasingly nostalgic for the clubs I'd loved and left, all that youth which had seen me through. All that running. I was at the age when settling-down occasionally felt like sinking, and I caught myself wondering if my past had ever actually happened. If only I could go back, check it was still there, maybe even play one more, one last game.

So that's what I decided to do, and in early September the Lomond road (the low one) left me in no doubt as to where I was. The dramatic highlands to the north of the loch loomed in green and brown, and signs by the roadside offered KILTS AND BAGPIPES 600 YARDS. Och aye. I was about to be a boy again, twenty-four and fresh of face.

I braked hard: a hitcher, just dying to share my mood and my plans. He was a young German with a rucksack the size of a house, which he toppled into the boot in exchange for my thoughts on the state of the union (it's my car, I'm giving the lift, this is how it works). By Tarbet, he had my considered opinion on rugby: the fast, compelling, TV-friendly combat sport in which sponsored gladiators are sold on their ability to crash into each other at speed, and sometimes even to avoid each other and score.

And then there was also rugger.

The word rugger is rarely heard these days, largely because it rhymes with bugger. This is inconvenient. However, for a long time rugger was the serious version of rugby, played by men on a mission. A mostly Christian mission, but also an educational one, and in 1944 in his no-nonsense *Rugger: The Man's Game*, the author E.H.D. Sewell proposed a post-war Ministry of Sport and Compulsory Rugger. 'For the good of the Empire.'

The ministry, alas, never came into existence. And look what happened to the Empire.

My German hitcher was such an appreciative listener that I agreed to take him via Crianlarich to Oban. It wasn't exactly on my route, but these things are all about give and take, and together the two of us were having a grand old time.

'Rugby, ja. It must be very violent.'

'Oh yes,' I replied, 'very.'

In the absence of dragons to slay and princesses to rescue, rugby football was once thought to inspire the cardinal British virtues of unselfishness, fearlessness, and self-control. It offered opportunities for struggle and sacrifice, but in the heat of battle it also relied on decency, self-discipline, and restraint. Otherwise, a game like that could be murderous.

I dropped my easy-going German by the Oban pier, exactly where he wanted to be, and felt virtuous, gentlemanly, a bit of a fraud. As I followed the coastal road back south, I convinced myself that it wasn't important for the German nation to know that rugby has a dark side. For a hundred years many boys had played rugby and made themselves into men. Others drank too much beer and took their trousers down in public places. The dark side of rugger the man-maker was the recidivist, the dreaded English rugger-bugger.

It was a contradiction at the heart of the English game. Sewell's amateur rugger was morally uplifting: 'It is something more than a mere game, is this man-maker.' However, it was also England on a fifty-year losing streak and Colin Smart tight on a pint of aftershave. It was taking care to leave Indian restaurants before the buggers came in. It was the common perception of marauding Old Boys in the south-east of England, a beer-swilling, guffawing circle of hell well-stuffed with solicitors, surveyors, and desperately small businessmen. They were unreflectively masculine and unthinkingly prejudiced. They were pissed young conservatives with muscles. It could hardly have been worse.

Recently, at the higher levels in England, rugby has been smothering both types of rugger, good and bad. Team England is currently run at peaks of efficiency and performance not normally associated with British sport, and thank Christ for that. Even so, traces of rugger still linger. The latest high-profile incident involved public schoolboy and England captain Lawrence Dallaglio (though how I wish it hadn't). He drank too much, went to a hotel-room with some new friends, and bragged about his sexual exploits and consumption of illegal drugs. I don't blame him: I could have done the same, probably have, though not to the *News of the World*.

It seemed there was no escape. Even the brightest English hero of the professional era was secretly a rugger-bugger, a weakness which simply didn't haunt the Springboks or All

Blacks. They might secretly be racists, or plain bores, but the rugger-bugger is all English. Dallaglio only wanted to fit in, he wanted to be part of the team, who on that occasion just happened to be a team of undercover journalists. He wanted to belong, to escape his mild, know-nothing, middle-class background. He'd therefore do anything, take on the risks of top-level rugby, drink aftershave, drop his trousers, invent a murky drug-dealing past.

Dallaglio was saved by rugby, the modern professional version. By way of penance, he made himself the standard pattern of the gym-built rugby warrior, though in some ways his sporting recovery is also a credit to E.H.D. Sewell's more positive concept of rugger: 'It inculcates self-control and discipline to a degree unknown in any other sport.' It made Dallaglio strong, made him a man. He could survive on the field, so he knew he could survive.

I felt much the same thing as I drove through Kilmore, then Kilninver and Kilmelford, closing in on the past. Not just in Argyll, but at all my former clubs in four different countries, I was hoping to witness the brotherhood of rugby in action. Or not. I wanted to see for myself whether the old heaving heart of the sport, rugger in both its forms, could still beat fiercely while professional rugby was twisting and straining into amenable shapes for the global sports commodity market.

I also wanted a game. I intended to turn up for training and present myself for selection, taking as my model Sean Fitzpatrick, the fearless hooker and long-time captain of the All Blacks, who aimed with all his considerable will to play in one last World Cup, in 1999. If Fitzy could hold on at the age of thirty-five for the All Blacks, then I could hold on for Mid-Argyll, and the SCUF in Paris, and Norwich and Geneva and Midsomer Norton. Of course I'd play a blinder every time (winning the princess, slaying the dragon), and everyone would think I was marvellous.

I'm married, I have some children. I therefore consider myself adult enough to accept the reality of change. I hadn't been back to Argyll since leaving the duchess eleven years earlier, and was prepared to find it substantially altered. Rugby had changed dramatically in the last ten years; so, probably, had everything else.

As an obvious example, I'd been able to book a room at Lunga Tower, in Mathilda's former apartments. The duchess died in 1997, and her rooms have since been taken over and let as bed and breakfast. I was headed for Lunga now, up the rutted track through rhododendron woods, and as I rounded the last bend before the house, I held my breath. I was hoping to make out at least a trace of our long-ago previous life.

I exhaled in relief. From the outside, Lunga looked just the same, the turrets and the towers, the dark Scottish stone. I knocked on the green door, thinking it must always have been green. No reply. The door always used to be open, so I pushed. It was open, and I went in, and my heart lurched. The dimly lit entrance-hall was exactly the same, and I was suddenly back in one of my lost lives, unled, mislaid. There were the same dark furnishings, the same rugs and bookcases, the same stags' heads and antlers on the wall. I'd forgotten the stags' heads, but they were definitely the same ones.

Up in the rooms, I recognised the pictures on the walls, and the elegant wallpaper hand-painted with a languid Japanese tree and cranes. In the old office I even found the familiar gold-framed mirror, into which I must have looked a thousand times, a young man of twenty-four in purple trousers and a green jumper knitted by my gran, wondering where, exactly, I thought I was heading. There was a bed now instead of a desk, but this was the only concession to bed and breakfast.

Every room was empty and available. I went up the final set of spiral stairs, up the remembered off-white carpet to the duchess's bedroom, right at the top of the Tower. It had a priceless view over Jura and the Corryvrecken, although whenever Mathilda felt poor we'd take sunset photographs from the window, and talk about selling them as postcards. The view was still basically priceless, and this room too was available.

I looked at Mathilda's bed, where she used to eat her five-course breakfast. She'd then stay there for the rest of the morning, reading or making phone-calls. Did I dare? For twenty quid a night I could sleep in the duchess's bed for a week. It was the same bed with the same four-poster drapes, in lace. They could have been the very same sheets.

Come on then, man or manservant? If I was a real man, I'd take Mathilda's bed to show that I'd changed, that I'd grown out of the past. I ought to take her bed on the simple manly principle that it disconcerted me even to consider it.

I took off my shoes and lay down on the bed, with the old crisp lace closing me in. I did think about it, I thought hard, but eventually decided on the bed in the room next door. This used to be Mathilda's upstairs sitting-room, where she'd call me in for dictation, and where we'd re-enact the events of her childhood in pre-war Paris, like the cruise-ship with a working carousel which carried her to safety in America.

I didn't want to flatten the past. I left Mathilda in her own bed with her complicated breakfasts, and dropped my bag in the room next door, conveniently on hand should she want to continue dictation. We'd probably start where we always left off, at the point where the grand old hard-up duke fell hopelessly in love with the young and innocent heiress.

So I wasn't man enough for Mathilda's bed. I did use her bathroom, though.

It was probably too much to hope that the Mid-Argyll rugby club was equally unchanged. In 1991, the popular perception of the English rugger-bugger was also my perception, and if I'd been in England when I saw England lose to New Zealand, I doubt I'd have borrowed the Mustang. But this was Scotland and way out on the west coast, and I wasn't with Englishmen but with Rhys Kelly from New Zealand, so I was hoping instead for some rugby. Or some rugger with the buggers taken out.

This was exactly what I got. With professionalism still distant, rugby was played on the mud of the infamous Mushroom Field for its own intrinsic worth. Mid-Argyll offered all the anecdotal delights of amateur rugger: a journey from changing room to pitch by open lorry; erecting the posts before the game; afterwards at the bar in Lochgilphead's Masonic Lodge (No. 754), fostering that other type of brotherhood, equally mysterious, between all players of the game.

Argyll is not a region with a strong rugby tradition, but the teams out here in the Wild West, with their unforgettable trips by boat to Mull or Bute, most closely resemble the earliest days of the union. I don't mean in the English public schools, where the game originated, but when it spread to outlying areas in Wales and south-west Ireland, to New Zealand and the African Cape.

The Celts and colonists appreciated rugby's emphasis on shared effort, and the game's rapid development showed how suited it was to expressing a certain form of rough and readiness. Under-equipped, ill-supported, tremendous fun, a group of convivial nineteenth-century tough guys with varying skills would arrange to meet a similar-sounding bunch from somewhere else. The numbers were fairly approximate, and the rules open to interpretation, but everyone loved it, and if a week later there wasn't another town or village with its own share of friendly tough guys, then we'd play this lot again, with the added spice of the cuts and grudges from the week before. Thus, in an alchemy of violent intent and good faith, the game began to take its shape.

Mid-Argyll proudly upheld this pioneer spirit. It had all the rough and the unflinching readiness, and the first time I was boshed in training by the woodsman Big Richard, by way of a 1991 welcome, I did wonder if this was really me.

The answer wasn't exactly difficult.

Without rugby I'd been in decline. My life as a failing novelist was a recent history of second-hand shoes, smoking, and not cleaning my teeth. Bad feet, bad teeth, bad lungs. With the energy left over from sitting still, I'd stay at home wondering, for a worrying length of time, what kind of shoes an ex-girlfriend was wearing. Right now. I started reading eco-pamphlets with titles like *Anger is Appropriate*, before coming to my senses and reminding myself that everything would turn out fine, or that's what I kept telling myself, because I am I am I. Which stopped when I had to ask: 'Am I?'

I needed fixed co-ordinates, and they came from an unlikely source. I could give rugby a go here. This wasn't England, and the sport had none of the deterrent associations of rugger. Rugby provided a direction, a beneficial distraction, as recognised more than a century earlier by the Victorians. In fact, none of the virtues which kept the nineteenth century solid were missing from the game of rugby. These included fair play, co-operation, dedication, enterprise, honesty, and of course pluck. There was also responsibility, decision-making, and patience. At that time, missing the point of my own life, I'd have settled for any credible combination of such fine qualities.

I was also sadly deluded. As well as picturing myself as a writer, I had an exalted vision of my own masculinity. At different moments I could suspect myself capable of every manly virtue, making it a safe bet that I'd immediately meet someone who surpassed me in all of them.

Rhys Kelly, for example, who came from New Zealand and lived two doors down in the village of Craobh Haven. While I was totally middle class and therefore wholly unskilled, Rhys used to pop back home to mend the dog. His dad was an All Black triallist, and he had a cat called Zinzan, but in those days Rhys was a mad punk rocker who'd recently been chased out of Hamilton. His set of interests was too wide, and despite his vigour in the tackle he'd made an early escape from the only country on earth where an annual bestseller is Bob Howitt's *New Zealand Rugby Greats*. Not just the first volume, but all three.

Mid-Argyll was like that. It was full of people who loved rugby but were wary of the worst of rugger attitudes. But God did we want to play. The game was as important to Rhys as it was to me, and his past explained why in the open Mustang on the way to training we always had to blast, at full volume, Rhys's favourite NZ punk bands, The Chills and The Irritants and The Wellington Hurricanes Are Gay. Among many others in the same alternative tradition.

In 2002, I went to find Rhys in his workshop on the hill above the seaside village of Ardfern. These days, Rhys makes doors and tables and pretty much anything you ask him to make. Staircases and attics and ocean-going liners. Like the stags' heads at Lunga, he hasn't changed much. He gives me a broad smile as he turns off the machines and effortlessly lifts a finished door onto a nearby pile. He's still a strong, hard-looking man, but one who's filled out a little and whose face is marked by the scars from more than a decade of highland battles.

I only mention the strength, and the hardness, because that was always part of what I wanted for myself. When I rediscovered rugby at Mid-Argyll, that was part of the urge to belong, not to a place, but to a certain idea of manliness. Even then, I knew that genuine physical and spiritual hardness could only come from fixed habits of life and work, and I was a white southern middle-class Englishman, along with a certain type of miniature Peruvian dog among the most pampered creatures on earth.

Even so, I soon realised that the mateship of rugby could transcend differences. I could never be as manly as Rhys (not as strong, not as hard), but I could play a game which embraced the notion of egalitarianism, of a team of hard strong men, a gathering of good honest blokes. That was me; that's what I wanted to be, and rugby famously had a welcome for everyone, short and tall, thin and fat, lightweight and overweight. The real man and the hopeless middle-class fantasist.

We'd planned to drive from Ardfern to training at Lochgilphead in Rhys's battered blue van, BUILDER, JOINER, GLAZIER. First though, while we caught up on each other's news, Rhys whipped out the engine, casually re-bored the pistons, then fixed the van back together again. He wiped his hands on his trousers, and we were away. Music on full, tumbling and rattling south through the dips and curves of the coastal road.

It turned out that the club captain, Big Richard, was injured. Rhys would therefore be in charge of training, and this Saturday's fixture was more important than usual because it was the first round of the BT Cellnet Scottish Cup.

'We're hoping to win, then?'

'No, mate. We're hoping to get the three hundred and eighty quid.'

Modern times. Mid-Argyll are in the bottom league of Scottish rugby, known for some reason as Glasgow and District League – Championship Group. We'd been drawn in the cup against Whitecraigs, a Glasgow club which was currently topping National Division Four. It was vital that Mid-Argyll fulfilled the fixture, not because there was any chance of winning, but because in the new professional dispensation there was money to be had. And £380 is a lot of money, especially for tackle-bags or new balls. Or shared at the end of the season among fifteen players and their families at the Argyll in Ardrishaig. Say.

It was a warm Tuesday evening in early September, with the sun still high in a blue sky and the Mushroom Field at its best and firmest after a hot dry August. Even now, the turf had a definite spring to it. In the winter, the club trains under lights at the Lochgilphead sports centre, but this still counted as summer training. Rhys therefore parked the van between the road and the field, and we changed in full view of the A816. It was easily warm enough for shorts and rolled-down socks, and in a puzzled way I watched as Rhys added track-suit trousers and a long-sleeved undershirt, and then an impermeable hooded rain-top. He pulled on gloves, a bala-clava, goggles.

I laughed at him. Of course I did. He looked ridiculous.

And then, as the sun hit the top of the nearest range of hills, the vicious midges came.

I didn't stop moving for the next hour and a half. In fact I jumped and hopped as high and youthfully as anyone, meaning all six of us, and among those six I include Rhys and myself, and Australian Tim who'd just started work at the Crinan Hotel. Even so, Rhys set out the poles and the tackle-shields, and in two groups of three we jinked and set up rucks, and kept on moving.

I was fit and ready for this, as I'd known for some time that

I'd need to be in good shape to score all those winning tries in the last minutes of games I was about to play for my former clubs. In my rigorous pre-season training programme, I'd even managed to win several of the prestigious Cornwall forty-yard beach dashes. And also a stage or two in the Tour de France, which uniquely for the greatest bike-race on earth was this year centred on the Mendip Hills. A typical day's racing would usually conclude after a punishing twenty miles or so near Shepton Mallet, where as the local favourite I'd edge out Armstrong and Cipollini in the sprint. Okay, so I wasn't in peak condition, but I wasn't a wreck either. I'd started the summer fat; now, after much running and cycling, I looked like a fit man going to seed.

After an hour or so of dodging the midges, we played a bit of tackling and supporting, and that was fun, and it was good to get an early bang to the face as a seasonal reminder that we don't just fall apart. Thanks, Iain. But six people. It was still light when we climbed into the van and set off back to Ardfern, and I agreed with Rhys that it didn't look good. There used to be twenty at training twice a week, and two teams, but the Mid-Argyll second team is a memory now, and even the first team's a struggle. I admired Rhys's loyalty, and that of the other guys, but still. I wondered how many newcomers, like we were eleven years ago, would gladly be back next week for games of touch three against three.

This needed discussing in the pub, and at the Galley of Lorne in Ardfern Rhys explained that the mini-rugby stopped at the age of thirteen. There was then no club rugby until sixteen, when any boys still interested were allowed to play in leagues with men. Mid-Argyll had no help from the Scottish

Rugby Union, not even now with the added competition from shinty. Shinty is an ancient highland game played with sticks.

'And let's face it, mate,' Rhys said, 'there's the women.'

The women *and* the kids, the whole catastrophe. Rhys has children, two girls, but somehow it doesn't apply to him. Fortunately, after a lager or two he seemed more cheery about the future. Then we had a think about some more lager, and I felt happy enough about keeping going because it wasn't long before closing. Only I'd forgotten that in Scotland, the bar wouldn't ever be closing.

So whatever Rhys told me that night – and he might have had the secret of the decline of west coast rugby in perfect perspective, and he might have told me what it was several times (and it wasn't *really* the women) – I was still going to have to ask someone else the same questions come the morning.

It may be, and this is a big claim, that the Scottish Rugby Union mismanaged the change to professionalism even more comprehensively than the Welsh. During the 1999 World Cup, as rugby's great modern chronicler Stephen Jones has pointed out, rugby in Scotland seemed to lose its public, its energy, and finally its team. There's no obvious sign of a Scottish recovery. They underperform in the European Cup. They're troubled by Italy in the Six Nations. Every second international player is actually from somewhere else, and second-rate Anzacs push out native loose-forwards when the scavenging Scots breakaways have rightly been feared since the dawn of national encounters.

However, it wouldn't be entirely fair to blame the hard

times of Mid-Argyll on the distant and snooty Scottish Union, though a decent national team would help. The west coast has little rugby heritage (no wonder the development officer never visits), but it's not just rugby which is suffering. Lochgilphead Redstar, the local soccer club, is also down to a single team.

By contrast, there's the heartening success story of shinty. This far north, it's shinty which is filling the games vacuum created in the 1990s when sport in schools was allowed to fade. It's the violence, apparently. Shinty's brutality holds a fascination for local adolescents, with the added advantage that you can use a stick.

In the week I visited, the *Oban Times* had two broadsheet pages of match and preview coverage, as well as a Spot the Shinty Ball competition (and not many papers can say that). The High School in Lochgilphead no longer offers either football or rugby, but it does have shinty teams at three different age groups.

I ask Ian Martin, manager of the Lochgilphead Sports Centre, if this is because it's a better game. I mean to play, of course, not morally. At Glencoe in 1692 the Campbells played shinty with the Macdonalds before massacring them, at night, in their sleep. Perhaps the kids prefer it that way?

'No,' he says, 'it's because they have a development officer. The lad comes in once a fortnight and gets teachers involved, and children are already playing when they come from primary school. And the kids do like a good run-around.'

After the sports centre, I browse the morning away on Argyll Street in Lochgilphead, and realise that in this part of the country sport can still mean shooting and fishing. A local sportsman is as likely to buy a rod or a gun as a shinty stick. I rummage in a charity shop, Scottish International Relief, and among the videos I find *Living with Lions*, the documentary of the 1997 British Lions in South Africa. So at least *someone* must be interested in rugby. Or used to be interested.

I then drive back up the main road towards Oban and take the turning for Craobh Haven, the unfinished village. The only street is exactly the same. The marina is full of boats, true enough, but it's still served by a one-street village and only imaginary adjuncts – pools, rinks, top-class hotels, all invisible. I'm overwhelmed by the stagnation, and the lack of change; it fills me with a deep, selfish joy.

And then, ambling towards the very end of the road, I see Welsh John the alcoholic electrician. He's thinner, his face even more lined, but he's still talking the same old nonsense. In our day, he was barred from the pub, but the Lord of the Isles has changed hands and now looks almost nice, and John's the old geezer allowed his own bar-stool in the fantasy corner of the bar.

'At lunchtime I only ever have one pint,' he says, as we settle in on the high stools. He lifts his glass and I see his hands are shaking. He tells me that Mathilda left him a thousand pounds in her will, and I can't think of any reason why he'd lie about that. As he talks, he blinks a lot. It's the most noticeable thing about him, along with an inexplicable remnant of rogueish charm. He was an engineer in the RAF, he sailed single-handed across the Atlantic, he invented the mobile telephone. And he blinks and blinks away as he talks, as if he doesn't quite believe that either he or anyone else is exactly who they say they are.

'I'm a writer, now,' I say. 'I do novels, mostly, but I'm writing a book about rugby.'

He finishes his beer. 'That's my one pint for the morning,' he says, rubbing his unsteady hands together and beaming his charming smile, 'but seeing as you're offering, I'll now have a dram.'

I buy him whisky, and it happens quicker than I expected. He's Welsh, you see, and soon drunk, and therefore once played full-back for Ebbw Vale. They used to find five-pound notes (and that was a lot of money in those days) tucked discreetly inside their boots. He played with Phil Bennett, and at school in the valleys they were punished for bringing in a round ball, righteously strapped across the backs of their legs.

'I hate soccer,' he says, a harmless Welsh drunk at the bar staring at the carpet and suddenly slouched with gloom and bitterness. 'Hate it.'

I imagine this happens a lot in Wales, and if you stacked up every Welshman who once played with Phil Bennett they'd probably reach the moon. However, it's a kind of rugby half-life which is rare in the western Highlands. In that sense, professionalism doesn't seem to have made much difference. There hasn't been any great outreach from the rugby strongholds in Edinburgh and the Borders, and if the game can't reach the coasts of Scotland, what hope does it have of conquering the world?

Or perhaps this part of the world is unconquerable, a jagged coastline of peninsulas lost in dreams of their own. I leave old Welsh John in the pub and use the pay-phone by the marina to call one of the founding directors of the original Craobh Haven development scheme. It's a bright, sunny day, and light beams from the bare aluminium masts of many expensive yachts.

'There are plans,' the man tells me, but it's all very complicated, all very unattributable. My man blames 'outside factors' as a terrible obstruction to forward planning, and the local wrangling sounds as confused and convoluted as an RFU board meeting. Not to mention as fiercely spun: in positive discussions with the council, everyone is agreed on the unlimited potential of the finest leisure-related development site in Europe. 'It's a potential goldmine.'

He may well be right, I think, looking from the under-developed village to the glittering sea in perfect early September sunshine. Forgetting for a moment the inevitable rain, the midges, and Craobh Haven's distance from the touristic mainstream. But look at the light; the stillness of the sea and the gaunt black mountains. It could happen.

And rugby could take over the world.

I want to talk to a rugby-playing Scot, and as it's lunchtime I go to see big Davy Anderson at the farm. In 1991, Davy was a rock of the Mid-Argyll first team, although even then he was forty-one years old. Davy'll set me straight, I think. Big Davy'll remind me what a great game rugby is and what a great club Mid-Argyll is and what a bright future it has as a rugby fortress in the west.

'I think it's going to fold,' he says, clearing a space in the paperwork on the table of his farmhouse kitchen. 'It can't go on and on.'

Davy Anderson the great back-row forward, latterly lock-forward, has a low brow, staunch eyebrows, big hands, big lugs. And the world is naught but sorrow. After thirteen seasons with Oban, he was one of five founder members of Mid-Argyll, in 1978. There were meant to be six of them, but one went to the wrong pub and never made it out again. They each put in five pounds, and made a winning start on an April evening away at Oban.

Heavily, at the table over tea and a biscuit, he tells me that the lowest point in the club's history is now.

'Come on, Davy, it can't be all bad.'

'It's never been worse, man.'

I change the subject, and ask him for the high point, which turns out to be the satisfaction of once sending a second team south to Newton Stewart, a five-hour drive.

'But back to the low point,' Davy says, leaning forward over his crossed arms. 'There's a lack of youngsters, and it's not as if they're playing other outdoor sports. They're just not there any more.'

Davy wants me to know the worst. There are two forty-nine-year-olds playing regularly for Mid-Argyll, men who were already old when I was young. Even at fifty-two, Davy himself still turns out when fit, only recently this hasn't been all that often. It's the hamstrings, and a quarrel with his sciatic nerve.

Big Davy blames a lot of things. It's a British problem (we're a race out of energy, because anyone with get up and go got up and went, mostly to Canada, but also to New Zealand and Australia). Or it's because the older folk can't communicate with the younger ones, or it's simply the money. The club used to make a habit of losing at least one weekend a year in Edinburgh, for a Five Nations international. The price of tickets now makes this impossible.

The professional players don't help, either. 'They're freaks of nature,' Davy complains, 'and you watch them on TV and think, not I can do that, but no way, I definitely *can't* do that.'

(And I think no Davy, not at fifty-two; you probably can't.)

Or it's the passive nature of today's youth, or the nanny state, which is the same as the Big Brother state, though I'm not immediately clear either about the details of this connection or its exact influence on rugby in Mid-Argyll. But after a little while, if nothing else, I'm fairly certain that the withered soul of this ungrateful state machine lies hidden somewhere deep and sinister inside the local government buildings on the outskirts of the town of Lochgilphead.

'They have no idea of a sports culture. No idea. They even asked the public for donations to save the swimming-pool! This is the background environment,' Davy says, 'and life's hard enough, in all conscience.'

Or it's simple geography. The nearest club to the south is at Lomond, and to the north Oban, and then Fort William. There's the expense of the travelling. And as for shinty . . .

'They *buy* the kids,' Davy says darkly, narrowing his eyes, knowingly lowering his brow.

'How's that then, Davy?'

'They give them a free stick.'

Rugby does nothing, and rugby is therefore dying. From his farm at Barneykill on the Crinan canal, big Davy turns out to be a firm admirer of those Scottish private schools where rugby is compulsory. The thought briefly seems to cheer him. Then he lapses once more into the arms of gloom.

'Where it's going, I don't know.'

I think it's fair to say that big Davy is not one of life's

optimists, and it isn't long before he starts in again on bureaucracy, and the government offices in Lochgilphead. They used to send out a few rugby players, but now the club doesn't have one single player from the council head-quarters, so what's the point of the bloody place? They prefer playing five-a-side football, and Davy groans at this, holding his ears in his hands and banging his head on the table.

'They have the choice of playing rugby, and they *prefer* soccer! And inside! With only five players on each team and with people they already know! They actually prefer playing indoors with nine people they already work with rather than taking the chance to get out and about in the fresh air with twenty-nine people they haven't yet met!'

By this time Davy's wife Sheila has walked past the table several times, often raising her eyes to heaven. She's also made us lunch. She's a nurse, and she knows how to cope.

'It's the increased professionalism of *life* that's the problem,' Davy complains, his knife and fork readied in his huge fists, 'never mind the rugby.'

He talks of feed reps who don't want to knock on doors with bruises and scars. Of fish-farmers who can't afford a day off from the platforms with injury. The managers these days simply don't have the time or incentives to be tolerant. Or even to be decent human beings.

And then he launches into a long story about rate assessors and a charge for a caravan on his farmland that was never actually there. Or having to get planning permission to change the hinges on a door. Or something. I'm finding it hard to follow.

In any case, the result is invariably depressing. Rugby's definitely going to the dogs. But then so is everything else.

This is quite possible, of course, and rugby at this humble level may be trapped in a fading order of outdated things. Times change, as do attitudes, and perhaps rugger is too twentieth century to survive. But then so is the Argyll café on Lochgilphead's high street, and that's doing well enough. Ten years ago, the Argyll café had nicotine-stained, suede-brown ceilings, and was full of people in coats sheltering from the rain. There was a handwritten sign on the toilet door which said WASH YOUR HANDS AFTER WORDS, but once inside, it was the kind of toilet where you wanted to wash the soap.

Nothing much has changed, except the ceiling's been painted. Or the old ceiling has been transferred to the floor, which is now brown and sticky. I was back in Lochgilphead in search of a shop called Undercover.Com, to see if attitudes had changed so radically that rugger could be cast adrift, a relic of the dowdy past with nothing to offer a bright new century.

First, though, I went back to the charity shop Scottish International Relief, to buy the video *Living with Lions*. I'd seen it before, but I wanted to watch Keith Wood winding himself up again, and Jim Telfer exploring the boundaries of the word fuck, and also Scott Gibbs bouncing those lardy Afrikaaners. I could justify this purchase by reasoning that the video would give me an insight into rugby's professional age in all its post-1995 glory, which I could then compare favourably or otherwise to the wind-ups and use of the word fuck at Mid-Argyll. Out of a sense of charity, I also thought it only right to make a contribution to the relief of Scottish internationals. They do have it hard, after all.

The video wasn't there. Some closet west coast rugby fan had already bought it, so perhaps there was more local interest than at first it seemed. I shuffled through other videos, including the dusty ones at the back without boxes. *Living with Lions* had definitely vanished, but I did find, boxless at the back underneath *Dirty Dancing*, *The Barbarians v. All Blacks 1973*. This match is a byword in the virtuous mythology of the great amateur game, so at fifty pence I took a chance and carried that one away with me instead.

In a more recent addition to the mythology of rugger, Mid-Argyll had spent the previous weekend in Edinburgh dressed as cavemen. Crossing the Erskine Bridge to Glasgow, they'd offered the toll money in pebbles, and the girl in the booth had sorted coolly through the stones with her finger. She'd looked up unfazed and said, 'Sorry, I can't change that.'

The men are still prehistoric, but the women are cool, even in the tollbooths on the Erskine Bridge. Even in Lochgilphead. It was a simple and unreconstructed world in the days when men would go to a rugby club for their dirty jokes. Now they're available from any number of outlets including, I'd been told, those on Argyll Street in Lochgilphead.

This obviously intrigued me, especially as ten years ago the most exotic consumer experience available in the town was provided by the bookshop. They'd place your new Anthony Burgess in a leopard-skin paper bag. That used to be as racy as it got, in Lochgilphead, but these days there's Undercover.Com, a high-street shop owned and run by local girl Sasha Hampton.

I used to know Sasha from parties on the beach, and when I eventually find the shop (it's the one with bras and pants and ejaculating penis key-rings in the window) I try to remind her it's me. She doesn't immediately make a connection.

'I'm sorry. Did we sleep together?'

Once we've sorted that one out, I tell her I'm now interested in men, if she sees what I mean, and she agrees to answer some questions. Sasha is small and curvy and has very shiny, very healthy-looking purple-coloured hair. She talks to me without blinking, as young and confident as blinking Welsh John is old and uncertain. Her blue eyes wide and innocent, she proposes I take a look at the bestseller from her cabinet of sex toys (PLEASE ASK TO BE SERVED, says a sign on the cabinet door). It is a battery-powered revolving tongue. She doesn't explain what this has to do with men.

However, nothing in the shop is quite as it seems. The main business is exotic lingerie, £20 for the cheapest bra-and-pants set up to about £60 for the PVC. I did ask. Except it wasn't always Sasha who answered. As we spoke, Rita was behind the changing-room curtain, trying on the exotic lingerie.

It was Rita the disembodied Scottish voice who let me know that it used to be a menswear shop, owned by local councillor Donny MacMillan. How things change, I thought, because as Rita said this Sasha was holding up her latest dildo design, known in prototype as the Mull of Kintyre. If all went well, the Mull of Kintyre would soon be in full production, manufactured from hypoallergenic rubber latex by a Lochgilphead factory currently specialising in acrylic toilet seats.

'It's about empowerment and feminine sexual confidence,' Rita called out, while Sasha gazed up at me winningly through her eyelashes and held out something pink and battery-powered which thrummed. I was embarrassed. I was so old-fashioned. Might just as well have spent the weekend in Edinburgh, indistinguishable from Cro-Magnon man.

Now more than ever, I thought, men need their own source of confidence. Rita swished the curtain to one side, and came smiling and blonde from the cubicle. She was fully dressed, but placed two pairs of satin briefs on the counter. I asked Sasha what she thought about the rugby club.

'Lovely, lovely blokes,' she said.

And I could have asked her other questions, but was frightened she'd know the answers.

'Are all men the same?'

The answer used to be: 'Yes, all men are the same. But rugby players are even worse.'

That was in the old days, and Sasha had assured me that she'd never in her life heard the term rugger-bugger. This seemed to prove, conclusively, its non-existence in this part of the world, of the combination of ideas, of the concept.

Back at the club, come training on Thursday, we were more concerned with the pressing issue of Saturday's cup match in Glasgow. And the £380 we'd forfeit if we couldn't raise a team. Rhys was hoping for a better turn-out, and this time the midges were waiting in force for the good food of all ten of us, including one youngster in a Spanish football shirt (long sleeves) with RAUL across the shoulders. Everyone called him Raul, though his real name was Scott.

While we warmed up, jogging and stretching, the club sorted out its admin. The Scottish Rugby Union had insisted, for the new season, that every affiliated club have a director of rugby, so the lads threw that one around and eventually decided on Brocken, one of Davy's 49-year-olds, and yet another survivor from '91. Brocken used to play flanker but had moved to the centre, and was suddenly the fittest 49-year-old director of rugby anywhere in Scotland, and I'd be prepared to have a bet on that.

In and around the tackle-bags, I mentioned my chat with Davy and the imminent demise of the club.

'Ach,' Brocken said, 'that's just Davy.'

Ian Malcolm even remembered the second-team trip to Newton Stewart. On the long journey home the team spent their petrol money at the George in Inveraray. Of course they then ran out of fuel, and had to push the minibus back into Lochgilphead in the early hours of the morning.

'Great days,' I said. 'You must miss them.'

'You weren't there. And nor was Davy. We pushed that bus for fucking miles.'

The numbers had nearly doubled since Tuesday, but ten on a sunny September evening was still not nearly enough (by about a third, in fact), and didn't bode well for the weekend. It was good news for me, on a purely selfish level, because it meant I was definitely in for the game. If we could raise fifteen, that was.

Rhys was confident. If all else failed, there was always a chance that from the shifting seasonal population a benevolent God would provide a batch of match-winning Australians. Last year it was Chad, Boomer, and Scottie, in from Tasmania to work on the fish-farms. And this year, though so far there was only Tim from the Crinan hotel, from that faraway sporting superpower there might well come another set of Boomers, Scotties, and Chads, identical in every way, equally enthusiastic, Australian to the core.

But on this particular Thursday so early in the season, there was as yet no obvious sign of salvation. We were struggling to make a team. In fact, several of the older players (though not Brocken, who was raring to go) had only come down for a run-out as a kind of fitness test. Yup. Not fit. They'd definitely be playing.

Anyone sane might have wondered why we bothered. Not just to turn up on evenings like this, but to face a guaranteed thrashing on the Saturday which we firmly expected to enjoy. What was it about rugby that clouded the judgement?

I think all rugby players believe, at varying depths of consciousness, that the game is impressive to women. We may be wrong, but that's not important. In a game which requires courage and manly endurance, we're addicted to showing we're the kind of men prepared to have a go, even if as it happens we don't always endure, and are not always entirely courageous.

Or it's simpler than that. Rugby is fast, fun, and violent. That's at least two advantages it has over shopping, and one over most other sports. It provides wincing collisions and an often brutal intensity. Admittedly, these aren't always attractive qualities to the participants themselves, but the mere possibility accords the game a halo, under which we the players can plausibly believe that this game and this game only makes us Saturday by Saturday into stronger and more admirable men.

Discussing these and other matters after training, I eventually made it home from the Galley of Lorne by 12.47 a.m. I didn't feel sleepy. I roamed Lunga, sniffing for memories, then realised that all the books in the Tower bookcases belonged to the duchess, and had never been moved away. I'd always blithely accepted the received wisdom that the past was lost. It was always lost. The best thing was to move on, and constantly moving on, I'd never looked back to check. But the past was still here, unchanged. It even had the same books.

I spent an hour checking for inscriptions – 'For Mathilda Argyll With All Best Wishes and Memories of Brion, William Burroughs' – and reflected that at about the time Mathilda was duchess over silver and lobsters at Inveraray Castle, Burroughs the beatnik writer was out to naked lunch taking potshots with a handgun at his wife.

Oh, I thought, what a wonderful world.

By Saturday, I was ready to believe I belonged. In fact, just as I'd done eleven years earlier, I allowed myself to feel a bit like a Celt, the glamour of it, forced to the edges of the nation. This might have been, now as then, the only workable justification for not being in London, getting serious about a career in fiction.

But it's difficult to take yourself seriously when you're a grown man waiting at the Lochgilphead bus-stop, desperately excited because you're about to travel three hours into Glasgow to play a ball-game designed for children. There was something regressive and adolescent about it, but then I liked to believe, even at my age, that I could live with that.

Adolescence was a time of blatant confusion. No, really, I *don't* understand, I *don't* feel comfortable in my skin. Anything else was pretence, and protracted youth a means of staying honest.

Having worked this out to my own satisfaction, I was then free to clear my mind for the game. I felt a bit sick. I also felt a responsibility. I wanted to play well for Rhys and the team. Partly, this would be a way of repaying their generosity, and among other qualities the game itself is very generous. On the pitch, it's possible to play generously by opening up space and opportunities for others, or simply by giving everything you have to the cause. Although it shares these qualities with other outdoor games, in rugby you know in advance that it's also going to hurt.

Nor was this the time for self-deprecation, humorous though it typically is. I had my pride, and since my last match for Mid-Argyll I'd been in and out of Europe and played some decent rugby at a much higher level. It was time to deliver. Like every Saturday.

This is what the elite players call mental preparation. However, the focus required to prepare while waiting at the Lochgilphead bus-stop requires a mental strength I didn't have. Rhys and the prop Corky Fraser, both former captains, were still on their phones pleading with strangers or haranguing relatives. We were up to fourteen, although only eight had actually arrived. No one knew how long this was going to take.

'A few more minutes,' Rhys said, dialling someone's cousin, but I wasn't born yesterday.

With time on my hands, I went into the nearby Tourist

Information. I asked lovely Catriona MacNeill (name-badge) what I could do for half an hour or so in the loch-side town of Lochgilphead. She raised her suggestive eyebrows and mentioned Sasha's shop. I'd already been.

'In that case,' she said, slender hands flat on the counter in front of her, 'there's nothing to do in the town of Lochgilphead.'

While official Information was being offered to tourists in this unusually frank manner, I decided to ask about the rugby club.

'Oh, them,' Catriona said, and I can only assume that this is the official and sanctioned view of the Highland and Islands Tourist Board: 'They're mad.'

I went back to the bus-stop and, still waiting for players to turn up, read the time-table. There were sometimes as many as three services a day, in one direction to Ardrishaig, Kilberry Road End, Tarbert (Turning Circle), Stronachullin, Kennacraig Road End, Tayinloan, and Campbeltown. About nine players now, maybe ten. In a more easterly direction, on a pre-planned outing from Lochgilphead, you could get to Lochgair, Minard, Furnace (War Memorial), Inveraray (Front Street), Dunoon (Ferry Terminal), and eventually, if you didn't mind the risk of being lost to the sinful city for ever, Glasgow Buchanan Bus Station.

In 1991, for away games in Glasgow, we used to take the council minibus. I remembered well the sense of relief and release in the sheer non-thought of those epic rugby journeys. It used to remind me of the Tibetan reaction to a sneeze – 'Congratulations!' – because in that one sneezed moment the brain is emptied of all rational thought. Congratulations.

Only those bus trips to Glasgow and back lasted a little while longer than a sneeze.

It turned out that the council eighteen-seater had been crashed the week before on the way home from Inverness by the junior shinty team. We were therefore travelling down in cars, and three cars would be enough. We were only fourteen, but it was getting late and Rhys decided to risk it. Maybe we could persuade a fifteenth by phone on the way down. Maybe one of the girls from the Erskine Bridge.

There was then a pre-match scuffle as everyone tried to avoid getting in a car with Big John. Along with Big Davy and Big Richard, Big John is big. He also talks a lot, Rhys telling me that only last weekend they'd had breakfast in Edinburgh together (dressed as cavemen), and Big John had even talked to his breakfast ('Good morning, Mr Beans, you're looking tasty this morning').

Shepherded to safety by Rhys, I therefore ended up one of five to a Vauxhall Vectra: me, Corky, James the driver, Rhys and Iain. I soon discovered that the diversity of the rugby world remains intact. And also its ability to talk nonsense. On the way down, through the glens and over the mountain passes, knees buckled up into the backs of the seats, we covered world terrorism, the fire brigade at Inveraray, the best way to get to Australia, and a former team-mate of ours still obsessed by the idea that somewhere in Edinburgh is a Chinese restaurant where the waitresses will serve you topless depending on what you order. The genius of this idea is that you're never in the wrong Chinese restaurant. You might be in the right place, but ordering the wrong dish. And, finally, professional rugby in Glasgow.

Amazingly, Corky and his Welsh girlfriend had bought season tickets for Glasgow Caledonians, and were prepared to drive three hours into Glasgow for Friday night or Sunday games. Despite the fact that a season ticket cost only £80, this was something of a victory for the professional game in Scotland, especially as the home supporters had never once seen their team win a fixture of any significance.

We waited on the Erskine Bridge for the other cars, but we were still only fourteen. Too late to turn back now. In convoy we moved slowly through Glasgow, and waiting for lights to change, I watched boys playing with broken glass in the lost concrete world beneath a junction of the M8. There must be better games to play on a Saturday.

At Whitecraigs Rugby Football Club, the true extent of the cup mismatch quickly becomes evident. As well as leading National Division Four, Whitecraigs have a clubhouse which is newer, bigger and by some margin more comfortable than the clubhouse at Bath. They have three flat, drained pitches, advertising hoardings, three XVs, and twenty-five players in an under-18 squad.

We have fourteen men. Luckily, we also have fourteen shirts, and Rhys decides it's probably best not to mention being one short, not yet. I resume my mental preparation by reminding myself, as I lace my boots and tape my socks, that these matches are contests, they're always tests, even if they're not internationals. Considering the two clubs and their relative position in the leagues, I also resign myself to a day of tackling and scrapping and let's face it, cheating. Or in other words, using my experience.

That's if we played at all. There was still some anxiety (no, really) that the referee wouldn't allow us to play with fourteen men. We ran out onto the pitch. We passed the ball a bit. We lined up for the ritual checking of the studs. And then I was lucky enough to remain in earshot as Rhys gently took the referee to one side.

It might have been my imagination, but I was sure Rhys was twanging that New Zealand accent of his as he explained to the ref, quietly but with the utmost sincerity, that the car containing our usual captain had broken down just shy of Lochgair. (Of course it had, what rugby team would arrive in only three cars?) They'd had to call the garage, and then didn't have time to organise a second vehicle. What was worse, not only did that car contain our captain, but also our young female physiotherapist, our seven allowable replace-ments, and a bucket-man.

On the bright side, we still had our director of rugby, who was forty-nine years old and playing in the centre.

The referee seemed convinced. The game was going to happen, and I was in at scrum-half. The game started happening, and I loved every minute of it. I'm not a bad tackler, as it happens, when I put my mind to it. And not a bad scrapper, either. And I'm a wily old cheat.

The referee, Ken Robertson, was a wise and impressive human being, and it's not often you hear that said about a referee. Not only did he frequently show pity for Whitecraigs by penalising them for their own safety, but it quickly became clear that he hadn't believed a word of Rhys's car story. He knew that we wanted to play a game of rugby, as did Whitecraigs, and therefore he was happy to have us play, ignoring the strict letter of the SRU regulations. Which, I think, is as it should be.

Rhys was typically uncompromising, and in true New Zealand fashion he never defended, just frenziedly attacked the man with the ball. In other areas, however, our defence was less than watertight, which is not necessarily a bad thing. An argument could even be made that at this level rugby as a spectacle is at its most attractive. The defence is not a solid wall spread across the pitch. At Mid-Argyll fixtures, you'll rarely hear a clamour for less congestion, fewer players on the field. In fact, we could have done with at least one more to make up the fifteen, and then a couple extra in addition to that.

As for those of us who were there on that famous day, we displayed all the enviable foolery and hardiness of Celts, ran until our lungs were sobbing and blunt, and tackled and bled in a derangement of all the senses. Rugby is an extreme sport. I even made a break, opening up the pitch, crashing through into the sudden silence and freedom of the wide-open spaces. I was just as quickly closed down, and crushed, but it was enough to remind me that the game also has joys in attack. I remembered the main reason I started playing again, all those years ago up on the coast: nothing complicated, I just really liked it.

At half-time Whitecraigs had a certain number of points. Then they brought on some replacements and started trying. As for my good intentions for influencing the game, rugby simply isn't like that. One person can only make all the difference if the teams are otherwise evenly matched. These teams were not evenly matched, and although we were committed to the struggle, and fought to the end, we finished both halves without threatening to score. At least we were consistent, but we'd have run them closer if we could have managed, I don't know, maybe another eighty points or so.

After the game, the wincing and the shaking hands and the pile of steaming shirts on the changing-room floor, the showers and borrowed hair-gel, we all sat in the huge upstairs room of the clubhouse with bowls of bread and mince. I couldn't speak. It would take a little while to stop shaking from the expense of physical effort. I had a swollen lip and a cut eye, and was fairly sure I'd broken my ear. But as we marvelled at the new clubhouse and watched the sexy young girls it seemed to attract, I was definitely feeling my age. This was nearly the end. Soon, there would be other things. But surely never again anything quite like this.

A couple of hours later outside Fast Freddie's Food Club in Govan we were close to winning, or we'd forgotten the score, I can't remember which. Anyway, it didn't matter. It was the middle of the evening and we were still two and a half hours from home. We bought some bottles and chips, and sat talking nonsense as the car sped along the banks of Loch Lomond (the low road again) with a double rainbow of Celtic brightness on the hills, the setting sun in a last rally against the darkness of approaching clouds.

James was not drinking and driving. I had the feeling that James always had to not drink and drive, just so the others could have the periodic pleasure of saying 'Home James, and don't spare the horses.' I sat in the back with my bunched knees and my bleeding eye, the skin gently swelling and seeping, certain that the secret to earthly happiness is a game of rugby and good companions and alcohol. Rugby is a game apart, distinctive and special, but I couldn't dwell on that because heading home from Glasgow we had the radio tuned to *Take the Floor* with Rabbie Shepherd ('Don't let me doon, Kenny!').

Rabbie's Saturday evening show is a timeless medley of Scots reels and laments, soundtracking the glory of the hills and water, water everywhere, in the black lochs and tumbling down the rock-sides, in the air, and up in the clouds always rolling in. The music is brilliant, it's truly awful, but it's the only station along the western roads with bearable reception.

We occasionally search for a few seconds of rave music, anything to escape from Rabbie, but Radio One cracks and fizzles. Radio Scotland and *Take the Floor*, however, is crystal clear all the way to Cromerty, reeling in the miles as night falls and mist rises off the spruce. As we climb Glen Croe towards the pass called Rest and Be Thankful, Corky develops a theory that Rabbie Shepherd in person spends his empty weekdays hiding transmitters behind rocks and trees in the Highlands. That way, he makes sure that come Saturday his is the only show anywhere from Glasgow to Skye. Fair play to the man. Shows initiative.

And then, for no particular reason, the boys from the lochs and hills burst into a rendition of 'Maybe It's Because I'm a Londoner', and I couldn't help but think that Mid-Argyll was a great club, a truly great club, possibly the finest band of men on the planet.

That may have been the alcopops talking. What with the tackles and the battering and the bruises, we'd decided on alcopops in the Govan off-license to make ourselves feel younger. We had them in Rusk flavour, and in Milk, and it was generally agreed we were getting younger all the time. By the George at Inveraray, they were even checking our age.

SCUF, Paris, 1992–4

'In rugby, because we are Parisians, we are all dogs! We are all homosexuals! This is very amusing to us. We enjoy the idea.'

Franck Mesnel

At Mid-Argyll, the forty-year-old full-back Dougie Johnson was a class act who'd represented West of Scotland with Peter Mackinnon, the finest player ever to turn out for Mid-Argyll. Mackinnon had once been Scotland's third best scrum-half, and was immunised and picked as standby for a national tour to the Far East. ('He had his *jags*, man,' big Davy told me, more than once, as if this was the most impressive rugby achievement he'd ever encountered, 'he'd had his *jags*!')

Fully immunised, Mackinnon was invited to Paris for a trial with the Second Division Sporting Club Universitaire de France (SCUF). He never came back.

In 1992, using the transfer system perfected over more than a century of amateur rugby, I moved to Paris from Argyll and gave Peter a call. He claimed to be retired, though he did play the occasional home game for the SCUF's veteran side, the *Trois Vieux*, but only if he was allowed to wear his track-suit trousers. At that time Mackinnon looked to be in his early thirties, still a young man, but then in 1992 I soon discovered that Paris was some distance from the hairy-legged machismo of the Highlands.

I also found out that the SCUF were no longer in the French Second Division. I arrived in late February '92 and went to see a Third Division match at the Stade Georges Carpentier in the 13th arrondissement. Barely within the periphérique, the stadium was hidden among streets lined with red and yellow restaurants and a million Chinese smelling of Gauloises. From the stand, it was evident that very soon the SCUF wouldn't be in the Third Division, either. They were getting thumped.

The Sporting Club Universitaire de France (est. 1895) is one of the oldest clubs in France, and true to the eccentric naming of French rugby clubs, it has no connection with any university. The club contested the final of the National Championship in both 1911 and 1912. On both occasions we failed to win the *Bouclier de Brennus*, the champion's shield, donated to the French Federation by the artist and sculptor Charles Brennus, himself an early *SCUFiste* and lifelong fanatic of the game.

It's no accident that for the biggest prize in French rugby Brennus designed a shield, as in Asterix. For the French, the shield is the privilege of the chief. An emblem of earned dominance, it denotes the superiority of one man over another, and therefore in Gallic eyes it was something of a disaster for a historic club like the SCUF to be slipping meekly and devoid of glory into the country's Fourth Division, known with cruel French gallantry as the *Championnat d'Honneur*.

Something had to be done. The club's president and Citroën's engineering director, Bruno Martin-Neuville, proclaimed in an open meeting that the honour of the SCUF, a club once the equal of Stade Français, demanded nothing less than an immediate recovery. The answer, as it would be several years later in every professional club in Europe, was a long summer of recruitment.

From the Paris Métro club, Bruno brought in coach and Darwinist philosopher Jean-Claude Soubras, as well as half the fearsome Métro pack, known at that time throughout Paris as 'the white wolves of the Ile de France'. I don't know why, because they were old, fat, and hard as Parisian lampposts. Uniformly, they liked to play with their shirt-sleeves rolled well above their rock-like biceps, and called each other Papa. To further strengthen the pack, Bruno imported some terrifying dogs of war from the road-ends of farms near Toulouse. And he flew in Trevor Wright, from Durban in South Africa.

This was in 1992, three years before the game officially went professional. And this wasn't even a national division, but the Parisian section of the *Championnat d'Honneur*. Trevor Wright, rugby player from Natal, was suddenly also Trevor Wright, astonishingly well-paid part-time barman and long-term rent-free tenant of a vice-president (plant and engineering) of Citroën.

One of the chronic problems of amateur rugby was that it was never entirely amateur, especially in France. As early as

1907, French clubs were advertising for half-backs in the national weekly rugby paper, the *Midi-Olympique*, and burly Welsh forwards were bribed out of coal-mines to pass on their skills in the sunny south-west.

By 1931, this semi-professionalism was such an open secret that the French were banned from the Five Nations, *Le Tournoi*, and only reinstated after sixteen years of exclusion. Since that time, with France an erratic but irrepressible force in world rugby, the French and the IRB had succeeded in maintaining an uneasy truce. By 1992, the Fédération Française was allowing clubs to register two foreign players, and keeping quiet about remuneration. I had a go at full-back, and along with Trevor Wright I was offered a job in an Irish bar. Fortunately, considering what was to happen to Trevor, I declined. I already had a job, in the National Library, where I made sure that the exit to an exhibition of Toulouse-Lautrec's drawings wasn't used as an entrance.

One of the highlights of the Lautrec exhibition was a looped tape from the 1890s of Yvette Guilbert singing her trademark naughty song: *'I 'ave a leetle cat,/ I'm very fond of zat.'* Even in 1890, this was a pussy joke. It was a rugby joke in the gallery of the National Library (which was also showing, among other rugby guffaws, Lautrec's sketches of a bar known as *Le Souris*, and its resident bulldog, Bouboule, who could identify lesbians before they reached the counter and tease them with a playful nip on the ankle). Elsewhere in the city, Jean-Pierre Rives, the heroic back-row forward and ex-French rugby captain, was exhibiting a very earnest installation of abstract sculpture, in blue steel.

Paris and Parisian rugby was a constant surprise; a century

of shamateurism had done nothing to suppress its singular spirit. In fact, the illegitimacy of the payments was a large part of rugby's underground charm. At the start of the 2002 season, back in Paris, I wanted to compare our bootleg days with pro rugby as it is now, with its official and glossy façade. Could the old, anarchic spirit of French rugby remain intact?

And could I? By the Tuesday after the Saturday defeat in Glasgow, I'd made it to Paris, but moving was still problematic. *Chewing* was problematic, and sneezing a complicated torture. Congratulations, I don't think, and so another season begins.

Luckily, Paris seemed to be its usual self, the policemen smoking cigarettes, young women crying on the early-morning Métro, and two blokes in raincoats snogging on the sunlit walkway beside the Seine. The city of light had so much to offer that I wondered why, when I first came here in 1992 as a curious 24-year-old, I'd called up Mackinnon. It wasn't clear what rugby could add to all this, to the boulevards and the demoiselles and books for sale under the chalk-white mottle of plane trees.

Initially overcome by the headiness of the city, and the idea of writing a novel in Paris, I did try for a short while to manage without rugby. But I soon discovered that the artistic life has its disadvantages, including in Paris a ridiculous side which can sap the will to live. At my lowest moment in the artistic demi-monde, I met a Japanese woman in a Burberry golf-hat who painted on canvas with cheese.

'I melt it,' she said.

'I see. How interesting.'

'Then I smear it on the canvas, and as it hardens it takes a shape. The shape it takes is the subject and meaning of my painting.'

'And what shape does the cheese usually take?'

'I do a lot of cats and dogs.'

Failing at the novel (I do a lot of cats and dogs), it wasn't long before I found myself haunting the underground system, watching out for blood-stains on the front of Métro trains. I had plenty of time to observe, in a detached way, that all over Paris there are lethal electrified pits into which people are hardly ever pushed. I was even missing the duchess, and her neat observation as I staggered under shopping bags that life is so much easier when there's two of one.

I needed to get out more. In Scotland, rugby had provided a sense of identity and belonging when I'd been living in a village of twelve inhabitants. This time, it would have to offer an unlikely source of comfort and co-ordinates in a city of two and a half million. I looked a little more closely. In France, the game was *le rugby*, and an equivalent word for rugger didn't seem to exist. As on the coast of Scotland, I felt I could try it out safe from my Englishman's fear of distinctively English idiots.

In fact, it was almost a different game. I already knew from the Five Nations that nowhere in Europe was rugby as openly romantic in its ambitions. The game here represented a way of life, a way of living. It presented itself as a kind of robust but eccentric family – exactly what I needed. As for the rugby itself, after Mid-Argyll I was full of confidence, although I soon found out why my playing triumphs in Scotland had seemed so effortless. In terms of playing standard, the only way was up.

As an added incentive, and for the first time in many years, there was an advantage to being English and a rugby player. I could turn up at the SCUF with some of the reflected national dog of Brian Moore, who'd so memorably buffeted the French in the epic 1991 World Cup quarter-final at the Parc des Princes. Brian Moore was consistently earning all England some respect, and that could only help.

So I went to the SCUF hoping for stability. That was not what the SCUF had to offer, and a week later, for my debut in the French championship, I travelled to Vincennes with a new identity. From now on, I would be known by the name on my playing licence, Yves Maréchal. Or at least until my official clearance came through from the RFU in London.

Yves Maréchal was not the most conscientious of writers, but he did enjoy his rugby. It was the game, and the people – men like club president Bruno Martin-Neuville, who I rang on the morning of my first day back in Paris in 2002. He asked me where in the city I was phoning from.

I looked at my map. 'The 7th arrondissement. Rue St Dominique.'

'Lunch, then. I know a place. It's just round the corner from where you're standing.'

No matter where I was in Paris, I suspect Bruno would have had a bistro to suggest, just round the corner. And in all those other bistros, as busy as this one on the rue Surcouf, the *patron* would also have rushed over with open arms and embraced him in the doorway and addressed him fondly as *Monsieur le Président*.

Bruno Martin-Neuville is a tall, shambling man, a slouched lock-forward in a sports jacket with unkempt grey hair and the light of kindness in the blue of his eyes. He's retired from Citroën now, and has taken up building steamboats, a placid enough pastime after all that rugby. He's also learning to paraglide. He's never been married, but he tells me he's engaged again, and as the delighted *patron* sends us over some complimentary kirs, he brings me up to date with the recent history of the SCUF.

Bruno handed on the presidency in 1995, after nearly twenty years (but as long as he lives he'll be *Monsieur le Président*). He's soon shaking his impressive old head, but smiling at the same time, as he breaks bread and tells me the story of the SCUF's decline. It turns out that the start of all the trouble was 1992/3, the season I arrived and played in the team. It was the first time the SCUF had recruited, and Trevor and the old warriors from the Métro and the Toulouse dogs of war and sometimes even me, we were all being paid by a shady character called Bouvron. Nobody ever said Monsieur Bouvron. I remember him as a thick-set man in an overcoat who used to stomp into the changing room on the rare occasions we lost, and with his hands in his pockets he'd glare and tell us we didn't resemble ourselves. He'd also mention that the sponsors weren't happy, then pause significantly, meaning our handouts and free *pastis* were no longer entirely secure.

In fact, Bouvron was the only sponsor, and his money came from speculation in real estate and a special relationship with communist city councils. A year after our triumphant 1993 promotion, Bouvron was in jail, the paid players drifted away, and the SCUF tumbled out of the Third Division and kept on falling. Thankfully we were now back in the

Championnat d'Honneur, where it had all started, but even that hadn't been easy.

'But God,' Bruno says – and he does actually say *Mon Dieu*. 'Mon Dieu!' he says, shaking his head, 'but that team of '93 was unlike any other.'

We reminisce about the promotion season, when in the first leg of the deciding play-off game Soubras the coach deliberately sent the forwards steaming into the tunnel ahead of the appointed time. He was hoping they'd collide with their opponents. The men from the south-west had been so alarmed that they reasserted their south-western sense of themselves by starting a fight. In the tunnel. At number fifteen, I was last out of the changing room, and the rest of the team came tumbling back in before I'd reached the door.

Personally, I didn't play well in that game. From the changing rooms under the stand we could hear compression horns, trumpets, drums. I was determined, in the half-remembered words of big-match commentators, not to let the occasion get to me. It didn't. I was in my own world. I played like a drain.

For the return leg, away in Alsace where we had to protect a narrow lead, I decided to let it get to me. That appeared the lesson to be learnt. In the fortnight between the two matches, I nurtured a motivating vision of retired and depressed sportsmen on tractor-mowers. They drove up and down, staring wistfully at the grass with tears in their eyes, wishing they'd let the occasion get to them, once at least, or at least a little more, every time. So for the away leg I let the whole occasion get to me, the compression horns and the trumpets and drums, and played as well as I knew I ever would.

Bruno tells me I'm remembered as the full-back who never made mistakes, but personally, from my own album of memories, I recall it being a lot more zingy than that.

As for Trevor Wright, there was no news. Bruno had no idea where he was, and hadn't heard a single word since the day Trevor left, and not even then. By 1994, Trevor was still playing but also running a bar by the Panthéon. After a series of arguments with the owner, an Irishman, he'd had to leave rapidly one morning in the back of a passing van, and was never seen again. I couldn't say I was surprised.

In 1992, Trevor Wright was greatness in waiting. He was twenty or twenty-one, had already played games at scrum-half for Natal, and he could run faster, tackle harder, and dodge more sharply than any player I've ever seen. He could also kick goals. In rugby at our level, he was therefore dynamite, and within a year he was finished.

These days, he'd be making a handsome living as a professional and eating as much carbohydrate as a man can stand. In those days, Paris was allowed to ruin him. We'd sometimes meet for a quiet drink, starting at about half-past seven in the Irish bar which paid his wages and where occasionally he actually worked. The first time I did this, I made a note of the fact that I was safely home on the dot of 6.12 a.m. At the time, those extra twelve minutes seemed highly significant, as if they alone could be blamed for the too much drink, the smoking, the hours lost in the suicidal *Violin Dingue*, and the translation of entire conversations about attack dogs from French into English and back again.

Before Christmas, still unbeaten, Trevor had twice been

engaged to be married. The SCUF supporters, of whom there were literally hundreds, loved him, and against the weaker sides we used to horse around in the fun tradition of Parisian rugby exemplified by the young Jacques Tati. During his long run in the third team of the Racing Club de Paris, and not only during lulls in play, Tati the great comedian used to test out his mime routines on scowling opposition wingers. He'd catch the ball, pretend to puff his pipe, wiggle his eyebrows, and then lope hard and fast for the corner.

The rugby in Paris was often full of charm, the French quickness of thought with the ball in hand a sporting version of wit, and their liberated approach to the game is reflected in the language. The fly-half is the *ouvreur*, who opens the game, in contrast to the dour English equivalent who closes it down with a fifty-metre punt. In France, the patterns of a match have none of the rigidity of the British version, and it's a commonplace that the game begins on the wing. Defences change rapidly from solid to liquid. Stone is suddenly paper, and cut to pieces. To ribbons.

This theatrical tradition of flair and disguise can be captivating, and in 2002 I was full of the joys of French rugby as I sat swaying on the Métro on the way to training, high on a dozen oysters and a litre of Bruno's Pouilly-Fumé. It may have been the wine, but I was feeling good about my chances of survival. The cut eye from Glasgow was now a decent buttery black, but nicely fringed with reddish brown, a real shiner, making me look less like me and more like a hard case from the SCUF's mercenary past. On the negative side, on the sober side, I still couldn't lift my arms above my shoulders.

I was prepared for changes. A club like the SCUF based in

a big city like Paris has a different character and different problems to a rural, community-based club like Mid-Argyll. For a start, the SCUF play their matches at the Stade Georges Carpentier, but they don't own it. And during the week they have to find other open spaces where they can train, a growing problem for an amateur club in an era when nothing is free or even cheap, especially open spaces in the centre of capital cities. It's also in the nature of a city club to have a higher turnover of players, making it unlikely there'd be many people I recognised. It was nearly ten years since I'd last trained there, after all.

I didn't let this worry me. An adopted country boy from Lochgilphead, I was now among the HLM and concrete on the inside lining of the periphérique of southern Paris. The training wouldn't be easy, I knew that, but I shared the deep British instinct that city life was effeminate and city comforts made men soft. I'd just come from Mid-Argyll, from the hills and the sodden flood-plains. I was an honorary sheep-shagger, and as hard as nails.

A large group of men wearing natty suits and toting black-and-white SCUF bags were hanging round the gates of an all-weather football pitch. There wasn't one face I recognised. I shook absolutely everybody by the hand anyway, because that's what the French do. Not one. I'd heard from Bruno that our team of mercenaries was not particularly well viewed by the club, but there was always the second and third teams. I ought to have recognised at least half a dozen old-timers.

My earlier confidence began to slip away. Despite the black-and-white SCUF jersey I'd retrieved from my cupboard of treasured objects, it was like joining a completely new club.

53

I then found out that the championship in France doesn't start until October. As it was mid-September, it was therefore like joining a new club still involved in pre-season fitness training. This is doubly unwise.

Unlike Mid-Argyll, the SCUF have no problem with numbers. There were at least fifty people out on the gravelly floodlit surface, though I stopped counting at twenty-nine or so because we were all running round and round in circles and I was getting dizzy.

I knew there'd be trouble as soon as I saw the coaches. There were two of them, both small and bald in ironed rugby shirts, and I recognised the littler of the two from '93. Soubras had sometimes let him wet the sponges. Both of them had clipboards *and* whistles *and* stopwatches. And also a tape-measure. The senior coach, who was marginally taller, had a neatly trimmed tonsure at the back of his head, and wore long shorts over his immaculate track-suit trousers, which in turn were primly tucked into his pulled-up socks. He unfolded a camping stool on which to sit and talk (and talk and talk), while the players sat on the ground around him. We then passed the ball meaninglessly in lines of four. One direction, stop, then the other. Repeat.

Later, we ran round in a circle roughly the size of the pitch, non-stop for thirty minutes, while the coach measured the white lines with the tape-measure. This was so that he'd know how far we'd run. He could then write this down on his clipboard.

Jean-Claude Soubras used to have us one-to-one wrestling, while insulting our mothers.

At the end of training I approached Monsieur Rausch, as

the senior coach was called, and of course complimented him fulsomely on what a very fine job he appeared to be doing. I then asked him politely if by any chance I might be able to get a game on the Sunday, which is always match-day in France.

Monsieur Rausch looked at me sternly, and told me the SCUF were off for a weekend's squad fitness session and pre-season practice match at Le Touquet-Paris-Plage, not far from Calais.

'Sounds like fun. What are my chances of a game?'

He frowned and referred to a small booklet, of which he had several, and not all of them small. He then said he doubted very much whether I'd be able to play, for complex reasons of insurance.

'How complex?'

'I'll need to refer to the Federation regulations.'

'Fine,' I said, and drifted off to the showers. People in rugby were increasingly saying such things, but I was sure that after another session on Thursday it would all seem easier. In fact, only the week before Brocken had been telling me about the time he and big Davy had come over, eight or nine years ago, and Peter Mackinnon had drafted them into an over-35s match on a Sunday morning. One of the SCUF props had then whistled the Scots round the Champs Elysée and the Eiffel Tower, wherever they wanted to go.

That's what rugby was all about, and that night I went to sleep dreaming of the beautiful game, particularly in France, where college professors publish books with titles like *Dans le Temple du Dieu Rugby*. To the French, of course, that deceptive, infuriating ball, which never bounces in the expected direction, just has to be a woman. She's unreliable, desirable, valuable, dangerous. She prefers a strong man with strong arms who knows how to hold her tight. But if he doesn't, if he takes her for granted, she'll soon move on to another . . . *putain*!

The French are essential to the global health of rugby union. They constantly bring fresh and surprising perspectives to the game, saving it from a slow death as an arcane celebration between former British colonies. They can also beat the All Blacks. Abdelatif Benazzi, for example, the immovable French forward with sixty-five caps (and twelve for Morocco), has personally beaten New Zealand the same number of times as the four home nations put together. I have a theory about this. The French can't be intimidated by sledging, by those gritty All-Black vowel sounds which remind the Brits of generations of All Black invincibles. The French don't understand a word. They just get on with it and win, and remain the best living proof that the game can transcend its Empire origins – we owe all our ambitions to them.

On the Wednesday morning I decided to track down Trevor Wright. In some ways, rugby friendships are superficial. At least that's how it seems, until I realised I had absolute confidence that if only I could find him, it'd be a hoot to speak to Trevor. And not just Trevor, or the white wolves of the Ile de France ('*Salut Papa!*'), but old friends and team-mates from all my clubs. I know them, and they know me. In some detail. And even those whose part in the battle I respected less, I still respect for being in the battle at all. If nothing else, they have the right intentions.

Admittedly, I was as close to Trevor as anyone on that

team of 1992/3. I was the only other English speaker, and even though at that time my French was imperfect, it was cheerful and always as fast as I could possibly make it. I was therefore the obvious choice as interpreter for Trevor, who never learnt a word. In the changing room before games, Soubras would rage and spit about the survival of the fittest, and destiny as strength through struggle. Trevor would lean over and ask me in a whisper what it was that Soubras was getting so worked up about, and I'd whisper back that it wasn't important.

Soubras would then come over and shake me violently by the shoulders, while fixing me fiercely in the eye.

'Does Trevor understand? Does Trevor understand?'

'He understands everything,' I'd say, as Soubras banged my head several times against the wall. 'Jean-Claude, really, let go. Everything is very clear to him.'

Trevor understood perfectly that it was his job, week in, week out, to win the game for us. Basically he couldn't win a game on his own. But if we were solid, he could do the rest.

Along with its charm, the French game can also be brutal, and French rugby has had to steal from English to accommodate the notion of *le fair play*. There is no equivalent word in the French vocabulary, and as the SCUF's best player, Trevor Wright was often knocked to bits. As well as being the finest broken-play runner ever to wait for me behind the posts, where he'd lob me the ball to gift me a score, he was also the first player I saw injected in the dressing room before a match. The needle went in the side of his knee, right behind the knee-cap. He was the club's investment. It was a crucial play-off game. *Bah voilà.*

However, not all the drugs in French rugby are in the trainer's bag (more commonly known as *la pharmacie*). In French-speaking countries, the game of rugby is cool. Cool in the rock-star sense. At a time when rugby and rugger were two of the most unfashionable words in the English language, in France *le rugby* was darkly seductive, a virile sport associated with manly combat, love of good food, and festivals (the riotous *bandas* of the south-west). The *Midi-Olympique* used to report on rugby in the winter and bull-fighting in the summer, *le rugbyman* as a winter matador, El Cordobes with the ears of the bull held aloft in his outstretched hands. He is *rugbyman*, a cartoon-book super-hero, and the clubs are full of *rugbymen*, entire graphic novels of them.

The French rugby player carries none of the rugger-bugger baggage which weighs so heavily, often with good reason, on the rounded shoulders of the English. He is an upright and heroic participant in a noble and dangerous enterprise which requires great courage and sacrifice of the self, and quite commonly also long hair and soft drugs and a two-tone VW camper van.

Ten years ago, it wasn't unusual for a clubhouse bar to empty while the young bloods from both teams reconvened on the benches in a steam-filled changing room. They would then inhale, and giggle through the nastier highlights of that day's game. In the etiquette of the day, the away team provided the dope. In some ways, I felt sorry for Trevor. He didn't stand a chance. This wasn't rugby as he knew it in South Africa. This was so new and bold and cool, it was almost writing.

In Paris, rugby provided all the experiences I'd fantasised

as a dividend of published fiction: long lunches in restaurants, cigarettes, late nights in dives, *pastis*, heated conversations about the essence of existence, and passing relationships with a huge range of interesting people, including François the front-row forward who tended the Shakespeare garden in the Bois du Boulogne. In Paris, even the ugly municipal gardeners have a series of breathtaking foreign girlfriends, the pick of the *jeune filles au pairs* who spend so much time wheeling rich French babies around public parks. As a mark of tender affection, François would sew his current girlfriend's national flag on the back of his denim work-jacket.

The last time I saw Trevor Wright, he was frazzled in a hospital bed in Montmartre with his entire right leg in plaster. He had his own room, but his main entertainment was zapping the TV in the room across the corridor. He was also newly engaged, to a Danish girl. At least he thought she was Danish, or possibly Greek. It was so hard to tell.

In 2002 I had no idea where to find him, but unlike ten years earlier there was now a web of information which stretched worldwide. I asked the Internet, which knows everything, to find me *Trevor Wright*, *Rugby*, and *South Africa*. Up came the results, and just from the heading I knew I had my man.

Natal Sharks Magazine Oct/Nov 1999. Trevor Wright is probably one of the most underrated rugby players around, and many believe had he not gone to France for three years he would have made it into the . . .

In a tortuous route involving the secretaries and coaches of various South African clubs, all of whom were only too happy to oblige, I eventually ended up with a number for Trevor. I rang him up.

'Rich, mate!'

It was the end of his day at an office at the bottom of a different continent, where Trevor sells windows. Not double-glazing, he tells me, just glass. And after marvelling at the fact that we're both still playing ('I tell you, mate, it's for the hot chicks that hang round the club'), I get some idea of what life was like as a travelling undercover rugby pro in 1992.

At that time in South Africa, Trevor was a Natal B regular and the Natal Under-21 Player of the Year. But he fancied a crack at Europe, and had a friend with a contact in France who was always looking for talented players. He was put in touch with the SCUF, who offered him 6,000 francs a month, about £150 a week including accommodation. It sounded good. As well as training and playing for the SCUF, Trevor worked three or four evenings a week in the Irish bar. That was one of the best bits.

'I like to keep busy,' Trevor says. 'Always have. And it was a good way to meet people.' Yes, I'd heard that, even at the time.

At first he lived with Bruno, but later, when Bruno lost count of the visitors to his spare room, Trevor moved to a ten-foot-square studio in the 4th arrondissement. He loved it, and the SCUF looked after him. When he had the knee injury he reminded me it wasn't only a single injection before the match, but two more at half-time. At half-time! But at least afterwards, and after his stint in the hospital in Montmartre, he was sent to recuperate at a specialist sports clinic somewhere warmer in the south.

The end of Trevor's SCUF career wasn't quite so simple. He played most of the next season, but with diminishing returns as his fitness and motivation faded. He was sent off for retaliation in a match of little importance. Then he had his disagreements with the Irish owner of the bar, who made accusations about disappearing stock which Trevor hotly disputes. After an altercation, during which various threats were made, Trevor left the bar vowing never to submit to physical intimidation. But luckily his brother was coming through the next morning in a camper van, and he picked Trevor up on his way to Germany.

'It was all a bit messy,' Trevor concludes thoughtfully.

He eventually made it back to South Africa, where he played in the national First Division with Harlequins, and now for the South Coast Warriors. He's paid a hundred rand a game, and a car. A hundred rand is an official wage cap, but Trevor tells me off the record that all the clubs in the division pay more. I tell him I'm not a journalist so there's no off the record. Then ask him if he has any regrets about his time in France.

'Yes,' he says. 'And no.'

If he'd stayed in Durban he might have played Super 12 for the Natal Sharks. But there again, in Paris he had a lot of fun, and met a lot of people. I know what he's saying; these are the vague, often repeated, immeasurable rugby virtues.

'I also regret not saying goodbye to Bruno,' Trevor tells me. 'I mean in the proper way. I never said thank you. You know what I mean.'

I promise I'll do it for him, while thinking how different Trevor's life could have been. It's worth comparing his strange and chaotic story with someone in a similar position today, now that rugby's money is safely out in the open. I'm in Paris, so I get in touch with South African Brian Liebenburg, centre three-quarter at Paris club Stade Français, recent French champions and finalists in the European Cup.

Brian is amenable, a helpful professional. He's twenty-two years old and his playing background is almost identical to Trevor's. He played for Natal under-21s, had a single game in the Currie Cup, but after missing out on a Super 12 contract with the Sharks he left South Africa for Italy. In Italy he was spotted by Diego Dominguez, the Argentinian-Italian with an odd nervous twitch which sends his neck into spasm, as if he's constantly flicking back his hair. Diego recommended Brian to Grenoble. At Grenoble, he started on a basic monthly wage of 20,000 francs (about £500 a week, or more than three times as much as Trevor). He then followed Dominguez to Stade Français, for a 'considerable' increase in salary.

This is at exactly the same age and background and talents as Trevor Wright, only ten years later. Brian Liebenburg was also offered a limitless number of French lessons, to reduce the danger of getting engaged by mistake. He didn't even have to work in an Irish bar, though he does have to abstain from parties and train Monday to Thursday, Saturday and Sunday, with Friday his solitary day off. That's five days a week of weights in the morning, and skills and drills in the afternoons.

'Is it a good experience?' I ask him, hardly convinced.

'It's up to the individual,' he replies sagely. 'Though I do sometimes manage to get out with some of the older players.'

I imagine young Brian Liebenburg in the midnight madness

of the *Violin Dingue* with a heavyweight Stade group including Peter de Villiers and Fabien Gaulthier and twitchy Dominguez himself. Ten years ago, you'd hope he came back alive. Now, you hope he comes back drunk, just a little bit, for the sake of old times rugger.

Despite this I'm in no doubt, comparing the abilities and careers of the two players, that Brian is getting the better deal. He's able to exploit his superior talent as a player of rugby for money, and knows he'll have something in the bank at the end of it. At any rate, it's unlikely he'll be fleeing Paris at dawn with a passing relative in a van. In this instance, rugby is providing this type of player with a much better chance at life than he'd ever have had with rugger. Brian's well-being is protected by the attitudes and knowledge of professionalism, while Trevor paid for his glory in blood and drugs and broken ligaments. Though he wouldn't want it forgotten that the rugger was loads of fun.

I'd like to talk it through with both of them, in more detail and with more jokes, but for that we really need a broad table, and a big meal, and some special *pichets* of wine chosen for the occasion by an acknowledged expert like Bruno. Nice as it is to talk on the phone, rugby works best at the level of real life.

Thursday night training is in the north of Paris, at a municipal stadium with a grass pitch inside a running-track. I recognise Lionel Busson and Jerome Hospital. They used to be law students. Now they're both married lawyers in their thirties. How did that happen? We promise to talk later, but first there's thirty minutes of semi-controlled tackling among the backs. The point of this exercise is to hone grudges for later, when we play thirty minutes' full contact and really develop those enmities to the full. I'd forgotten that every week during training in France, as well as whanging the ball about with abandon, they also have a full-contact match.

As the teams line up (and somehow I'm in at scrum-half again) I'm reminded that there's a throat-drying seriousness about rugby, the game itself, the match on match-day. This has a lot to do with the risk of serious physical injury. There *is* the larking about, but usually only afterwards.

In the first few minutes of this unexpected and abrasive practice match, I get it wrong. I try not to try too hard, conscious that I'm a visitor, an amateur, a dilettante. But everyone else is trying like fuck, and it turns out that city life is not effeminate and that the advance of material comforts has not made men soft. I'm slammed back into the middle of last week, where I see again that this isn't the time for self-deprecation. It's time to get stuck in, a weekly rite of passage in which I reassert my manliness and solid self-reliance.

In France, this assertion of manliness is closely bound up with the concept of *castagne*, of the size of the fight in the man. A rugby match is perceived to be noble and improving like the medieval tournaments which originated in France in the eleventh century. These allowed knights to display skill and courage with blunted weapons in mock battles known as *mêlées*, the same word used today in rugby for scrums. And in medieval tournaments, too, the contestants sometimes got hurt.

Pinetree Colin Meads, the sixties All Black captain who trained with a sheep under each arm, judged that the French were the most brutal of all the nations, even worse than the Springboks. Violence has always been part of their game, and I played my first matches on French soil as a schoolboy on tour to Toulouse in 1984. I was grateful for that early introduction to French rugby: the fantastic kit, the Wallaby balls, the dugouts, the floodlights. That particular French habit of standing side-on in team photos with crossed arms while looking down your nose. But it made me laugh when I read, much later, that 'total rugby and the idea that a prop could act like a centre was introduced by Toulouse in 1985'.

When we went, in December 1984, there was still the idea that a prop could act like a pathological lunatic. Late into the night after the game, the Toulouse junior front row were binding together and rushing aluminium garage doors with their heads. I'd never seen anything like it. It was brilliant.

In recent years, the French have been trying to calm themselves down. They want to avoid the kind of spiral of violence which led in 1927 to a player being killed in the deep-south derby between Quilan and Perpignan. Another player was killed in a match in 1930, and it perhaps wasn't a coincidence that the Five Nations ban would quickly follow. Shamateurs, yes. Intensely frightening, even more so.

And that's just the players. Before a local grudge match at Mont de Marsan, the great Michel Crauste had his cat returned to his home in a bag. In pieces. And the last time statistics were collated for foul play at all levels of the French championship, 18.6% of infringements were due to aggression by spectators.

Yet after the full-contact training, and after a final thirty minutes' mindless running in circles round the athletics track,

Monsieur Rausch in his ironed track-suit and long stripy socks, with his whistle and his stopwatch and his clipboard, was adamant that I still couldn't play on Sunday. For reasons, 'as previously stated', of insurance.

'It would be unreasonable to play,' he added sniffily.

Of course it would be unreasonable to play, you moron, and dangerous, too. It was French rugby. People get hurt. People *die*. What else did he think I was expecting?

He hid behind his handbook and the safety of his clipboard. There was no persuading him. So I grumped off with Lionel and Jerome to a café by Notre Dame, and for a while they did little to alleviate my gloom. They ordered salad. I couldn't believe it.

And then, joshing me on the shoulder, they ordered chicken and chips and several jugs of extra-strong beer. You have to laugh. We remembered the promotion match all those years ago and Frédéric Butez (artist, photographer, centre three-quarter) dancing on the roof of the bus when we stopped at a *péage* on the autoroute. He'd scored two cracking tries that day, but then the police arrived. We should all have been arrested.

I also asked them about Trevor, and the legend of Trevor Wright remains intact. Especially as a bar-manager, Jerome tells me; Trevor knew how to make a fellow *SCUFiste* welcome. I don't mention his amazement at the mysterious disappearance of the bar-stock.

Not that I wanted to go to Le Touquet anyway. Frankly, Monsieur Rausch, I didn't fancy two days of running in circles being stopwatched and clipboarded just to get a pre-season game. However, if I was barred from playing at the weekend, I'd have to make alternative plans. First, though, I shouldn't forget where I was. This was Paris. I decided to go out for lunch.

Jean Hospital suggested the 9th arrondissement. He knew a bar and a decent place to eat. Jean was a prop in the SCUF team of the late sixties and early seventies, when the other prop was his brother Michel, who in 1995 took over the presidency from Bruno, who played in the same team. Together, the front-row brothers Jean and Michel were known in their playing days as *les Hospitaux*. My friend the lawyer from last night, Jerome Hospital, is Jean's nephew and Michel's son, and Jerome's son is Victor Hospital, but he's only twelve months old so he's yet to pull on the jersey. Though apparently he *looks* like a front-row Hospital.

Jean is retired now and writing a book called *Le Rugby et le SCUF, 1895–2002: Une certaine idée du sport*. We go to the bar, and there are SCUF stickers on the espresso machines, and a room out the back where Jean settles his prop-forward's body at a narrow table and buys me a magnificent lunch. He tells me the history of the SCUF. It's important, he says. The history of the SCUF *is* the SCUF.

The club was founded in 1895 by Charles Brennus. Up until 1914, in the glory years, the SCUF played in front of 10,000 people at the Stade Colombes, a stadium they owned and which would later become the home of the French national team. Then the war. By 1918, the SCUF had four surviving players. They had no team, and therefore no income. They sold Colombes to the Racing Club, and since then the SCUF has never owned its own ground.

Ironically, this may have saved us. In the last ten years, many of the Parisian clubs with their own grounds have disappeared. They were unlucky: they found they had something to mortgage to pay for players. They did that, and nothing much came of it but losing the money, and now the grounds and the clubs are gone – the ASPP (the former gendarmerie club), CASG (merged with Stade Français), Métro (merged with the Racing Club) and the ASPTT – all gone.

I know this because I sat at lunch for many hours with Jean Hospital, enjoying the food he recommended, drinking the wine he selected, talking rugby.

These days the SCUF still play their matches at the Stade Georges Carpentier, which is fitting, as Carpentier the dashing heavyweight boxer once played rugby for the SCUF. When he wasn't boxing Jack Dempsey or powering the SCUF at scrums, Georges 'The Orchid Man' Carpentier was having a long affair with the little sparrow, the Parisian chanteuse Edith Piaf. I'd only recently listened to her greatest hits on the old valve gramophone where I was staying, and I could understand if sometimes, when Edith came down to breakfast in her dressing-gown, humming with tears in her eyes 'A Quoi Ça Sert L'Amour?', Georges looked at her, not without tenderness, and said, 'I really don't know, love, I'm off to the rugby.'

Anyway, she always let him go, and as an example to all women everywhere with rugby-playing partners, Edith famously never regretted anything.

After the First World War, the SCUF couldn't recover their eminence. Their most recent brush with the elite was a brief visit to the Second Division in the 1980s, when Mackinnon was invited over. The SCUF had, however, provided three presidents to the FFR, and also Dr Martin, president of the SCUF 1951–67 and team doctor to the folklore French teams of the fifties and sixties. Jean Hospital has some admirable black-and-white photographs of Dr Martin nonchalantly stitching head-wounds on the side of the pitch at Colombes. He has one hand on the player's head, the other tugging on the needle, and a lit cigarette in his mouth.

Jean Hospital is a player with a sense of gratitude to the game, an awareness of debts unpaid. He credits Dr Martin with introducing him to sturdy Anglo-Saxon attitudes to sport. He means fair play, fraternisation, and drinking to excess. He's also forever grateful to the doctor for organising games away in the mornings of the misty Five Nations of long ago. To Blackrock College Dublin (fourteen pitches!), to Lasswade, to Porthcawl, often staying in the French team hotel just one floor above heroes like Rives and Cholley and Maso, who of course weren't a patch on the giants of an earlier age like Prat and Spanghero and the heavenly Boniface brothers, the gods, the Thors and Mercurys of all French rugby nostalgics and dreamers.

And it occurs to me as we talk that I love the French niceties at table. While lunching, the host in France takes his validating sip of wine, even at the start of the third bottle. Oh yes, he says, lightly smacking his lips, that one too seems just about perfect.

As for the future, Jean has confidence in the SCUF, but not in rugby. The SCUF can raise four teams, but then have no one to play against. They have a thriving Ecole de Rugby, and this year the under-14s beat everyone out of sight, including Stade Français. Since the error of the season of mercenaries, 70% of the SCUF first XV now come through the juniors, but the Federation aren't making survival any easier. The reserves play twelve a side, for example, after an unpopular federal edict which few of the clubs understand. Why twelve? In another unilateral edict, the Federation has declared that first teams must play their matches with a minimum of four replacements. It's hardly surprising, Jean says, that many clubs have decided to reduce numbers to a group of twenty-five players and no more.

'That's not a club!' he splutters. 'It's a team!'

The SCUF have already tried and failed with recruitment, and financially they can't compete. They may soon have to pay players simply to stand still, but the club's entire working budget is 40,000 euros. This is less than the yearly salary of one so-so player, and a lot less than today's equivalent for a barnstormer like Brian Liebenburg, or Trevor Wright. Even the dapper Monsieur Rausch comes at a price: £4,000 a year for two evenings a week and Sunday. Even at this level, no one would coach for less.

Not surprisingly, the SCUF are attempting to promote a different model for survival. It will be familiar to anyone, like Jean Hospital, with a knowledge of the early days of the game. In a city like Paris, rugby struggles to exploit the sense of ritual which unites men who belong to the same local environment, the same provincial community. Instead, it can turn to an ideal of sportsmanship, revisiting those *rugbyman* origins which once privileged sociability over belonging to the same class or town, or age group.

It's a distinction not unlike the one between rugby and rugger. Denis Lalanne, author of the finest ever rugby tour book, *Le Grand Combat du XV de France*, identifies the two versions of the French game. There is *le neo-rugby*, a game played by professionals in the market economy of global sport. And then there's *le rugby bohème* (nothing as prosaic as *rugger*), and this is the game played by the rest of us. It's rugby as a morality, a way of living, and my lunch with Jean is not a pleasant dividend from my former association with the SCUF. This spontaneous generosity is an expression of the club's philosophy, now and for ever. Towards the end of the third bottle of wine, looking through old SCUF photos of many men in moustaches, I think truly that the SCUF is a grand club, a great club, historically among the finest band of men on the planet.

Unusually for me in September – in fact any time between September and April – I had nothing planned for Saturday afternoon. The SCUF were in Le Touquet-Paris-Plage having their times for running in circles recorded by M. Rausch. Stade Français were away at Grenoble. Hankering for some action, I decided on a nostalgic visit to the Parc.

After the soccer World Cup in '98, with the gleaming Stade de France beckoning from the other side of Paris, French rugby deserted the Parc des Princes. As a rugby stadium, the Parc had developed a formidable reputation as one of the toughest places in the world to come and play. It was always the 'cauldron' of the Parc des Princes, the *chaudron*, the hot place. Partly this was because of its two concrete tiers, both of which bounce the noise back to the crowd, and presumably the players as well. It was also the difference of the pitch, which was hard, and the grass, which was short, and the balls, which were rounder and brown with black tips. And the players too, of course, who were sweaty and psychotic, and that was just for the anthems.

The Parc des Princes isn't used for rugby any more. It's now home to the Paris Saint-Germain association football team. I rang the box-office, and as luck would have it that Saturday there was an evening match between PSG and Strasbourg. I therefore discussed buying a ticket with the friendly man at the end of the phone. He asked me where I wanted to sit, but as the last football match I paid to see was Swindon v. Swansea in 1983, I didn't really know.

'The middle, maybe,' I suggested. 'Or the end. What's the middle like?'

For that match at Swindon's County Ground, Dad and me and Tim were standing in the away supporters' end. We weren't regulars, and it must have been a busy day in the season, like Boxing Day. At some point during the game, an injured Swansea fan was lifted down over our heads to the goal-line. He was bleeding from a face-wound, and he dripped on us as he did on everyone else below him, but he was still clutching his match programme and screaming his heart out for Swansea. Down at the Town End, jubilant and scuffling teenagers were led away one at a time at intervals of about ten minutes, or as soon as the police could get there.

'It's your ticket. Where would you *like* to sit?'

I didn't want to get involved in any fighting. Did they have fighting at French First Division football matches? I'd gone out almost every Saturday for the last fifteen years for a kind of stylised fight, and now I was faced with a soccer match and was frightened of going. Being a rugby man, of course, I overcame that fear and pushed on anyway. I cleared my throat.

'I don't know. Where would *you* sit?'

'Well, personally,' the very nice and mild-sounding telephone operator said, 'I like a bit of atmosphere.'

In Paris the first time round, I discovered there were various ways of being a man. Recently, those variations have increasingly become an acceptable field of interest. In fact, during my 2002 week in Paris, many of the cinemas were showing Nick Hornby's *Comme un Garçon* starring Hugh Grant, a film about a handsome French waiter with a nice life and a beautiful girlfriend who feels compelled to visit drive-by prostitutes for blow-jobs.

No, it isn't really; it's much less interesting than that. But if Hugh Grant was one conundrum, and Nick Hornby another, there remained more reliable role models like Rhys Kelly, working with his hands and fixing stuff. Then there was Trevor Wright, heroically picking from five different girls who'd wait for him outside his Irish bar at closing time (or so Jerome Hospital assures me, and he's a lawyer so it must be true). It seemed that not all men were the same, not even all rugby players, and I took advantage of my free Saturday to see a Robert Rauschenburg exhibition at the little-known Musée Maillol. Actually.

Rauschenburg's art is the scavenge of bits and scraps, which he then tacks together. It's not as interesting as it sounds in the listings magazine, so I search through for

73

something else. For purely aesthetic reasons, I choose another exhibition in another gallery: *The Nude in Contemporary Czech Photography*. Which is exactly what it says on the tin, and the photos involve much exercise of what art and cinema critics call the male gaze. I honestly don't think we can help it. In any case, by about half-past three my male gaze was elsewhere in a bar called Le Recrutement, watching Canal+ and the second half of Mont de Marsan against Toulouse.

Unlike Lochgilphead, Paris is a rugby town and the bar had four screens, all of them showing the match. I took my place at the zinc, and with the score at 35–6 to Stade Toulousain, the ladies behind the counter started dancing half-turns with raised arms while trilling strange, Spanish-sounding songs.

They encouraged me to join them, the union of rugby union in action, and it was some time before I escaped into the warm Parisian evening. I stretched my shoulders and checked my map. Then, before setting out for the Parc des Princes, I stopped at a phone-box and rang my friends and family. I told them where I was going and how much I loved them. Yes, Mum, I'm wearing my running shoes. I know I might need to run. No, Mum, and I'm sure I'll be fine. And then I set out for the Parc.

On my way, and fresh from celebrating Toulouse's victory with strangers, I allowed myself to wonder whether rugby was inherently superior to all other games. But in particular to football, association football, soccer. This debate has been going on, mostly in whispers, ever since the separation of Britain's original winter ball-games into two codes in the third quarter of the nineteenth century. More often than not, the rugby fraternity has taken the moral high ground, confident that our version of the game is something special. If this attitude was limited to Britain it could be dismissed as upper-class posturing, along with civility and the stiff upper lip. However, it's interesting to see that as the game spread to France, its perceived values travelled with it.

Even in the shamateur years, the money was secondary. In another of Lalanne's engaging rugby books, *Le Temps des Bonis*, he elegantly repulses British attacks on paid French players by citing a meeting between Horatio Nelson and Admiral Surcouf, somewhere in the Indian Ocean. Nelson accuses the French of knowing only how to fight for money. The English, on the other hand, fight for honour.

'Monsieur,' replies the haughty French admiral, 'people will only fight for what they do not already have.'

French rugby had honour to spare. The game required it and created it, and in the south-west rugby embodied not only honour but unity, courage, loyalty, all the positive values of community. In Paris, it added a kind of artistic freedom to the mix, self-expression and poetry to soften the menace. This was best displayed by the great Racing Club teams of the eighties and early nineties, who once drank champagne at half-time during the bruising final of a national championship.

'Even in Paris, where you have theatre and cinema and jazz and literature,' Franck Mesnel has said, 'rugby also exists.'

Mesnel played at centre for the Racing Club and France. When his playing career came to an end he founded Eden Park, an upmarket clothing boutique named after the stadium in New Zealand where France won a momentous World Cup semi-final against Australia. Franck initially sold fancy rugby shirts, with the distinctive values of rugby sewn into his added-value brand. There are now more than fifty Eden Park shops in thirteen countries, all branded with photos of the Racing Club, old leather rugby balls, international match programmes. Eden Park has moved on from rugby shirts, but the branding remains. They sell tailored menswear. This spring, they'll be launching a range of Eden Park kitchen implements.

Now. Franck Mesnel played some good rugby, and he was central to the Racing Club mythology. But Franck. Franck. It wasn't all just for the selling of an egg-whisk, was it, Franck? Was it? A spatula imbued with the distinctive spirit and added value of more than a century of our special game. Oh, Franck.

Perhaps no sport is superior to any other, and it's more helpful to see sporting differences as variant maps of the mind. The secret to falling in love with a game is to find the sport which best maps the inside of yours. Some of us need external co-ordinates to an instinct for honour and fair play. At the same time, I also think of life in terms of confrontation and sporadic bursts of intense activity. I can relate to the importance of defence. There's the true-seeming unpredictability of rugby, and on my own personal mind-map the world is marked as a dangerous place, best controlled by co-operating with others. It's also possible in rugby, occasionally, to rest and to hide. And at the end of all that mind-mapping, I often like to forget orienteering altogether for a good laugh among humorous people who also like to drink too much.

In that sense, at least, sporting spectators have an

advantage over participants. They can do their drinking beforehand. As I walked past Princess Diana's underpass at Alma Marceau, the crowds heading towards the Parc were beginning to swell, young men in red-and-blue PSG shirts taking over the pavements on a warm Paris evening. In no time at all I realised that the Coca-Cola corporation is sadly deluded. In Paris like everywhere else it's Eat Football, Sleep Football, Drink Beer. And lots of it.

I've seen the Boks at the Parc, and my final visit was to see the Welsh. I took a girl who laughed at the over-sized leeks and daffodils, and then cried when the Welsh supporters, whose players were visibly smaller and less athletic, filled the stadium's harsh concrete bowl with the hwyl of 'Land of My Fathers'. The hopeless glory of all that sung hope was as rousing a moment as I've ever experienced in a stadium. It had nothing to do with the match.

I was about to experience something similar, because these days, with the PSG at the Parc, no one in their right mind can think the game on the pitch nearly as interesting as events going off in the stands. My nice telephone friend from the box-office, who personally liked a bit of atmosphere with his football, had found me a seat in the home curve of the stadium right at the top of the second tier. I was more or less opposite where the English backs had whacked Blanco in the first minute of the 1991 World Cup quarter-final. It was a mark of respect, Serge.

Up here, I was also about ten seats from the outside edge of the PSG Ultras, the mob of Parisian hooligans whose motif is a straight-on view of clenched knuckles. Fortunately, the Ultras were caged in, or I was caged in. In any case, there was a fence between us. Welcome to the Parc des Princes. At my first ever big soccer match, now, I remembered being a teenager at my first ever big rock concert (Motorhead, as it happens), with no idea what came next or what I was supposed to be doing. But whatever it was, I was clenched and self-conscious about doing it wrong. I was a white middle-class rugby player from England, and unlike many of my peers I'd never chosen the football stands as an adopted habitat. Among the more established categories of football followers, there are also many mild boys who regret going to private school. They now love soccer, with a passion.

I wasn't one of them, and I was back in all the worst bits of Swindon against Swansea, except instead of the County Ground this was Paris and the Parc des Princes. The Parc keeps noise in, and the noise was building as I discovered the main advantage of being right at the top of the second tier. No one could throw anything down on me from above, like paper darts or cigarette-ends or smouldering roaches. The bomb of choice was the burning programme. The complimentary programmes were thoughtfully supplied in advance, tucked behind every seat, so all the supporters needed to add was the flame. They look after their own at PSG.

I missed the kick-off, because to my right and also to my left, in the Kop de Boulogne, there was an eruption of purple and orange flares, the smoke hazing the pitch and obscuring the game for at least ten minutes. I sat there blinded and braced to run, just about able to make out the magnesium core of the waving flares. And I thought, by golly, they didn't use to do this on their biannual jolly to the Parc, not the committee men from the Old Caterhamians.

The PSG supporters went mad. They were off their heads, and encouraged in their frenzy by two or three shirtless orchestrating imps. These lads were even barmier than the rest, and didn't face the game on the pitch for one second. They stood up on the edge of the parapet between tiers, and danced and megaphoned and banged on drums. At a given signal, they paused for fifteen minutes, then they went insane again for another forty-five. The sport they loved wasn't football but the fervour of the mob; that was the map of the inside of their minds, which personally I found quite scary. Wanting to be objective, remembering why I was here, I tried to spot the difference between the Parc now and the Parc then.

For the rugby, they never had huge reinforced steel barriers to separate the supporters. I'm just saying. And however modern and up-to-date pro rugby may become, I can't imagine an ordinary Saturday league match at Welford Road containing so much nervosity and menace as the PSG supporters can generate at the Parc. The cauldron is still a hot place; it's also an evil pit. Three weeks later, for a home game against Olympique Marseilles, the Parc was allocated 2,000 uniformed riot police. Forty-two Ultras were arrested for carrying weapons, including metal bars, bottles, and chains.

Back at the game, the Parisians scored their third goal shortly after the Strasbourg fans set fire to their seats, effectively ending the match as a contest. Alone among the home supporters, I wanted Strasbourg to score, just to see the reaction, but then I felt the people around me suspicious of what I was thinking. It wasn't a comfortable sensation, so I cheered when the crowd cheered, even though the game itself was hardly compelling. Maybe it was too easy a win, and I'm no judge of soccer quality, but that Ronaldinho looked like one day he might come to something.

Otherwise, I wasn't captivated by this other code of football, the kicking and dribbling code, the diving and play-acting code. I'm a generally sane, curious human being, and therefore found the crowd much more interesting than the football. Admittedly, I do spend a lot of time on my own, inside behind a desk, but PSG had two LeRoys playing (Laurent and Jerome), and I loved it every time 40,000 stoned, drunk Parisians bayed out madly for 'LeRoy! LeRoy!', pronounced in the way of the French, '*Le roi! Le roi!*'

Right until the end, shirtless, sweating, in the sick purple haze of the flares, the PSG imp-spirits with their megaphones exhorted the Parisian faithful. You'd have to have been desensitised for quite some time to think that the match is of anywhere near comparable intensity, interest, or importance. This show is not on television. The cameras deliberately avoid lingering, and that's the secret of its excitement. It's not on the TV. The drugs and the burning bombs and the metal bars are not in the shops, or in an advert near you. It's an unmediated experience, and it's breeding and living in the Parc des Princes.

Thankfully.

I'd thought beforehand that football was all Mastercard and David Beckham, the pampered and sponsored rubbish I'd seen on *Match of the Day*. But in the crowd it's better than that. You have to be there. Like in scrums and under rucks, and on unmediated sports fields everywhere. They can't take that away, at least not yet.

At the end of the match, the PSG players walked off the pitch without any acknowledgement of the madness they'd nominally inspired. Not even a wave. One of the Strasbourg players ran over to the away fans, who were hopping about to avoid stewards brandishing fire extinguishers, and threw them his sweaty shirt.

With the SCUF in Le Touquet-Paris-Plage, if I'd been allowed, I'd have spent this evening preparing for tomorrow's match. I'd have had an early night, possibly. Although I wouldn't have started Sunday's game, not after only a single week's training, out of loyalty to old times Rausch would have named me among the replacements. On a breezy seaside Sunday afternoon I could easily imagine the score reaching something like Le Touquet 13 SCUF 0, with about five minutes of the match remaining. I'd still be on the sidelines, nervy, waiting, until suddenly the club as a kind of living organism would realise how much it had missed me, not just in this match, but in every match of every season for the past ten years.

Rausch lets slip a wry smile and says, 'What the hell!' He throws down his clipboard and untucks his track-suit from his socks. He sends me on. I immediately catch the ball in open play and jink and dodge and sprint and score. The kicker's been hopeless all afternoon, so I also pop over the conversion. Le Touquet 13 SCUF 7. For nostalgic reasons, the next time I have the ball I indulge in a little horseplay in the comic tradition of Jacques Tati. I evade a tackler or two by pretending to be blown this way and that by the gusting breeze. I then catch a whisper passed from player to player that I ought to be elected trainer. However, as it happens, I've already been spotted by the wily Diego Dominguez. He waves and calls out to me from behind the posts, flicking his hair back and begging me to sign for the Stade, but under the bright sea-skies of Le Touquet I have to say sorry, sorry Diego, but I've a Nobel Prize to win, and in literature that takes a lifetime of unswerving commitment.

I continue to toy with the opposition, wondering whether to score those winning seven points, and one of their larger players is not amused. He's charging straight at me. I'm about to be whacked and buried at the bottom of a ruck. It occurs to me, as I suddenly realise there's nowhere left to dodge, that rugby is hard, and dangerous. Without the mandatory FFR insurance, I could possibly be about to suffer long-term catastrophic neck trauma, or permanent injury to the brain as its soft tissues are bounced against the skull. At any moment I could be among the 70% of rugby players with a damaged cervical spinal cord to suffer permanent neurological deficit. Complete tetraplegia.

Monsieur Rausch and his booklets and the mean FFR regulations would therefore have been right all along. And then I'd be sorry.

Radley College, Abingdon, 1983/4

'Through sport, boys acquire virtues which no books can give them, not merely daring and endurance, but, better still, temper, self-restraint, fairness, honour, unenvious approbation of another's success, and all that "give and take" of life which stand a man in good stead when he goes forth into the world, and without which, indeed, his success is always maimed and partial.'

Charles Kingsley

Rugby puts hairs on your chest. It makes you a better man, a better person. This belief in rugby union as a character builder, a proven and reliable man-maker, has been a part of the game since its very earliest days. To understand why, we have to go back to school, to the public schools of the mid-nineteenth century.

The ancient and venerable private schools, such as Winchester (est. 1382) and Charterhouse (est. 1611) preferred the simpler version of football called soccer, as did the common people, and they cheerfully carried on playing it. The new Victorian public schools, the parvenus and arrivistes, were less confident of their social status. They therefore adopted the more exclusive form of football pioneered at Rugby (est. 1567), precisely because it wasn't soccer.

There were alternatives, and more convenient ones. As well as the variant form of football played at Rugby, there were others at Shrewsbury (est. 1552), Harrow (est. 1571), and Eton (est. 1440). It wasn't even as if the rules or equipment of these other games were prohibitive: all you needed for the Eton game was a wall. Despite this, the new public schools seized on the all-handling, all-scrumming version from Rugby, which as well as not being soccer had other distinct advantages.

It kept a large number of boys safely occupied in a restricted space for hours at a time. In the beginning, up to a hundred boys could play in a single match, as reported in *Tom Brown's Schooldays*. This was a significant consideration, especially when the sports rugby replaced included poaching, baiting the local tradesmen, and attempting to burn down the school. The teachers blamed the bad example of the French Revolution, but there was nothing like a mass game of rugby to keep Frenchified hands off the candles.

In addition to these practical benefits, there was already a sense that the rigours of rugby football had a specific moral worth. At that time, with its huge pile-ups and vicious hackings, the game observably encouraged delinquency, as it sometimes does today. Yet it was delinquency within the boundaries of a playing area, a confined space in which to monitor and encourage the formation of character.

It's tempting to be cynical about this. The new public

schools wanted to co-opt games as a tool both of recreation and control. However, they also needed to counter the lingering Puritan conviction that amusements were simply *wrong*. The most confident way to do this was to claim that exactly the opposite was true, and organised games were intrinsically right. The game was no longer just a game. It suddenly became so much more than that.

This isn't to suggest that the early schoolmasters who promoted the game were insincere. Perhaps thinking partly of their own safety, they hoped with a passion that rugby could turn boyish nature, and its love of tumult, into manly culture and a respect for others (especially schoolmasters). The game of rugby was also in a good position to benefit from the arguments of Charles Darwin. Rugby was a tough game. A fit and toughened boy was, by the popular conception of Darwinism, more likely to survive. Hardiness could therefore be seen as a gift from the school, a preparation for life, while at the same time helping to save on the heating.

In an ideal Victorian world, public schoolboys would turn out muscular and Christian. Rugby was the forge, and what had once been little more than a free-for-all between two sides, where a boy could make a name for himself by his pluck, gradually became the testing-ground of character. Defeat would teach pride, and victory humility. Boys would learn courage in pursuit of glory, teamwork in adversity, and a stoical reaction to physical pain. The ultimate test of character was to stand up and be counted, not to flinch, to run the ball hard and straight at the opposition and then stand and tackle, when in their turn as they were bound to do they fiercely ran it back.

It seems likely that this attitude, endemic in an officer-class recruited primarily from public schools, made its full contribution to the stupidity of the First World War. While morally inferior soccer players were still getting excited about a cup final in 1915, entire rugby clubs had joined up en masse, and rugger could soon boast its very own war heroes. Like Edgar Mobbs of Northampton and England, over age but raising his own sportsmen's company, who used to punt a rugger ball into no-man's land ahead of the attack. And Ronald Poulton-Palmer, of Huntley and Palmer's biscuits, an England international who scored four tries in the last game of 1914, but gave it all up for the 4th Royal Berkshires.

Mobbs was killed in 1917 at Ypres, while following up the ball. Of course he was. Silly bugger.

Poulton-Palmer was shot dead in 1915 in Belgium, one among millions.

It could have been different. In the two years leading up to the Somme, at the expense of many *SCUFistes* and other brave men, the French Army had learnt important lessons during their own great battle at Verdun. They told the British that many lives could be saved, when going over the top, by dodging, by varying the lines of running. The English refused to believe it, and continued rigidly with their unflinching and fatal approach. The British officers had pluck, they had bottom; they had blood. They now also have the Memorial Ground at Bristol, dedicated 'to those who played the Great Game during season 1914–1918'.

It's enough to make a grown man weep.

*

It was unlikely I'd get a game with schoolboys, even though I'd once been one myself. The days of men against boys survive only in the phrases of lazy sportswriters, although between the wars a standard public school fixture list might have included Harlequins, Rosslyn Park, and the Oxford Colonial Club. These days that kind of thing isn't allowed, so I'd asked Mr Greed, master in charge of rugby at the boys' boarding school Radley College (est. 1847), if I could get a game as a referee. The school proudly claims that on a good day it can send out twenty-two separate rugby teams, and I was hoping that a volunteer referee for the under-14 fifths might always come in handy.

Radley College is hidden away on a 700-acre campus not far from Oxford. Between 1980 and 1984, I was regularly withdrawn from everyday life for months on end, as if abducted by aliens, and brought to live here instead. At the time, I blamed the parents.

For a while, through the sixties and seventies, my dad and his brother were making serious money as builders in Swindon, at that time the fastest growing town in Europe. In fact, this was its only distinction, especially since the collapse of the rail-works. One of the most obvious benefits to the family of Swindon's prosperity was the financial clout to avoid Swindon's schools, and eventually, in Dad's considerate foresight for his own children, the town of Swindon itself.

Presumably it was also the people. The eminent Victorian and games enthusiast Charles Kingsley wrote letters to Thomas Hughes (among others) on the effeminacy of the shop-keeping class, the class below his own: 'I find that even in the prime of youth they shrink from, and are unable to bear

87

. . . fatigue, danger, pain, which would be considered as sport by an average public schoolboy.'

Fatigue, danger, pain. There you have it. All the advantages of private education, but of the many private boarding schools within driving distance of the town, I still don't know why Dad chose this one. I suspect it was the rugby. The family had originally moved to Swindon from the Forest of Dean, a rugby fastness in Gloucestershire, and Dad was always keen. At the Swindon club, in his twenties, he'd founded a third XV to be sure of getting a game. And he must have seen that Radley was firmly among those arriviste schools which clutched the games-playing philosophy to heart. The first XV pitch is even named Bigside, after the original pitch at Rugby School famously described in *Tom Brown's Schooldays*. They were all in it together.

As it turned out, in my four interrupted years at one of England's pre-eminent rugby-playing public schools, I was saved by rugby. I was good at it, which meant that whenever they sent me home they always allowed me back again. Others were less fortunate, but at the time I was ignorant of Dr Arnold, and the ethos of the public school sports-field. Rugby was *designed* as a salvation, a manly pursuit which would instil in me the virtues of muscular Christianity, while as a useful side-effect using up energy I might otherwise be saving for masturbation.

I hadn't set foot inside the gates of Radley College for eighteen years, and arriving from Paris with a vicious common cold, my expectations were mixed. In my day, because rugby built character, it was compulsory. Which hardly explained the case of Roderick and Mark Newall, direct contemporaries of mine at the school, who despite years of compulsory rugby murdered their parents in 1987 with a Chinese rice-flail. They then cut up and buried the bodies, and evaded conviction for several years.

Rugby was fallible, but in the 1983 and '84 seasons, it was undeniable that the first XV was the highest available honour at this particular school. In those days, while the Newall brothers were experimenting after rugby with martial arts, the first XV had their smug caricatures posted on the school's main notice-board. On Friday evenings before a match, while the Newalls flicked through weapons catalogues, we the team were eating steak and chips in a segregated dining room. It was desperately unfair. If you were in the team, it was fantastic.

The school was merely sustaining the games ethic, with the same intention as a hundred years previously. It was celebrating manliness, hardiness, and endurance as products of austere training and testing on the games-field. Although in truth the testing was more pervasive than that, in the dormitories and the classrooms and also in the very early morning before it was even light, with punitive cold baths and endless runs in the lung-busting dark. Ah, those were the days!

I was not feeling entirely at ease as I walked up the drive with my rucksack. Eighteen years was long enough to hope that many things had changed, but as I passed the science-block and then the tuck-shop, I found I was still anxious about doing something wrong. I had a book to write, and didn't want to get sent away, like the last time. All Dad had said when he came to pick me up was: 'We'll say no more about it.' And we sat in silence in the new Jag past Abingdon, Kingston Bagpuize, Stratton St Margaret, all the way back to Swindon and saying no more about it. Now I come to think of it, we've never said anything about it, not once in all the time since. Which is about as manly as I suppose it gets.

I was expecting changes. As part of the gift of making us tough, we rugby players used to spend a week in early September at the paratroop barracks in Aldershot. The army instructors would begin each exercise by making us shout 'I'm a cunt'. Louder, man, can't hear you. Nowadays, the boys go touring in South Africa and Australia, and come back bronzed and full of tellable stories. I'd already been sent the tour brochures, and felt slightly overwhelmed by the gloss and professionalism.

Despite the commonness of my cold, I was determined to approach the week with as open a mind as my education allowed. I'd already established that rugby retained its importance. It had its own master-in-charge, and at Radley, physical education and games are the same thing. There is no separate class or instruction in what is elsewhere known as PE. The games themselves take on all of the educational burden, and I sensed there might still be agreement here with the doughty Sewell of *Rugger: The Man's Game*. Sewell thought that a rugby ball should be reclassified in schools as an Educational Appliance.

Mr Richard 'Greedy' Greed was taking me to lunch in the clatter and scram of the school's wood-panelled dining-hall. In his late thirties, Greedy is tall and fit and looks like a runner of fast half-marathons. It soon becomes clear that he's also one among many on the Radley staff who are used to getting things right on a regular basis. Not just can do, but will do, have done, and what's next. He's also steeped in rugby. He's a rugby evangelist, an apostle. There's a fellowship about him, an openness, and I'm soon convinced by his big soulful eyes, windows on a big rugby soul.

He started his own rugby in a harsher environment than this one, playing his first game for the Wellington club in Somerset at sixteen, and then turning out for Wiveliscombe on the Sunday. That's committed rugby: there are no friendlies in front of the single wooden stand at Wiveliscombe.

'Ah,' he says longingly, glancing across the tables at certain of his colleagues, 'at school in those days you did sport and they left you alone.'

But it's Monday and lunch is for wimps and we've many things to do. Greedy takes me to his classroom in the History block to watch the video debrief of Saturday's match. This wasn't a common feature of the grand old game in 1914, or indeed in 1984. The boys, though, the public schoolboys, I guess they're much the same.

The room is full of handsome, arrogant, brittle, fearless young men, in sloppy ties and jackets. They laugh and rock back on their plastic chairs. I see they've kept me my usual place, and I sit at the back of the class watching the boys watch themselves on the screen.

Mr Greed in teacher's mode has already warned me that this is about the best attention they can offer, and the video debrief is more for fun than a training tool. The boys like to see how they look to others, out on the grass of Bigside. They then guffaw hopelessly at the puny legs of the other team's winger. The match is Radley College v. Abingdon School, a fixture only adopted in 1966, so the newcomers were never really in it.

I'm transfixed. On the television screen Radley run Mensa attacking patterns at high speed, and tackle their hearts out. As I watch them tear into rucks and expertly recycle ball, I see that this is top-class rugby Greedy has them playing, and nothing even close to rugger.

I was wrong about the refereeing. Volunteer referees for the under-14 fifths are very welcome, but only if they're passed in advance as competent. Greedy had therefore set up a test for me on a junior boys' game somewhere out on the distant pitches, but it hadn't rained for a month and all contact matches were off. I was glad to see that this didn't excuse any of the boys from rugby. They played games of touch instead, or sped through passing drills, and I spent the afternoon jogging round the fields on a random tour of the two astroturfs and the ten grass pitches, every one of them better than the best pitch in the Somerset Premier League.

I was hopelessly won over. It was like a nature reserve, or a national park. Of limited relevance but heartening all the same, and a very beautifully preserved acreage of England.

The boys in their red and white hoops seemed happy, and the best players at every age still clustered close to the scrum-half, eager for action. Others inched out towards the wings, where they wouldn't get in the way. Unless they were big, of course, in which case they had to go in the scrum. The Golden Age of rugby, when no one cheated or talked back to the ref, was alive and well – it's how small private schoolboys play the game.

It was noticeable that the ferocity increased with age, as the latent energy for rebellion took that much more effort to work away. But as the first Warden of Radley, the Reverend Robert Singleton, once said, 'the great thing was to be always employed, the devil hated industry'.

I jogged past state-of-the-art Silver Fern scrum machines, piles of tackle-bags, legions of armoured suits, and full sets of size 4 balls for the younger boys (to give an idea of the scale of the school-club, Radley has more than sixty armoured suits and only that September the club had ordered 187 brand-new balls). There were countless cones, and cricket pavilions full of tackle-shields and kicking tees. If you like rugby, I thought, you'll love this school.

The sun was shining, which may have helped, but here were 600 boys liking their rugby very much, even touch rugby on rock-hard pitches. And why not? I did, when it was my turn, with not a thought for the invisible flag flying over each run and tackle, rugby as a preparation for the greater game of life. Nor, at that age, did I ever wonder whether it was only the intensity of rugby that could hope to distract from the absence of a mother's love.

Dad used to watch all the matches against other schools, without fail. And usually Mum would come too, and bring a cake. Maybe they did drive all that way, sometimes twice a week, to watch rugby. Or rugby was just the excuse, so God knows how we'd have managed if I hadn't made the team. But I don't think that was it. The rugby was real and enjoyable enough, for all three of us. It was the cake which was the substitute.

As background to all the activity on the pitches, the sound

of the pipes was skirling from the music school, a reminder that there was more to Radley in the twenty-first century than sport. In fact, there was no end to the lengths they'd gone to impress me. The arts block is a model of excellence, and the screens and machines in the electronics department are astonishing. There's a new swimming pool, and indoor cricket nets, and a separate room with a long bank of rowing machines. The boys can use all or any of these after games, even though most of these activities are classed as hobbies. Games are still games.

Rugby is no longer entirely compulsory. Monday is even academic precedence day, which means that work comes first, but only if strictly necessary. Our 1980s Mondays were spent running up and down the pitch for hours, working on fitness and, even though we hardly needed it, discipline. I'm a cunt.

I jogged down to the golf-course and watched a foursome of boys playing golf. There's something about little boys playing golf, in their V-neck sweaters and two-tone shoes, observing the golfing etiquette, which is simply wrong. The game is taking the boy and making him into a man, but a middle-aged man with all the wrong ambitions.

Earlier in the day, I'd watched the maintenance staff cruising round the campus in milk-floats, adding to the impression that Radley is a very expensive theme-park, in which rugby is the fastest ride. Just like a theme-park, it doesn't seem real. It's better than that, and it's tempting to believe that the school succeeds and prospers because God likes it best.

Of course, I go looking for the edges of the illusion. As the school stretches and grows, it has the theme-park problem of maintaining the dream, keeping distant and invisible the outside world. I disturb a huddle of Canada geese on the 7th tee by what used to be the pond, but is now the water hazard. So much land has been cleared for the golf-course that from the furthest end you can just about make out the chimneys of Didcot power station. In my four years here as a boy I had no idea you could see the power station from the school. And I always had a soft spot for the Didcot smoke-stacks.

Running back to the first XV, I had to admit that all this was better, shinier, more robust and full of health than I remembered. It was an enclosed world and I was here for a week; I'd been abducted by enlightened aliens. Morale is high, order prevails, and to make the world as universally right as it is at Radley would require only unlimited resources, communities in almost penal isolation, and the exclusion of one half of the population. And, of course, a healthy respect for rugby.

I was impressed.

Back at their training session, the first-team squad were eagerly boshing tackle-shields and urging each other on like professionals. Rugby more than most activities is a central part of the shop window for this type of school, and as the headmaster Angus MacPhail told me, 'Whatever we do, it must be perceived that we're doing it well.' Which is surely a decent objective, and a sound philosophy, but a maxim less urgently applied, I should imagine, to the Radley College kite-flying club.

Having said that, these boys with rugby talent are preparing and playing to a level of excellence. They have shoulder-pads and headguards and mitts, all the equipment that money can buy. They're such able and committed young men it seems a dreadful waste that within three months they'll never play together ever again, and the majority of them will never play another game.

In any sport, wherever there's a genuine quest for excellence, there's likely to be an Australian. Greedy met Shona Sundaraj during Radley's pre-season tour to Australia, at the Drummoyne rugby club in Sydney. She's twenty-three years old, a qualified physiotherapist from Sydney University, and she is achingly pretty. And I say that as a 35-year-old. If I was seventeen again, or sixteen, and trapped on this campus without women, oh the ache, the ache. Or maybe not, after all that rugby.

I feel that possibly, despite the high standards set by the school, Shona is a test too far. She gave up a couple of Australian Football League teams to come to Radley to help with the rugby during the winter term, and guess what? A school like this one, with its emphasis on games and attention to detail, is very like Australia. Except it's Shona's fifth week, and already she finds we're way behind in our attitudes. It's all a bit technical, injuries and conditioning and stretching, but I stare into her dark and earnest Australian eyes and hang on every word.

I ask if after five weeks she sees these boys being made into better men, through sport. Sure, she says. It's the teamwork, and the fellowship. And it forms tougher men, too, by the sound of it. Shona hasn't yet put anyone off games, not one.

On a need-to-know basis, I ask her if any of the boys have made a pass at her.

They have. Thank God, I think, thank God for that.

And then I think: get a grip, man. Forget rugby for a moment. Be intelligent. It's not rugby which is inspiring and encouraging manliness in this closeted world without women. It's far more likely to be Shona. Be manly, play well, behave well, be good. Anything to impress her. Trembling, one of the first XV boys watches longingly as Shona rummages with her delicate fingers among heat-creams and cold-sprays. He eventually finds the courage to make some clumsy remark and closes his eyes, straining for a positive response. Shona turns and firmly knocks him back. The schoolboy, the trainee man, has to blink his eyes open, re-set his jaw, and get straight back up. That's the real school of educational knocks, for which not even the master-in-charge Mr Greed has a list of preparatory drills.

I took a cold shower. I went to Chapel. Every evening at ten past seven, five days a week, the 600 boys in the school go to Chapel. All afternoon I'd seen the durability of the muscular side of muscular Christianity. If the link had been broken (the grumpy chaplain would later tell me that rugger 'bred narrow-minded, thuggish boys' and that muscular Christianity was an 'incompatible phrase') then the Christianity in its separate sphere seemed just as resilient as the muscles.

I stood with the teachers at the back of the banked wooden pews, which face each other down the long narrow building. During the reading, I calculated that in the space of four years I must have attended this chapel about 800 times. At roughly ten minutes a service, this was many more man-hours than I'd spent learning to catch and punt and spin a pass off both hands. So when, in Argyll, that first pass had stuck and I knew that an instinct for rugby was fixed inside me, then this also, the life everlasting, must be rooted equally deep.

Chapel is even more compulsory than rugby. Six hundred boys as young as thirteen, many of them looking like Prince Harry in his gawky phase, were costumed as men in jackets and ties. They stood for the hymns, they knelt for the prayers; I hoped they were giving thanks for games. Games are one way of staying boyish, of insisting on boyishness – an escape from this older type of imposture.

These days, whatever its man-making qualities, rugby can also provide more concrete benefits. On long Sunday afternoons, I used to take a ball out to the fields and practise snap drop-goals, pretending to be Ireland's Tony Ward, or Scotland's John Rutherford, or even Gareth Davies. There was nobody worth imitating in English rugby, not like today, when it's plausible to imagine England as champions of the world. Today's youngsters are offered heroes, opportunities, an entire career path.

The next afternoon at the school (in my kit again, the inner child gleefully turning inside out), I met up with Nick Wood, nineteen-year-old Oxford undergraduate, recent Radley College schoolboy, and last year's loose-head prop for England under-18s. He comes back to help with coaching four or five times a term, out of a sense of gratitude.

'I was a fat boy,' Nick tells me, 'but with Mr Greed's encouragement . . .'

Nick Wood is a clever boy, studying Spanish and German

at Brasenose College, Oxford. He's also six foot one and 110 kilos, and has an Academy contract with Gloucester. When he left on England's six-and-a-half-week tour to the southern hemisphere, he was the only toff in the 28-strong squad, and he's in no doubt that rugby has made him a better person, a better man, mostly by allowing him to mix with a wider range of people. He means by making friends with oiks and commoners, and other good men on the broader horizons.

'I also learnt to respect fellow players whether I like them or not.'

Yes, yes, I think, all very admirable. But like the boys in the video debriefing, I'm trying to find the me in this. I'm trying to see how I look to others, out on the grass of Bigside. I ask Nick how long he was in the school's first XV. Two years. Ah-ha. And only a couple of the boys went straight up from the under-16s, which frankly as far as I'm concerned is excellent news.

From the years in which I played, two of Radley's first XV went on to higher things. Whispering Ash Johnson had several seasons with Northampton, and then one at Gloucester, where on a memorable *Rugby Special* from the early nineties I saw him comprehensively lamped by Chris Sheasby, at number eight for Harlequins. Sheasby later played for Wasps in the year they won the championship, and also for the London Irish team which lifted the 2002 National Powergen Cup. He has eight England caps, and was vice-captain of the World-Cup winning England sevens team in 1993 (while the SCUF were edging back into the French Third Division, and smoking dope in changing rooms).

Sheasby, I think it's fair to say, has had a tremendously

impressive career as a rugby player, and I have nothing but respect for his achievements. Indeed, as the only other sixteen-year-old in 1983 to move straight from the colts into the first XV, he and I have a meaningful rugby connection, although as outside-half I feel that my achievement was probably the greater.

After insisting on this small but nevertheless significant point, I begin to wonder how Sheasby's rugby might have made him the man he is today. Chris Sheasby is a highly paid professional rugby player who's won a World Cup and every available domestic honour. He's also a disappointment to the *Daily Mail*. He is a public cad, a bounder, who occasionally features in the Nigel Dempster column with almost famous blondes, one of whom is the single mother of his child (which Dempster always mentions, as if this alone makes Sheasby a rat). I know this because my friend at the *Daily Mail* sent me the cuttings, and I have them in a folder in my bag.

Sheasby is often linked with Will Carling, a team-mate from their seasons together at Harlequins. In another spectacular failure for rugger the man's game, consider Will Carling, public schoolboy and throughout the nineties the most famous rugby man on the planet. Until his fiancée and the mother of his small baby found out from a press release that she was about to be rudely ditched. This wasn't the kind of manly character Dr Arnold or E.H.D. Sewell had in mind.

They were thinking more along the lines of Eric H. Liddell, who won seven caps for Scotland before retiring from the game in 1923. The next year in Paris he became Olympic champion at 400 metres. The Olympic gold I see as his one allowable indulgence, because this frivolity aside, rugby had prepared him for a lifetime of work as a Christian missionary in China. He was later to die in a Japanese prisoner-of-war camp.

More immediately, the kind of manly man Sewell was thinking of could still be found at Radley College, in the person of the school archivist Tony Money. Tony had kindly searched out for me the hand-written reports of all Radley's rugby matches between 1914 and the early thirties. It was from these that I learnt how the boys themselves revered 'dash' and 'ginger', 'vigour' and 'bustle', the refrain of each season that next year 'harder play and better tackling are essential'. I also came across methods for selecting teams in the years before regular fixtures against outside schools. Light Hair would play against Dark Hair, Tall against Short, or A to G versus H to Z. My own personal favourite was Disyllables v. the Rest of the World, which produced match reports with a curious, puzzle-like quality: 'The Disyllables proved much the stronger, with Pearson, Deacon, Edgell and Mitchell conspicuous, and Cholmondeley for the Rest.'

Tony Money was a boy at Radley from 1934 to 1938, and describes his time at the school as a course in survival. He remembers once being flogged for saying 'Damn you!', and then feeling rather pleased with himself because until that point everyone else had been flogged but him. He was full-back in the third XV. He was also at the Allied landings in Italy, and I felt sure he'd be able to help me. Did the playing of rugby at school lead him to behave with greater courage and manliness during the stiffest challenges of war?

Tony is wearing a pale blue shirt, a claret tie, and a grey, mud-coloured sports jacket. He has big, square, tortoiseshell glasses and a high domed head. He's a handsome, small man, in grey school trousers, and his look is somewhere between Denis Thatcher and Michael Foot, as if even between right and left he's settled on the wiser position of compromise. He talks round his teeth a little, and in the way of brave, direct men, he refuses to answer silly questions. I want to know if the non-games players were, basically, more cowardly. Lesser men and soldiers.

'Everyone I knew played games.'

He's also reluctant, as a genuine hero, to talk about his heroism. In the army Tony became a captain, though he claims not to be a natural leader, and before Italy he served in North Africa where he was awarded the Military Cross. He rugby-tackled a German, and his platoon started shooting. Unfortunately, they shot both men at the same time. And then the grenade exploded.

'They threw a grenade at you?'

'No, I threw the grenade, earlier on. Then it rolled back down the hill.'

He's uncomfortable and picks at his trousers when talking about the war. But I've heard enough, and just as I'm about to claim Tony as the genuine article, an actual decorated hero formed and moulded in the public schools of England by the great game of rugby, he confesses that actually he's always preferred soccer.

This is all wrong. It's *Rugby* The Man's Game. I've read my E.H.D. Sewell and he refers to rugby as The Man's Game throughout, as if each time punching the reader's arm, eh? Eh? Other football sports are plainly inferior – 'American football is only another form of kiss in the ring' – and if

Roosevelt introduced rugby, gridiron would 'be forgotten in a night'. Soccer isn't worth a mention, not even the time of day.

After the war, Tony Money wrote to Harlequins asking for a game. They never wrote back, and Tony therefore resumed his love affair with Arsenal unhindered by rival claims from a rugby club.

He remembers 70,000 at Highbury in the thirties, and fainting boys passed down to the front from hand to hand. He remembers hearing the word fuck and the instant remonstration, ''Alf a mo, chum, there's ladies 'ere.' And he mentions, referring to the Arsenal crowds he now sees on television, that many of them would clearly benefit from playing some kind of game themselves.

Tony Money grins with mischief. He's an unlikely rebel, his own man. While Radley was for ever eulogising and elevating the status of its rugger players, Tony was quietly but subversively running a soccer club, which he kept alive for twenty-five years.

I cough into my hand, look at my notepad for inspiration, and ask him if rugby men are more reliable.

'They tend to come from a higher class.'

'But are they more reliable?'

He smiles, and I know what he means. Okay, forget that. Forget the prepared questions. I try to salvage an essential connection between rugby and the Military Cross by asking if he remembers any games of rugby from during the war.

'We played once at Cassino,' Tony recalls, picking at his trousers but then stopping. This is a story against himself, so he's much more comfortable telling it. 'We arranged a game between the Fifth Battalion The Buffs and the Sixth Battalion The Royal West Kents. All I can remember was a huge crowd of New Zealanders packing the touchlines. They jeered throughout. Especially at me.'

Tony doggedly refuses to be anything but wise, though I do get him to agree that rugby is a tougher game than football. But only on the condition I accept that soccer has its own horrific injuries.

As we're speaking, a TV producer knocks and enters, and asks Tony in his role as archivist a few questions about the comedian Peter Cook, another of the school's old boys. 'Not a rugby man,' Tony confides as the producer leaves, which at least demonstrates that compulsory rugby didn't exclusively churn out rugger-buggers. Peter Cook would have played, would have had no choice, and the game must have given him some of the qualities which made him successful as Peter Cook.

'The game itself doesn't matter,' Tony tells me, and this is knowledge which comes from fifty years in teaching, more than forty of them at Radley. 'Any sport will do, but everyone should play a game. It's the best way of channelling aggression, and football and rugby are the easiest games to organise. Personally, I was rather fond of boxing.'

He mentions in passing that on the whole boxers didn't make the best of soldiers. 'And don't forget how important sport is for the boys. It keeps them busy. And exhausts them so they don't get sexy. It does do that.'

In Tony Money's archives I'd come across another alleged advantage of the amateur game, as an agent of social cohesion.

The memory of shared sports, it was claimed, together with nostalgia for lost youth, would hold men together twenty, thirty, and forty years on.

I had a clear image of my own contemporaries as boys, but no idea what had later become of them. Except the Newalls, of course. And Chris Sheasby. After several false starts, which put some strain on the idea of a truly global rugby brother-hood, we agreed to meet at the London Irish training ground in Sunbury. In a way, rugby had held us together, because I'd intermittently followed Sheasby's progress in the papers and on television. He used to feature frequently on the old *Rugby Special*, especially when Nigel Starmer-Smith was doing the commentary. The programme was so amateurish, like the game it was covering, that you could always hear the cold in Starmer-Smith's voice, but the wonder of *Rugby Special* was the glimpse of untidy and open grounds, often swathed in mist or the steam rising from crowd and players alike. It was *Rugby Special* that coloured in the idea of Pontypool, Melrose, Kingsholm, the rugby towns and grounds easily as compelling as any players or match.

My last actual memory of Sheasby was on a muddy pitch in Toulouse on that schoolboy tour to France. The mayhem had just started, and Sheasby's opposite number at the back of the line-out turned and bopped him on the nose. Sheasby looked entirely bemused. Whereas the prop Gary Denman, who sometimes did press-ups on his knuckles with the Newall brothers, was far less diffident.

Although these memories fell short of nostalgia for lost youth, I found myself on a sunny Friday morning sitting in the stand at Sunbury, waiting for the arrival of professional rugby player Chris Sheasby. And then waiting some more.

London Irish were leaving that afternoon for the next day's Premiership match against Sale. I was still waiting. I watched the team coach arrive from the depot and reverse delicately towards the stand, bleating. I moved to the press seats, with their folding table-tops, and sat in the sunshine as the automatic sprinkler rolled itself slowly along the training-pitch.

He was now an hour and a half late. In their sponsored track-suits and T-shirts, the London Irish squad were beginning to assemble. I'd already established in the portakabin office that Sheasby wasn't playing in Saturday's game, was not travelling on the coach, and was not answering his mobile. This I already knew, and I was getting increasingly frustrated when one of the props, Neal Hatley, spotted me up in the stand and asked me who I was waiting for.

I tell him, and with a South African accent he shouts back up, 'Are you going to write about what a twat he is?'

Well, Hats, an hour and a half ago that wasn't *necessarily* the idea.

I talk to Hatley instead, and to Paul Sackey, Irish's 22-year-old wing who's been on the fringes of the England team. Sheasby isn't really a twat. This is what's known in the sporting world as banter. Neal is squat and square, and from South Africa. Paul is tall and sleek, and he's black. These two extreme physical types join me in the stand and agree that Sheasby is a truly awesome player. I ask them other questions, about money, but none of the players knows what any of the others are earning. They say they prefer it that way, as long as the win bonus is the same for everyone.

Other players gather round, and because I'm sitting and they're standing, I suddenly feel very small. I *am* very small. I'm surrounded.

The players at London Irish, like their professional colleagues the world over, have huge, cartoon faces. All the features are exaggerated, but especially the cheekbones and jaw. And the ears. Rob Hardwick, another prop, tells me he wears a scrum-cap because a bang on his damaged and cauliflowered ear leaves him in screaming pain for a year.

I get to the point, and everyone automatically agrees that rugby makes them better as people. There's the teamwork, and the communication. Most of all (they tell me as rap music blares from the gym), there's the discipline. They all nod and agree on that, and as I look from face to face, they suddenly make me think of boy scouts. There's something over-earnest about their total and worthy professionalism. *It's a game*, I want to say, but don't. The scouts should be encouraged, even if you never fancied joining yourself.

Still no sign of Sheasby, and, irritably, I assume he must have missed out on the discipline. He's late because he's a cad, I remind myself, and an exception to the rugby rule. He's simply not going to turn up. And it's only because I'm one of the good guys, tolerance and patience just two of my virtues shaped by rugby, that I decide to give him a chance by hanging around a little longer. London Irish set off for Sale on the bus, leaving me in the empty stand at the nearly empty club, feeling a total prat.

I think warmly of my cuttings from the *Sun* and the *Daily Mail*. If Sheasby doesn't show, these are my primary sources of information about *a serial philanderer and former England rugby star.* It could have been different. If he'd turned up on time, I'd have had a better idea of who he was, I mean as well as being described as a *love-rat, slippery, over-the-top,* a *rugby rat,* a TRIPLE *love cheat,* a *compulsive liar,* a *creep,* the *scrum of the earth* and the *biggest cheat in Britain.* Who according to the *News of the World* worries about the size of his penis. That's not what *I* think, of course it isn't, but Sheasby's not here to set straight the record.

He's also a *great lover,* but I think this might be a formula. However vicious a *News of the World* kiss 'n' tell turns out to be, the kisser 'n' teller usually mentions the incomparable stamina and love technique of the lover. I suspect this makes the victim less likely to sue, but they can't all be great lovers, surely? I lean back in the sunshine and wonder about the comparative rattiness of a rugby-rat in the *Sun* against a love-rat in the *Mail,* and it's about then that Chris Sheasby sweeps into the empty London Irish car-park.

In a red 1970s Ford Mustang.

Yeah, yeah, Chris. It's only a fucking Mustang. We've *all* had a Mustang.

And out he steps, in his suede loafers, no socks, tailored black trousers and long-sleeved white T-shirt. What a chump. What a big, fit, athletic, high-achieving chump of a rugby bloke.

Chris is due to have physiotherapy on his injured knee. I chase him around for a while as he looks for the physiotherapist, and I'm thinking: you *chump,* Chris, I'm writing a *book,* don't you know the *power* I have? And all you have is, well, pretty much everything I ever wanted. Aged thirteen.

For many years I've secretly been proud of Chris Sheasby,

and I've made a failed sportsman's associative link in my mind. It goes like this:

'Did you hear about Beard?'

'What about him?'

'He played with Sheasby.'

'So?'

'Sheasby played for England.'

Which becomes, with very little effort:

'Did you hear about Beard?'

'What about him?'

'He played for England.'

'Did he?'

'Well, no, but he did play with Sheasby.'

Sometimes, I can convince myself that I always knew I'd never run out at Twickenham, but when I was young it wouldn't have *surprised* me if that had been what I ended up doing. At several stages in my life I believed I could have done a job, however ridiculous such an idea might have been. And at Lord's, too, and the very next day if necessary. So why, then, did I never play for England?

Nobody ever asked.

I eventually get to talk to Sheasby while the physio has him on the table, massaging his knee. Sheasby claims the injury has nothing to do with age. I then calm down, and ask some less belligerent questions. Sheasby already knows the answers, as I thought he might, because he's been asked these questions many times before. I therefore wait patiently as he flips through his practised media responses.

At the top for eighteen years, still feels good, always ahead of the game, no need for drugs, high on life, a winner.

His exaggerated cheekbones and jaw shine with robust good health, and he promises the truth of stories that I suspect are not entirely true. (Eighteen years at the top? I was *playing* with him eighteen years ago, and was never aware of having even one year at the top.) He has grey beginning to show at the temples, and bitchily I wonder if when he's playing he dyes it, like the football veteran Tony Cascarino used to do. Perceptions prolong careers.

When I ask Chris why he didn't win more England caps (me! asking him that!), I begin to think that his supreme, path-clearing self-confidence might be driven by a great pumping engine of resentment. He describes some of the ups and downs of top-level sport, and I'm made to feel how dreadfully arbitrary it all is, and not just rugby. I should probably mention that every time I've seen Sheasby play, and despite wanting on principle to disagree with Starmer-Smith, he's unfailingly been among the best players on the pitch. He has the talent and the attitude and the physical power to have played fifty games for England, to be up there in the pantheon with the great marauding and power-play forwards of the age.

I'm the one saying this, unprompted, it's not him. Yet an untimely change of national coach, a bout of flu, a selectors' unkept promise at a crucial time, and suddenly all Chris's glory is stolen and squandered by others.

Sheasby is often 'totally vindicated'. In being selected for England within three games of leaving Harlequins for Wasps. In leaving Harlequins a second time because of the inadequacies of good old Zinzan, the living legend who later had to resign to stop the club imploding. Chris wants to be remembered as a great player. He's angry, and frustrated, but he mentions again that he's a winner, and if a winner is someone who frequently plays in a winning team, then undoubtedly he is. Bizarrely, he then lists all his wins, ever, including an obscure cup among the colleges of London University.

'Are you now, or have you ever been,' I ask, 'related to Nigel Starmer-Smith?'

'No.'

'Really?'

'He's been very kind.'

'Has rugby made you a better person?'

'Yes, definitely.'

The physiotherapist has moved on, and we're sitting in the entrance to the clubhouse, both of us side by side on big stacks of plastic chairs. I'm talking to an England rugby player and swinging my legs. Putting my notepad aside (a low and old trick, this one), I say, 'Tell me about the *Sun*.' And after a short pause, in which Sheasby looks at me closely and licks his lips, he's off again.

'What did I do *wrong*?' he asks, several times, but I don't think he's inviting an answer. 'No one was hurt, there weren't any children involved.'

'Actually Chris, there were,' and I know this because I've re-read the cuttings while waiting in the stand. Several times, actually.

He looks at me now with narrower eyes, dangerous, quite nasty, and says apart from his daughter, who is wonderful. He then says he was only in the paper because at the time both he and the girls were in the public eye, and he lists five or six women whose names I don't recognise, though several times he stops to call his current girlfriend on the mobile. Her name is recognisably Darling.

He has big open hands. I wonder if he'll drop the phone and punch me.

'Rugby is a great game for its friendships,' he says, but like me, he hasn't a single friend from the rugby at Radley. I aim for safer territory, and ask him what he intends to do next. Coaching, maybe, and possibly play on to the age of thirty-eight.

We wrap it up, and I walk with Chris to the convertible red Mustang with the white roof, where he pulls out his kit for a session in the gym. I've ended up warming to him, and find something defiant and admirable in the burnished chrome of his self-belief. At seventeen, this undaunted confidence could make him seem a bit of a fool, but there's something determined and heroic in keeping the shine on the façade at the age of thirty-five. It is the fool persisting in his folly, becoming wise. The chumpishness has been going for so long, and with such bravado, that gradually he's turning from a chump to a character. In fact, I'd go as far as to say that he's something of a genius, at thirty-five his self-belief so strong that physical realities fade and disappear.

I wish him well. We are thirty-five years old. He's putting on shorts and going to the gym, as if his life depended on it.

I'd been looking forward to my plain yellow shirt and referee's platitudes. I'd even been practising them.

'Gentlemen, we can do this all day . . .'

'If *you* want to referee, *you* take the whistle.'

'Look, sunshine, I've had just about enough of you.'

As many others have observed before me, there was no referee when Webb Ellis allegedly picked up the ball and ran. In fact, the presence of a referee would have stopped the game being invented ('Now then, Ellis, let's not be silly, shall we?'). The ref has therefore always had an equivocal role as the guardian of rugby's injustices and uncertainties.

In the nineteenth century, when referees were first introduced both to soccer and rugby, the true amateur was still privately obliged to police himself. Inconveniently, the best example of this comes from soccer. The former public schoolboys of the Corinthian Casuals would withdraw their goalkeeper if a penalty was awarded against them. It was a matter of principle: it would be wrong not to accept the consequences of a foul, even if accidental.

Now, in both codes, playing without a referee is unimaginable. Who else is going to decide how much cheating counts as too much?

I'd been hoping to officiate the under-14 fifths as a way of judging today's sense of fair play among boys. But the weather held and the pitches were unyielding, hard and crazed like cricket wickets. It didn't look good. Greedy was going to have to cancel all home matches except the second XV, who were playing on the watered grass of Bigside.

Sissies. In my opinion, from the perspective of the last century and the one before that, a cracked head and cut knees were valuable lessons in a public school preparation for life. A bit of grazing and scabbing would have reassured me that boys were being made into men. Fatigue, that's what they needed. Danger. Pain. But the old virtues seemed to have gone out of fashion.

I bet Tony Money would have played. I even asked him, but he was ready for me and retaliated with a passage in the match reports from 1921/2, when 'owing to the prolonged drought it has been impossible to play football at all as yet'. In 1921 they had their first match on 22 October, still weeks away, and then only after 'a great effort was made to flood Bigside in order to make it soft enough to play on. This was done by means of a sixteen-hand fire engine, hired from Abingdon Fire Brigade. The hose was very leaky, but all concerned did their best to make it a success.'

Never underestimate an archivist. It seemed that they weren't as tough as they liked everyone to think, those old boys with leather skin reminiscing from their fireside chairs at the snug East India. Sissies.

Deprived of my chance, whistle in hand, to penalise cowardice and reward virtue, I spent my last night in the school at dinner with Greedy. He was a good man to ask for an opinion on what I'd hoped to referee for myself, because there wasn't much he hadn't seen. As a young marauding full-back, he'd moved through the great clubs of Somerset and Avon, from Taunton to Bridgwater to Bristol, playing for the county, 'fully embracing the amateur ethos'. I take this to mean he had a few beers.

You can tell he's originally from the south-west because in his house there's only one photo of him playing rugby. You can't actually see it's him. He's making a tackle.

After Loughborough, and a UAU final win against Swansea, he joined Bedford and helped them into the newly formed professional Premier League. Like many elite players who started out in the amateur era, Greedy was organised and busy. He was teaching at Bedford School, coaching Bedfordshire under-16s, then Midland Schools, then England Schools. He had a part-time job as assistant coach to Paul Turner at Bedford. He's seen rugby from all sides, coaching and playing, amateur and professional, from top to bottom, at all ages.

'The biggest advance of professionalism is the coaching,' he says firmly, and looking at the training videos stacked beside the TV, I believe him.

Despite the videos, and the state-of-the-art coaching methods, and his experience at Bedford, Greedy is a rugger man. I mean that as a compliment. He wants the game to embody a healthy as opposed to Hobbesian competitiveness, in which life is like a Gloucester prop, nasty, brutish, and short.

He remembers Dick Best at Bedford referring to professional players as cattle, and points out that money can distort the values of any sport, even rugby. 'Different sports do have different core values,' he says, and Greedy is not a man who needs to be asked twice for an opinion. 'In our game, it's the confrontation and teamwork which make it distinct. It's also more *natural* than soccer, to pick up a ball and run. Think about it. It's the most natural way to move a thing from A to B.'

Yes, I think, and we walk it through with an empty bottle, from the lounge to the kitchen. It's not our first instinct, either then or coming back with a fresh one, to kick it.

'Trust is a core value. It may be that training is, too. In rugby, you can't just turn up. Commitment. Shared responsibility. Think of soccer again. It's a game with limited areas of responsibility – the centre-forward, the goalkeeper. We don't have that in the same way.'

Greedy is a purist. He's opposed to sports scholarships, widely available in the sixth forms at private schools aware of the public relations value of a successful XV. He suspends boys for foul play, he consoles them with the importance of losing. It doesn't take long as I listen to Greedy, as I drink his wine, before I begin to feel that Radley College is a grand rugby school, a truly great place to start out in the game, one of the finest forges of men on the planet.

Why haven't more people, while welcoming the new rigour and excitement of rugby the professional sport, not pointed out that the earlier vision of rugby as rugger was fine and proper? Restraint in victory and good humour in defeat, a conviction that rules should be freely accepted and the referee's decision final, a belief that the team is more important than the individual, what exactly was wrong with all of that?

So the implementation of the vision was never perfect. The same is true of the professional game, though its aims and ambitions, to become a going concern, are far more earthbound.

The influence of public schools on the development of rugby is often misjudged, especially when attention is limited to the worst aspects of rugger, and the sink of the RFU committees. Until recently it was generally agreed that the RFU, traditional bastion of old school old boys, was a byword for treachery, hypocrisy, and intransigence. These, of course, are the other lessons of the public school, the ones taught elsewhere in the curriculum, and need not concern us here.

*

The next day, match-day, I stood in the sunshine with my hands in my pockets and watched the second XV take on Cheltenham College. This fixture was first played in 1942, and neither school can claim historical prominence over the other; they're both solidly in the band of reformed public schools which did so much to develop the game, and Cheltenham were the first school to win away at Rugby, in 1896.

Shona had travelled with the Radley first XV, so as the seconds ran out in the last unsponsored shirts in either hemisphere, I was confident I was about to see schoolboy rugby in all its purity. I was looking forward to manliness unconfused by sexuality, a moral and physical demonstration of what manliness could mean. I was expecting fireworks.

The ferocity of the contact was tremendous, and there was no shirking from any of the boys on either side. The Radley lads had better skills, and scored first. In fact, they were much better all round, but I could see they didn't really believe it, and I found myself hoping that Cheltenham would score. I wanted to see the character of the Radley boys tested. After all, that's what it's supposed to be about. Cheltenham scored. Radley were tested. They argued with the referee and were penalised ten yards. Not good, chaps, not virtuous. But finally they rose to the challenge and came through by ten points to five, and it's another Saturday triumph for Mr Richard 'Greedy' Greed.

At the end, there are three cheers each for two fine teams and applause for a jolly good match. I'm proud of the game I love and what it's offering these boys, and feel grateful that once upon a time, a long time ago, it saved a boy like me.

Pembroke College, Cambridge, 1985–8

'Deep down, most good rugby players are free-spirited.'

Jeremy Guscott

Grow up, go to college, make mistakes. Most of them won't matter, because life hasn't really started yet, and college rugby can be explained away as further preparation for life. In the early years, when the sport was first popular among boys and students, the pain and endurance were training for something else, something grander, such as managing textile workers in Burnley, or ruling India. Rugby was like Latin grammar, useful for many secondary reasons, but never intended as an end in itself.

Nevertheless, I hadn't imagined playing rugby at university. The intellectual and liberal assumption, which I fully intended to adopt as my own, pinned rugby at a boys' boarding school as an outlet for frustrated sexuality. The greater the love of closeted boys for sport, the more intense their frustration. However, as in many other areas, Cambridge turned out to be more interesting than that. I started having regular sex. *And* I still loved rugby.

At Cambridge, I soon realised that I was never going to get the sheer exhilaration I knew from school of being among the chosen. The last great amateur fixture is the Varsity Match at Twickenham, a contest untouched by the meritocracy of leagues and cups. And one which at that time regularly attracted more than 50,000 paying spectators, as well as providing a kind of unofficial trial for the brightest of home nation talents.

I wasn't big enough, for a start. And I was in competition with a fully grown man I only ever knew as 'England's Mark Bailey'. There was also a youngish Gavin Hastings, a full-back and fifteen stones. Fifteen! How we marvelled, blind to the monsters just around the corner. Injured by my lack of prospects, I entered an aesthetic phase where winning and losing as concepts were simply too absurd, too exhausting to contemplate.

As a first-generation student, I missed out on my parents and their closest friends telling hilarious stories about that mad and disposable idealist phase before they all buckled down as accountants. World peace, universal justice, what larks! I was therefore dense enough to believe that a life exalting literature was actually possible. I would live the life of the artist, not just now as a student, but for always. And if that sounded pretentious, then rugby football would keep my feet firmly on the ground, my studs secure in the turf.

I therefore went back to play for Pembroke College, where the psychological injuries inflicted by fat Gav and England's Mark Bailey allowed me to do everything I'd always done, except kick. It was a matter of principle: I was an artist. I therefore became a menace of an outside-half, almost French.

I *never* kicked, and in that year we won the First Division of the colleges' championship, but with a negative points-difference (we beat five or six other teams by the odd point, but the game we lost was with utter brilliance, by over forty points to nothing).

Our team was the sportsman's poison cocktail of too much talent and not enough work. At least, it's poisonous if you want to play for England, and by this stage it was either that or the Nobel Prize for Literature, but probably not both. And anyway, I preferred to spend my time with a swirling, bewildering club of Kates and Christines rather than any number of high-cheeked Blues.

Edward Lytellton, the Edwardian headmaster of Eton, once claimed in a letter to *The Times* 'that in proportion as the adolescent mind gets absorbed in sex questions, wreckage of life ensues'. In a move which I think would have placated even him, I made regular visits to the playing-fields of Cambridge for hard bouts of moral rehabilitation and direction. For the first and only time in my life, I really didn't have to be anywhere I didn't want to be, do anything I didn't want to do. Yet I did feel like training on Sunday mornings and playing during the week, often twice.

It was basically schools rugby, but with beer, and at that time it was rugby at universities which did so much to distort popular conceptions of the sport. Not many university rugby clubs have their own clubhouse, so bad behaviour is always out in the open, and otherwise innocent students all over the country have at some stage encountered the worst of rugger in the Student Union. They witness the rugger-buggers in horrific action, up close and ugly, and the more sharp-minded among them end up as investigative journalists on the *News of the World*, making Lawrence Dallaglio their mission. The problem, of course, is students, and not the game of rugby. Although admittedly, the combination of the two can be deadly.

I hadn't played a match since Mid-Argyll's spectacular trouncing in Glasgow, but felt confident I could get a game. Pembroke College had always promised lifetime membership, and although I'd never tested this in practice, in my mind it qualified me for selection. I wasn't going to cheat. To make it fair, I would of course present myself at training.

Only I was far too early, because students in these enlightened days train on Sunday afternoons, and not in the mornings. I therefore had some free time to roam the city centre, and get sentimental in the midday rain.

My first instinct in all of these remembered places, out of insecurity, has been to adopt an inner attitude of superiority. In Cambridge it was no different. It wasn't so much that I wanted to feel superior to the place itself, as to my own former self. It seemed vitally important that I was better, wiser, simply *more* now than I had been then. Which is how I found myself in a corner of the market-square trying to feel superior to the young, clever, good-looking students laughing and strolling arm in arm under confidently shared umbrellas. It didn't, couldn't work. I was jealous, and wished that when I'd been here I could have known better the terror of not being here. My second thought about these enviable strangers was that if they were lucky, really lucky as I had been, these years of their lives would have little to do with study, or getting on, or even sport. In all their lives to come, if they were very lucky, they'd never again love so fiercely, or be so fiercely loved.

This may not have been the ideal frame of mind in which to arrive at training.

At Pembroke College rugby club, everything devolves to the captain, from buying a ball to fostering team spirit to recruitment and selection. In return, the vice-captain washes the shirts. He sits there in the college laundry, watching the swirl and tumble of all those navy and pale-blue hoops. This is a very important role. It reminds the captain that things could be worse.

The captain in 2002/3 is James Stevenson, a gangly and personable chap in the fourth year of an Engineering degree. He's a public schoolboy, a former third XV man like Tony Money, but he knows the game and he's an enthusiast. He's also very apologetic, and wishes it wasn't so, but Pembroke rugby isn't healthy. Two seasons ago the team was relegated from the First Division of the colleges' championship. Last season the team was relegated again, from the second. I had no idea there was anywhere lower to go, but only a late restructuring of the leagues saved Pembroke from the joke of the colleges' Third Division. Apparently it exists.

Instead, thanks to that timely reprieve, we were now in League 2b, a nicely academic euphemism which didn't mean the lean years were over. At the end of the previous season, several games were forfeited because Pembroke couldn't raise a team, not even for the Easter Sevens tournament. The college has 400 undergraduates, about 250 of them young men. Graduates are also allowed to play, and Pembroke couldn't find seven rugby players among them. There was even talk that the club would have to disband.

Rugby isn't the only sport in trouble. The soccer eleven has also been relegated, and in the week before I arrived the hockey team had lost the first match of term by eight goals to nil (and to prove that the problem is students, and not rugby, the players then went out and drank a pint for every goal conceded).

Pembroke College has extensive and attractive sports-fields. As well as pitches for hockey, rugby and soccer, there's a cricket square once famous for the evenness of its bounce. There are also six grass tennis courts, and squash courts attached to the pavilion in which eight of us are now pulling on our boots on a rainy Sunday afternoon for the first training session of the season. Seven undergraduates, and me. James had apologised for the numbers in advance, but I'm not that old and it seemed only recently that the college could assemble three complete teams of fifteen. Eight players, in total. I wonder how this can be, especially when the Pembroke prospectus promises 'education in the broadest sense, as well as a degree'. Perhaps education in the broadest sense no longer includes sport, but that idea seems so absurd I just have to pull up my socks and go outside for a run-around.

James is in charge. The college owns some tackle-bags, he thinks, and maybe some cones, but last year's captain forgot to hand on the key to the locker, wherever that may be. James organises us with commendable good humour, and very much in the tradition of the gentleman amateur, as if practising with too much verve might compromise our natural talent. He then sets up a scrum, with the flankers binding on the number eight. Nobody has packed down like this for years, and I tell James it's wrong, probably even illegal.

'Oh,' James says, 'that. I probably should have mentioned it earlier, but we'll be playing by our own special rules.'

It was in Cambridge, in 1863, that the original rules of the game were first codified, although in every club in the land you'll find some corner bore who'll tell you they're not rules, they're *laws*. But in 1863 the first code of rules drawn up by a committee of schoolmasters was called the Cambridge Rules. The main change was over hacking, which gave players licence to kick each other's shins at will, and its prohibition led to a predictable outcry that the game had gone soft and was now worse than useless.

These Cambridge Rules at least provided a reasonable basis for agreement. If nothing else, they rationalised the vocabulary of the game, because until then a scrum had variously been called a hot, a bully, a rouge, a squash, a shindy, a grovel, a gutter, and a pudding. The rules were, however, formulated by a committee. Consequently, they turned out to be unsatisfactory in all sorts of predictable ways. To this day, it's accepted that the laws of rugby are open to interpretation, both by players and referee. You only know which rules you're playing in the line-out, or the tackle situation, or rucks and mauls, after the match actually starts. Some people think this is a ridiculous way for a sport to carry on. I disagree. It's just another feature of the test that is rugby union, a trial of every player's ability to adapt.

This vagueness about what's actually allowed is partly responsible for the game's special character. The rules and scoring system of soccer are so simple and well thought through that the letter of the law is clear and unequivocal. The rugby law-book is slightly more tricky:

> Law 11.4: In general play, a player can be put on-side either by an action of a team-mate or by an action of an opponent. However, the off-side player cannot be put on-side if the off-side player interferes with play, or moves forward, towards the ball, or fails to comply with the 10-metre law.

None of this is important, because it's overruled anyway by rugby's code of honour. Rugby thrives on the *unwritten* rule. The players and referees make their own decisions about what's allowed, and so they must, because the laws themselves are sometimes of limited assistance. Law 14: 'A player must not make the ball unplayable by falling down.'

On this wet Sunday afternoon with the sky grey like sodden kitchen-roll, I find out that Cambridge is still at the centre of law development. The university rugby club is home to the grandly named Rugby Football Union Law Laboratory at Cambridge University. No less. What this means in practice is that every winter while the rest of us are enjoying a game which vaguely resembles the one England play on the telly, there are many students on the games-fields of Cambridge playing totally bonkers rugby.

The Cambridge College Leagues, uniquely in the rugby-playing world, are used by the RFU to test out ideas for new laws. The games are therefore experiments, contraptions. They're the pet machines of mad professors.

The colleges recently played a season where a penalty kick was worth eight points. This stopped working when the referees realised there was nothing to be gained from the law of advantage. Eight points was the biggest advantage possible. In another year, the team scoring a try could decide where to take the conversion, with more points on offer for a kick from the touchlines. Everyone took the kicks from the middle, and no one chased back to catch a try-scoring wing. One season, every college in Cambridge played with the offside line ten yards behind the back foot of the scrum. Designed for safety, it gave the attacking back row a chance to build up some serious steam, thereby imperilling already battered centres and increasing the risk of injury. I think it only right to thank those students on everyone's behalf for finding this out the hard way.

Not all the Cambridge experiments have failed. James Stevenson tells me with some pride that a captain of Pembroke College was the first player in English rugby union to be sent to the sin-bin.

As we huddle round in the softly falling rain, James tells us that for the coming season we shall be beagling two alternative rules. All defenders have to stay at least one metre behind the back foot. More challengingly, the set scrum will no longer bind in a 3–4–1 formation. The flankers have to put their shoulders on the second rows, effectively making the formation 3–2–3.

We play around with this for a while, all eight of us, working out the consequences. My first instinct is to look for ways it can help us cheat, but then I remember that although this isn't school, it's still the cradle of sport. Instead of actually trying stuff out, binding and packing down and running lines of defence, James and his pals hypothesise. They muse and deliberate, chins in hand, and it's an intellectual approach that suits us. We do it very well. We then play some rapid and energetic touch in the soft rain which slicks the grass and makes it fun for diving and sliding.

When we've had enough, we pack up and cycle back across Lammas Land to Pembroke. In a recent *Pembroke Gazette*, the annual report on the rugby season mentioned sponsorship, and I'd been preparing myself for branded team strips and track-suits, a corporate involvement seeping even as deep as this. There's no sign it actually has.

I thank James for the loan of a bike, and as we stack it with hundreds of others, he admits he's struggling to get fifteen players for the midweek match. This is the first league fixture of the season, and it's the beginning of term, when enthusiasm is supposed to be highest.

It's a crying shame, and I wonder if it has to be like this. James shrugs, and suggests I speak to Dick Tilley, who'll be able to tell me everything.

Dick Tilley, as well as being Cambridge's director of rugby and therefore caretaker of the College Leagues, is also director of the Laws Laboratory. This is based in the members' stand at the university ground at Grange Road.

As I walked there the next morning, through Clare College and past the library, I imagined how the lab might look. The inside of the Grange Road stand is more like a cricket pavilion, with wooden rolls of honour commemorating former Blues, and vast open fireplaces. The lab would be out of place, and therefore hidden away somewhere in a sound-proofed room behind a panelled door. Inside, it would be gleaming, sterile, with technicians in lab-coats and safety glasses poring over scrum machines and complex spring mechanisms. There would be crash-test dummies dressed in the latest protective helmets and body armour, the small ones in mitts testing crash-balls at speed on a six-foot-five, eighteen-stone tackler made out of tungsten. Which the techies referred to as Jonah.

And Dick Tilley would preside in a white coat and small round glasses, laughing madly as he fired Jonah into walls and concocted laws from the bits to be stapled back together.

Dick Tilley is a welcoming white-haired hard man with a tan. He has neither glasses nor a white coat, but an open-necked shirt and a relaxed, informal style. He too is a lifelong prop giving back to the game. A former teacher in a Corby comprehensive, and a coach at Northampton, England Schools, and Bedford, he arrived in Cambridge in 1995 with the remit to improve college rugby. It was a seasonal job. Now, he's all year round and director of everything.

We start with the Laws Lab, which like so much in rugby was formulated over a good lunch. The RFU's head of laws and some senior referees were bemoaning the lack of a trial period for new rules, so Dick offered them the closed world of the Cambridge colleges. This would enable the lawmakers to be clearer about what they were trying to achieve, and it was soon agreed that any new law should conform to three ideal criteria: making the game safer, more enjoyable, and easier to referee. This year, for example, the revised scrum is intended to reduce the compressional forces on the props from today's huge flankers. It's also designed to revive the art of the specialist hooker. I don't know how. It's all part of the mystery of the front row, but Dick is passionate about preserving the role of the short, fat boys. So he should be, because without them there'd be no Corky Frasers, no Hospitaux, no Dick Tilleys, none of the dogged enthusiasts to keep rugby honest in its undetermined future.

'It helps that the players are intelligent,' Dick adds. 'It accelerates the development period.'

He remembers an experiment which required all players to tackle below the waist. It started well, with the students scything each other down. Then the attackers started to run lower. Clever boys.

The defence tackled lower.

The attackers dropped their shoulders and ran even lower.

In the end, the attackers were on their knees, and it was impossible to stop them without conceding a penalty. Evidence of intelligence; end of experiment.

Dick is also proud of increasing the number of matches played against Oxford, so there are now firsts, seconds, under-21s, under-21 As, and a pick-up team from the colleges. However, the under-21 teams have made the gulf in standard between college sides and the Blues even wider. Nor is this helped by the recruitment of graduate players for the university first team, which this season includes two 32-year-olds (really? I might still have a chance!). At Twickenham, Cambridge University will probably field only one under-graduate, two at the most.

It's true, as Dick points out, that Cambridge is in a strange position, balanced awkwardly between other universities and the clubs. The bald economic fact is that by far the largest part of CURFC's £500,000 revenue (which also funds college rugby) is generated by the 50,000 attendance at Twickenham for the Varsity match. If the quality of rugby slips, if it becomes rugger and the attendance falls, then rugby at Cambridge could well be endangered.

'But it's not exactly high quality anyway, is it?' I say, as if it's any business of mine. 'The young Hastings and Rob Andrews aren't here any more, they're being paid to play in the Premiership.'

Dick admits the quality isn't high, especially compared to the internationals and European matches on offer to rugby fans the rest of the year. But Dick's an optimist, as most people who work full-time in rugby have to be. He sees a future when Cambridge University welcomes the best and brightest who aren't going to make it as professionals. These clever, talented lads will then pioneer innovative match-play patterns and techniques, as a lesson to everyone else.

Which is all very praiseworthy, and may stay the execution of Cambridge v. Oxford at Twickenham, but why is rugby in Pembroke so rubbish?

Dick starts with the facts. In state schools, along with all sports, rugby has suffered. For years teachers have been withdrawing their unpaid labour as coaches, or having the playing-fields sold out from beneath them to Tesco. In Cambridge University, public school entry has dropped. As has the intake of men. There are therefore fewer students arriving at the colleges who already know the game. Dick adds that at Cambridge, freshers arrive from school wanting to try something new. Many of the rugby players are lost to international bungee jumping or the Green Carnation Society. Whereas the women's section grows with every year, for exactly the same reason. It's something new. The women try it, they like it, and before they know it they're growing as people and taping up their ears.

This doesn't quite add up. If students like trying new things, which I'm sure they do, then all those male students who've never played should be giving rugby a go. I'd already suggested this to James Stevenson, when he was worrying about raising a team, but he told me it wasn't that simple. Everyone had heard of the Varsity match, and newcomers were scared that Pembroke rugby would be equally serious.

The women, however, had no such preconceptions, and quickly realised that rugby's a laugh. And then fairly soon after, much more fun even than that.

'It gets worse,' Dick says.

College rugby needed saving because the afternoons at Cambridge are no longer sacred. It used to be a morning place, five mornings a week ample for the discovery of DNA or the writing of the *Tractatus logico-philosophicus*. But these days it's a competitive world out there. Cambridge University is an academic hothouse. There are afternoon lectures, afternoon classes, and no safeguards for sports. Or indeed for anything else.

'Then there's admissions.'

Dick tells me that certain colleges will still accept intelligent students who happen to be good at sport. If an applicant has an interest or talent for games, it's probably best to identify these sympathetic colleges in advance.

I raise my eyebrows, and he tells it to me straight.
'Pembroke isn't one of them.'

In no time at all, because midweek games always creep up like this, it's the day of the match. James has eventually found fifteen players, but only by begging on his knees in the Engineering faculty and selling his soul to some chums from the soccer team. He's also included me. As for the standard, I'd asked Dick Tilley what to expect.

'It's true to the spirit of the game,' he'd said loyally, adding with a glint in his eye which I didn't really appreciate, 'and believe me, the tackling's not a problem.'

Perhaps it was this, and the lingering cold I still had from Radley, but I suddenly felt my age. As the team cycled in convoy along the Barton Road to the Queens' College pitches, I made some depressing calculations. If someone like me had turned up doing something like this when I was an undergraduate, he'd have first played for Pembroke in 1968. *Nineteen sixty-eight.* For Christ's sake. That was thirty-four years ago, when I was only one. That was ancient history, and in 1985 what would *we* have made of an aged geezer from 1968? It was as if I'd finally managed to get my trip in perspective, and putting it like that, I felt not only old but also a bit of a weirdo.

As we undressed, it started to rain in blocks, rebounding hard off the corrugated roof of the changing room. I tried to pump myself up for the game, reminding myself that I was older and stronger than these young people, these youngsters, these boys. It didn't really work. Something had happened at Radley which I didn't want to mention, but it came back to me now. On my tour of the school, I'd stopped at the fully equipped gym. The school's number eight, who the year before had played for England under-16s, was in there working his pecs on some chest weights. He reached back, grabbed the pads, slammed them closed in front of him. Repeat, about twenty times. Once, I kidded myself, me and Sheasby were as good as this, and now we're eighteen years stronger. I could have played for England, you know.

The boy stood up and I sat at his machine: I couldn't shift the weights. I couldn't bring the pads together, not even once.

'Of course,' the boy said, looking down at me as he brushed powder on his hands, 'I usually lift more, but I've been injured.'

Yeah, yeah. You should take a closer look at Nick Wood, my son. He played for England under-18s but he's already a crock. He had the best possible background and made all the sensible choices, but he has constant discomfort in his shoulder, problems with his ankles, neck pains. All part and parcel of the professional approach. You want to watch out, mate.

Back in Cambridge, changing for the game, I couldn't muster the same bravado. As I waited for James to hand out the shirts I checked myself over, which I'd learnt from *Big Brother* was common behaviour as part of an identity crisis. My upper body was fine. It was my lower upper body that worried me, especially after the weeks of hospitality I'd dutifully accepted in the name of rugby. Or rugger. Rhys Kelly and Jean Hospital and Richard Greedy Greed had *dissolved* my pre-season fitness.

The worst thing about ageing and sport is not that you

can't perform any more. You can be as good as you've ever been, only not always, not every time. Most sports people can accept that. The problem comes when you realise you won't have any idea exactly how old you are today until the game actually starts.

As a general rule, though, I think it's safe to say that after a certain age if it's hurting, it isn't working. At this point in a sportsman's career, looking the part suddenly becomes essential. I'd therefore bought myself some spanking new Pembroke rugby socks, and I secured them neatly below the knee with tape. Even so, I could still see myself for what I was. A 35-year-old man with a fading black eye hoping to impress some students. Wearing only shorts and long blue socks. At least the others could claim that rugby was just a small part of their elite preparation for life. For me, this *was* life. This is what I do. I'm a half-dressed weirdo in a rickety pavilion on Cambridge's Barton Road.

This process of thought is not recommended as ideal preparation for a game of rugby. I ditched the defeatism, and told myself that I did not lack imagination (that wasn't why I was still here, still doing this after all these years), nor did I have a sad and barren existence. In other words, and in capital letters, I AM NOT OLD.

It worked pretty well until James looked up from the shirt-bag and apologised. I knew by now that this was a bad sign. He then told me that due to the shortage of experienced players (neither his engineering nor his soccer pals had ever played before), I would be filling in at blind-side wing-forward.

In most other games, a change of position is fairly easy

to accommodate. And I felt confident that with all my experience I could fill every position in the back line, at 9 or any of the double-digit numbers from 10 to 15. But James was asking me to play in the forwards, at number 6. He threw me a well-washed shirt and the single digit on the back seemed lonely, unprotected. Shouldn't there be another digit back there? Some mistake, surely, but I could also play 16, if that's what he wanted. That wasn't what James wanted, even though the forwards played a different game. It was basically like this: the backs are fly-boys and the forwards are nutters.

Of course I didn't say any of this. I grunted and pulled on the shirt, because I AM NOT OLD. The positional change put me in the forefront of the new scrum rule from the Laws Lab, but I have no fear of the edge, because I AM NOT OLD.

Alert to the difference between forwards and backs, I ran out onto the lush grass of the pitch with my knuckles low to the ground. I thought I could deal with this, but almost immediately learnt my rugby limits when James politely suggested I could jump in the line-out.

'Why me, James?'

'You're the only forward with proper shorts.'

It wasn't *fair*. I only had the proper shorts because at my age it's important to look the part. James was now proposing that his fellow students lift a 35-year-old man high in the air by his shorts. Ah, I see. I began to suspect some of that old-time student humour. Ho ho.

In the spirit of utilitarian sacrifice, stoicism, and the team ethic (all the rugger virtues), I was prepared to suffer. I knew what I had to do, and I'd even trained with the army. 'I'm a cunt,' I said quietly to myself, and stepped up. I clenched my buttocks and closed my eyes, but was miraculously saved at the last minute by the loping arrival of our only tall forward. Who wasn't wearing the right shorts either, but hey, it wasn't my place to point that out.

And then we were away, and the ball slapped into my hands almost from the kick-off. I caromed and beamed in the wet. Even though there was something pathetic about a fully grown man playing rugby with boys, as if I too were still a boy, I did feel very boyish as I ran around out there in my blue and blue hoops, disguised to look like the other boys.

The referees in Cambridge are briefed in advance about the experimental laws, and what they're aiming to achieve. These games therefore involve a certain amount of coaching as well as refereeing. Nevertheless, the matches remain competitive, and there's no lack of passion, and just as Dick Tilley had promised me, the tackling was uniformly fierce. Almost mad, in fact. These students must think they'll live for ever.

After Mid-Argyll, I was keen to make up some of the points difference on my tour's aggregate score. At the very least, I wanted to win. Unfortunately, after looking lively for about ten minutes, I found out why forwards are always complaining. It's exhausting to play like that, knuckles on the ground, falling down, getting up, falling down. I wheezed behind the play as we went 12–0 behind, then came back to 12–7 (only seventy-eight points to go!).

My fading contribution to the game was occasionally punctuated by a skirmish I was having with one of the Queens' College centres. He'd introduced himself at an early ruck by saying, 'Do that again and I'll break your neck.' As all I'd done was tackle him, I thought, 'Hello, you're a bit of an idiot.' This was clearly a job for Rugby Union Man. The boy was only an apprentice idiot, about twenty, and the next time he tried to get my hands off the ball by snapping my fingers I took a pace back and called him over, as if I was the referee. I did that beckoning thing with the finger, and he came immediately, though looking confused. I told him I was monitoring the game, and had my eye on him. I looked at him sternly out of one eye only, and he visibly wilted. He was still a schoolboy, eager to please, and suddenly afraid I might be a *teacher*.

It was sad, really, to find out how easy it was to subdue him. But who knows? Maybe at least one foolish boy learnt a lesson that day, and became less foolish, and let's face facts, due to a game of rugger an improved human being.

But enough of that. I had the game to save, and this was no time for self-deprecation. In the heat of a match it hardly ever is. Summoning all my experience and skill, that afternoon I personally delivered Pembroke's first league victory in over twelve months of trying. No false modesty, please. It was the final minute of the game, 12–7 to Queens'. Breaking out wide, sprinting hard for the side-line, I dragged all the defence with me before contriving a miracle overhead sling-pass to set the supporting scrum-half free for a score beneath the posts. If anyone tells you different, then check that they were there.

The nerveless James Stevenson converted. Queens' College 12 Pembroke College 14. The whistle went for the end of the game. It was a famous victory, and all the Pembroke men clung to each other and jumped up and down in a little circle, enough to warm my dry old heart. But not as much as feeling an honorary nineteen years old. Or even the knowledge that we'd won that match because we were the better men. Boys. Men and boys. Yah boo sucks.

I'd survived my pre-match old-age crisis, but this was no time for complacency. I had the good sense to realise there was something even more worrying about a 35-year-old man going to the Cross Keys and playing drinking games with students until he was sick. Fortunately, on this occasion, that wasn't part of James's plan. Otherwise I'd almost certainly have done it.

For the end of the match, the Queens' groundsman had prepared trays of half-pints of shandy, but most of the team were already bustling off to lectures. A small group would be meeting up later, in the Hat and Feathers, but only because Newcastle United were playing on satellite in the Champions League.

When I joined them scrubbed and glowing later that evening, they were all behaving impeccably. There wasn't a rugger-bugger in sight and Newcastle were winning. It therefore counted as a good night out, apparently, though I did manage to distract James long enough to ask him how he felt about being used as a guinea-pig for Dick Tilley's Laws Lab.

'I don't like it,' he said, interrupting himself to admire some Shearer pantomime magic. He tripped over an invisible leg. 'I'm trying to introduce players to the game, but they don't know what game they're learning. Maybe it works better at a higher standard, where all the players already know how to play.'

But I doubted that Dick Tilley's Laws Lab was entirely to

blame. On an impulse, I decided to stay a few more days in Cambridge. I wanted to find out why, out of 250 young men, Pembroke College, a stand-alone club within the RFU, couldn't muster fifteen players once a week for a fun game of rugger. It was pathetic.

This was partly a sentimental reaction, and there's a living strain of sentimentality at all levels of the rugby universe. It's a side-effect of epic encounters and lost vitality, and in the corner of every club-bar in every land a gnarled ex-forward is codgering on about the '55 Lions or the Welsh peeing in your pocket on the terraces of the old Arms Park. Great days. Like the ones at Pembroke College which I loved, partly because of the rugby in the days when college rugby had so much more to offer. I wanted to find out what had happened to Pembroke.

It may have been, quite simply, that the decline in rugger left no place in modern rugby for a student club like this one. But I couldn't see why that should be. It seemed more likely that there had been some change in the college itself, or perhaps the university as a whole. In my opinion, as I watched Shearer recover within seconds from a badly fractured skull, it mattered whether students were encouraged to participate in sport, any sport. If they weren't, it suggested a downgrading in the role of games in education, and a significant shift from the philosophy of the nineteenth century: 'Their education was by no means confined to the school-room; but a serious part of it was carried on in their play-hours; a healthy play was equally necessary with close study to the advance of virtue.'

The Reverend Singleton again, in 1848. This wasn't a

belief-system that could be discounted between the school and university gates. Even today in its prospectus, Pembroke College has its share of standard pieties about the education of the whole student. 'There is plenty to get involved with at Pembroke – including splendid facilities for rugby [. . .] What are we looking for? We look for evidence that you will contribute, both academically and in other ways, to the life of the College.'

Just at the moment, those other ways don't seem to include college sport.

I want to make some comparisons here between Pembroke College and rugby union. It's a kind of surprise scissors move, requiring speed and sleight of hand, but I want to pass from one to the other, and then back again. It's a double-switch, and it starts with those in English rugby who feel that the special and distinctive qualities of the game have been under threat since 1987, when competitive leagues were first introduced. The imperative to win, it was thought, would impose itself at the expense of other aspects of the game, notably fair play and the broader experience offered by woozy social interaction after matches.

The University of Cambridge, rather like rugby union, is also proud of its special and distinctive qualities. It isn't just the learning, it's the whole experience: the sport, the music, the punting, that woozy social interaction. These are also under threat. Academic league tables for college performance were first calculated in 1980.

Pembroke College, as it happens, is currently top of the Tompkins Table for academic performance, and rightly proud of that. Pembroke is the Leicester Tigers of superbrain students. Unfortunately, it's also currently the Walkington Rovers (bottom of Yorkshire League 6, points for 39, points against 305) of college sport. It seems only reasonable to ask whether the two things might be connected, and then to wonder whether the college is a poorer or richer place of learning as a result.

All week, the feeling had been creeping over me that Pembroke was the most beautiful, the most boring of colleges. I didn't want to believe it, but it seemed to be true. Then I discovered that there wasn't a single Geography student anywhere in Pembroke, not one. Ah, I thought, that would partly explain it.

Apparently Pembroke couldn't find either the teachers or the applicants in Geography to maintain the academic averages. They therefore scrapped the subject, even though Geography students have traditionally made up in extra-curricular energy what they may sometimes have lacked in academic rigour. So, as the prospectus cheerfully admits, we *obviously want to encourage good candidates from all backgrounds to apply for all subjects (except Geography)*. That's it in a two-word bracket. No more rampaging Ian Wilmshursts, ever.

But Geography is only a part of the answer. I popped into the admissions office, with a straightforward request for available statistics about public school admissions. I meant to be thorough, and I could see that a reduction in admissions from private schools would affect some sports more than others, notably rugby. That's how the sport came to be so prominent in Oxford and Cambridge in the first place. It established itself more strongly than soccer because the Oxbridge intake in the late nineteenth and early twentieth centuries was mostly middle-class men from rugby-playing schools.

I also wanted to know the current proportion of men to women in the college. Pembroke was one of the last male colleges to go mixed, in 1984, and men's sports could expect a slight decline as the number of available players decreased. In the last two years, in which Pembroke had struggled to raise a sevens team let alone a XV, the intake in each year had been 77–58 and 73–57, in favour of the men. Including the third-year students, this meant the college still had about 220 men to pick a team from, not counting the fourth years and graduates. The proportion of these 220 students from private schools is about 48%, though this seems less important than whether the intake are generally of a curious and active disposition (we only need *fifteen*, for God's sake).

Innocent that I am, I raised the issue in a chatty way with the senior tutor, who happened to be in the outer office of admissions at the same time as I was. He was youngish, much the same age as me, and also in the business of English literature. I thought we might be friends, but he was strangely defensive. Or aggressive. He was aggressively defensive, attacking the man with the ball.

'I get many phone-calls,' he said, turning to a desk and straightening some papers with real determination, 'mostly from old members, asking about our anti-sports admissions policy.'

'*Is* there one?' I asked, wide-eyed, astonished, shocked to hear it put so bluntly (I'm not *that* innocent).

'Of course there isn't.'

It was a mistimed tackle, but it still took me some time to

recover from the implication that I, like those other con-cerned old members on the end of the phone, was some kind of reactionary stick-in-the-mud toss-pot. The senior tutor then told me that college statistics were not available to people like me, and anyway, the most obvious reason for the decline in sport at Pembroke was the arrival of women. Old members never thought of that.

Ah, I see. Not only reactionary in an armchair with nothing better to do. But sexist too.

In Pembroke, and for all I know elsewhere in the university, the sports-playing students used to be dismissed by the intellectuals as 'hearties'. I know, because I was in both camps, and I wasn't going to become a hearty by default and lazy association.

'Look at the rowing,' the senior tutor said, now sorting viciously through a filing cabinet. 'The women were head of the river.'

Yes, in 1998. As a modern kind of chap, wary of sexism and reaction (natural instincts though they may be), I'd already checked this out. The women's victory in rowing was already a former glory. And even though I was dudgeoned generally by the senior tutor's tone, I refrained from mentioning that women's rugby, just as an example, was flourishing in the university as a whole but not at all in Pembroke. And that's a fact, even if one out of three Pembroke students gets a first-class degree.

The senior tutor had implied that my reaction to the decline in Pembroke sport was a mixture of sentimental recollection and gender blindness, nothing but profound and personal failings of character. Me? It wasn't easy, but I shied away from full combat because possibly we were both mistaken. Pembroke rugby was in decline because these days the students were more secure about their masculinity. Possible, if difficult to measure. I decided to ask a student who was actively involved.

So actively, in fact, that in her four years at Cambridge Cory Birdsall has represented Pembroke at football, tennis, squash, swimming and rugby. She's also played pool against Oxford, and that counts. Like James Stevenson, she's an Engineering student. Unlike him, she's small and well made, and has deep, dark eyes. We go for coffee in a shop off the market, and Cory points out without rancour that my impression of sport in decline is misleading. Actually, it's much worse than it looks.

This is because the same people tend to do all the sports. There are therefore even fewer participants than it appears from the limited number of teams the college sends out. Cory does everything in women's sport, and she tells me that James also plays midfield in the soccer team and is captain of squash and tennis.

Cory and James are both fourth years and therefore about to graduate. Cory tells me that in the last two years there have been no freshers entering the women's sports, and that there's a perception among the students themselves, both men and women, that Pembroke has an anti-sports admissions policy. Ah-ha! Even better, a friend of Cory's had courageously raised the subject with my testy senior tutor, the man himself. He'd apparently deflected her with talk about cycles, as if the college had no control over its own admissions policy. And although an occasional poor year might be inevitable, two consecutive years suggested that either the imbalance hadn't been identified, or no priority had been given to redressing it.

It's not just me. This is what the students think. And if this perception of Pembroke is correct, then at the champion academic college at the University of Cambridge sport is no longer valued as an educational benefit. The muscular optimism of the nineteenth century, the healthy mind and healthy body, has been replaced by swotting. The university experience is exclusively about results, and the rest suffers, and the college fills with the kind of students who buy college scarves and wear them in public. I saw them; they do.

In this new educational model, in which Pembroke is a droning hive producing great networks of first-class degrees, rugby fades as surely as Latin, once the cornerstone of a sound education. It starts to seem eccentric, as if all these years we've only been playing a game.

Cory says it's not just sport. The first-year students don't even use the bar.

'Why wouldn't they use the bar?' she asks me, opening her hands, utterly bemused. 'It's *there*.'

It used to be Christ's College, Cory says, but Pembroke is fast closing in on the title of Most Boring College in Cambridge. Cory wants to play rugby, but at the Freshers Fair no new students showed an interest. There weren't any freshers for soccer, either, or for any of Cory's other sports, and Cory really wants to play, and not for the university but for Pembroke.

Cory Birdsall has a high 2:1. James Stevenson has a first. Neither of them damaged the college averages, but just now there are no new Corys or Jameses. Why should this matter?

Pembroke barely has one rugby team, soon there may be none. Perhaps this signifies a lack of demand, and students simply don't want to play games any more. Or more likely, without a rugby team, Pembroke is denying its students the opportunity to give the game a go at an accessible level among friends.

It's not possible for an unskilled enthusiast to play instead for the university. Whatever lofty position Pembroke achieves in academic league tables, it fails its students by neglecting to maintain a balance of activity, including the chance to participate in college sport with college friends. With four applicants for every place, it's within Pembroke's power to redress this imbalance, and genuinely offer the range of education boasted in the prospectus.

It's not up to James, or to Cory, it's the responsibility of the people in charge. Although just at the moment they don't seem to think it is.

By now, I was pretty hot under the collar. Suddenly I could see all sorts of ways in which this new Cambridge held up an eerie mirror to many of the changes in rugby since the game went professional. Perhaps I shouldn't have been surprised: both are subject to the conformity of the age. On the surface, certain things seem unchanged, like the soap-coloured walls of the Pembroke guest-rooms, like the itch of expectation before a big international. But Pembroke College is commercialising as surely as rugby. The college has gone professional.

The teaching fellows wear sponsored shirts. There's the Warwick Hotels Fellow in Economics, the Pfizer Fellow in

Engineering, and the SmithKline Beecham Fellow in Neuro-
biology. There's a Unilever Fellow and an Anglian Water
Senior Research Fellow, and Pembroke pays its own
undergraduates an hourly rate to cold-call former students
for contributions. (Like any newly professional rugby club,
they claim to need more money to improve the facilities to
attract the best people.)

Maybe they had to do this. Until recently, as in rugby, there
was probably no great call to abandon an essentially middle-
class Englishness of approach, and its slightly bumbling
ethos. Maybe the pressure accumulated, and without league
victories and sponsored gowns the college would have
floundered like the English teams of the seventies, fat and
drunk and good for nothing.

In rugby, it's now understood that the commercialisation
of the sport involves the inevitable acquisition of business
principles and modes of behaviour. These may be introduced
to the detriment of what formerly existed, and in rugby as in
a Cambridge college. One favoured principle of business is
that measurable results come first, and yielding to the ruthless
logic of the market, it's the invisible benefits and fragile items
of extra value that are soonest sacrificed.

Here's the scissors move again, the double-switch back to
rugby. In its professional infancy, rugby as a commodity had
seemingly limitless market potential. The model rugger man,
who from now on would be lured by a fast and compelling
spectacle known exclusively as rugby, was perceived as an
affluent middle-class wage-earner, a regular consumer
(mainly of drinks), predictably masculine and conservative.

In short, he had the consumer profile and the disposable

cash, and all those flush public school and Oxbridge lawyers would surely buy into the successful commodification of the professional game. It was sweets from a baby, a simple matching of commercial sponsor to receptive audience. Listen to Taka Furuhashi, senior promotions executive of NEC, on the straightforward reasoning behind his corporation's eager sponsorship of Harlequins: 'many of our products are business orientated, and the rugby crowd is primarily in business'. What a great market, or as a director of Barclays stockbrokers expressed it more succinctly, 'a bunch of Jeremys in their Rover Discoverys'.

In which case, why hasn't it worked out quite as neatly as the commercial managers projected? They were wrong, that's all. Their view of the typical rugby man was in fact a prejudice, and a long way wide of the truth. In my experience, rugby encourages diversity, and even at Pembroke the rugby club was a natural home for some of the more diverse characters the college once admitted. We had Paul Farquhar-Smith, who had a name like a camp tailor but was as uncompromising a centre as you'd ever hope to meet (and who liked to eat red-hot chilli peppers as if they were tomatoes). We also had vets and natural scientists and economists and historians and lawyers and yes, geographers, quiet lads and noisy ones, Scots and Irish, a paratrooper on secondment and a graduate Geordie research chemist. No one could agree on anything, and we were as happy as could be.

Unusually for a team sport, rugby subverts notions of conformity, of the need for every team player to take the same view. Forwards are not the same as backs. They set themselves different objectives, which they perform with an attitude all their own. The diversity of tasks on the pitch also encourages a broad tolerance of error. Unlike footballers or a badminton doubles pair, for example, we can't all do, pretty much, the same things. It therefore shouldn't have been so surprising that in rugby there was no unanimous stampede to conform to the commercial age.

At the amateur level, rugby sets the players at odds with society. Doing *anything* not for money is odd, but we're doing something seriously and not for money, with the risk of getting hurt, and not for money. And until very recently that was true of every rugby union player in the country. It's this subversive grounding in free thought which corporate sponsors often find troublesome (and it would be nice to think the same could be said of sponsored academics). Professional sport seeks to celebrate capitalist values such as competition, discipline, and results. At the student and amateur level, these values are not always apparent. Unlike the spectator (the consumer) of sport, the amateur participant remains free to explore his or her game as something other than a drive for efficiency and maximum production.

How else to explain the love for rugby of Ernesto 'Che' Guevara, who despite crippling asthma attacks played while a student in Argentina as a coughing scrum-half? For several years he even had a rugby column in his local Buenos Aires newspaper, and he'd surely have used it to denounce those professional owners and executives who constantly whine that rugby must exist, like every other aspect of society (including universities! I hear the senior tutor cry), in the 'real, unforgiving world'. That isn't what most players (or students) want, in fact quite the opposite. They want the unreal, forgiving world of rugby (student life) at its most flexible, and the club (the college) at its most tolerant. Amateur rugby players, like students, offer impenetrable pockets of resistance. We're not prepared to give everything to win. We won't sacrifice the sport for the result.

The affinity between rugby and non-conformism is a pattern repeated in the history of the game. This is less unlikely than it sounds. Rugby football once forged muscular Christians to withstand foreign threats to colonial and commercial dominance. It taught its players independence, and to stand up for themselves in the manner of William Webb Ellis, who in 1823 first took the ball in his arms 'with a fine disregard for the rules'. Think Che having a dart down the blind side, picking up tactical awareness and leadership skills, but also a love of tumult.

The rugby developed in the public schools of England changed when adopted by men from very different environments. Welsh rugby, for example, was always a means of expressing non-conformity against the English. In Australia and New Zealand, rugby plays a powerful dissenting role against the creeping Americanisation of those cultures, and if we're lucky the same resistance may even develop here. In France, rugby was embraced in the south-west as an unbending symbol of defiance to the central authority of Paris, and in the USA, rugby in higher education was historically a player-led rebellion against the coach-dominated US gridiron code. College boys all along the West Coast exchanged the authoritarian rationality of playbooks for the unpredictability of rugby, the braveheart of contact sports, for freedom.

This isn't a rule without exceptions. There's the problematic use of rugby to instil moral discipline in unruly but homogeneous groups, like schoolboys, or Afrikaaners. There's Che on the one hand, but Benito Mussolini and Idi Amin on the other. Both men were known to have enjoyed their rugby, though probably not on the left wing. The attempt by Mussolini to co-opt rugby as a vehicle for fascist unity is instructive.

First, he claimed rugby as an evolution of the Roman games *feninda* and *harpastum*. This made it Italian, and therefore acceptable. Then, from 1927, he gave the game its very own propaganda committee. Rugby was going to revitalise Italian masculinity while teaching co-operation, self-discipline and the subjugation of the individual to the needs of the group. Rugby wouldn't oblige; it favoured individuals and individualism, the Webb Ellises of Il Duce's neo-Roman Italy. Mussolini dropped the sport in disgust, and adopted *volata* instead, a pliant and meaningless kind of handball.

Rugby was too rich for Mussolini, too resistant to authority, an unofficial carnival realm where the social order is mocked and where after the game drinking, laughter and singing offer the temporary release which makes life worth living. These interludes are as important today as they ever were, especially in places like Pembroke College, where the recruitment posters in the Student Union aren't offering much in the way of carnival.

So you're thinking of a career in financial services?

They're students, for God's sake, they're players of rugby. Drink, laugh, sing.

*

Women who play rugby are in the honourable front rank of rugby subversives. I think it's fair to suggest that rugby is a sport for women of a non-conformist cast of mind. As early as 1891, a group of feisty New Zealanders attempted an overseas tour, but they were deemed too independent for their own good and the tour was cancelled. Rugby and resistance were again linked in 1930 by the Sydney Women's Rugby League, which staged a charity match in aid of the unemployed, or specifically the city's women unemployed.

If rugby is sometimes thought to be manly, it's a small step to think it 'unwomanly'. Resistant to such an entrenched set of opposites, women's rugby has become one of the fastest growing sports in the world. It's this sense of resilience, of the game suiting so many disparate and determined people, which gives it much of its special quality.

Inspired by the living idea of the individualism of women's rugby, I ended up at the Fountain Inn, near Downing College. Hayley Moore, captain of the Cambridge University Women's Rugby Club, was already there. The pub was her idea.

Hayley used to play club hockey in Leicester, her home town, but found it boring. Always a fan of the Tigers, she arrived in Cambridge and decided to give rugby a go. The university has two women's squads, and every year more students are taking up the game (though not from Pembroke). As for the playing standard, it's rising all the time because increasing numbers of freshers have played before, in mini-rugby at their local home clubs. They love the game, Hayley loves the game, we all do.

Hayley has sparky brown eyes and an intelligent brow, and she's studying Medicine. She still finds time for playing or training five days a week, usually at second row or hooker, and in the last three years she's broken her nose, her fingers, and she's been concussed. And obviously, she says, I've pulled muscles and twisted things.

'I just strap up and get on with it.'

She has lovely teeth, and I ask her if by any chance she's related to another hooker, Brian Moore. No, I didn't really think so. Her hero is Martin Johnson. I ask if she's ever embarrassed by being a rugby player, because at certain moments most of the rest of us are.

'It's not something I always volunteer immediately,' she replies, but not because she has any doubts about the special qualities of the game. 'I think it's a way of life.'

Quite.

'You really bond with your team-mates, you feel part of a team.'

Exactly.

'And the socials are all a part of it.'

Hayley, a reflective person, has thought about this before, often. She's attracted strongly to the notion of support in the game, of the need for each player to look after the others, and the team ethic generally. She explains all this with the passion of a rugby man from the valleys in about 1970, and it occurs to me that the future of the game is in good hands. Hayley suggests, unprompted, that all girls should have a year or two of compulsory rugby, in between some occasional netball and hockey. She'll be agreeing with E.H.D. Sewell next, and introducing it by law.

I ask her the question about manliness, though starting with male rugby players and what she makes of them. It sounds as if I'm flirting, and that's because I am. She expects rugby players to be more manly, she says, but only in the ruff 'n' tuff sense, more masculine.

'That's not really what I meant,' I say archly. 'Are they better men? Are they more reliable as people?'

She laughs out loud, and nearly spills her pint. 'Definitely not.'

'If it's not making men from boys, what about women from girls?'

'That will already have happened,' Hayley says, as if this ought to have been evident. She explains that rugby doesn't attract girlie-girls, and mentions make-up and hair. Yuck, I say. It attracts a certain type of woman, but they're like that already. It isn't the game that made them that way.

'What type of woman?'

'Some people expect us to act like men, but I have no desire whatsoever to be a man.'

The most common question Hayley is asked by the less enlightened of male rugby players is, 'Why do you want to play rugby?' To which she answers, 'Why do *you* want to play?'

That's the exact point I'm trying to make. Because it's the best outdoors team-game on earth. Because she and her team-mates learn the value of stoicism, perseverance, endurance, teamwork, resilience, and drinking laughing and singing. They experience the same values in the sport as men do, and the result isn't manliness, it's a mixture of these other qualities we can all share together. No need to keep them to ourselves.

'I'd spend my whole life doing rugby-related things if I could. But it wouldn't get me anywhere.'

Hayley is making me very happy. I know she's already among the converted, but it's a common rugby failing to want to be generous with the game we love. As Stephen Jones has eloquently written, 'I wanted others to realise we hold it so dear to our hearts because of what it is and what it does to our senses, not just because we were born in a certain place or class and are therefore stuck with it.'

Although I was, and I am. And Jones is too; he's Welsh. But Hayley is neither and she loves the game; all the girls love the game. She'll keep playing during her hospital training, if she has time, and many of the Cambridge players move on to Saracens or Richmond. Hayley has already played in a tournament with some of the England forwards, and says they're much bigger, and a class apart. But if she moves permanently to hooker, and puts on some muscle . . . although first there's the all-important Varsity match next March. The average age of the team will be twenty-four, with only five graduates among them.

Undergraduate rugby is alive and well in the University of Cambridge, only not where you'd expect to find it. I have another pint with Hayley and decide the women's club is a grand club, a great club of the future, and a band of the finest women on the planet.

It was my last night in Cambridge, and later that evening I went back to Pembroke and walked round the gardens in the dark. Just as I was deciding once and for all that there was no place quite so calm and dull anywhere within the city limits,

I came across a man in a wetsuit. He was from California. He had flippers on his feet and a mask on his head. He may have been drinking.

'Pembroke rocks,' he said, and promised me a party.

We couldn't find a party. The best he could do was a brightly lit room where seven people in black polo-necks were discussing Cherie Blair. Everyone else was safely in bed, and what kind of preparation for life was that?

Earlier on, after Hayley had brightened my world, I'd gone looking for rugger-buggers and bad student behaviour. My eventual reward was Anglia University rugby club at the White Swan on Mill Road.

There were about twenty-five of them, men and women, starting the evening as they meant to go on. Vodka Reef. Snakebite and black. And the same for my friend. I sat quietly in a corner and watched them as they settled round their table and did the traditional things. No pointing allowed (pointing with the elbow only). Drinking with the right hand. They also had a pack of pornographic playing cards. Whenever anyone qualified for a drinking penalty, they had to draw a card at random. If a horse was involved, the penalty was doubled.

I bet Anglia University accepts students for Geography.

Luckily, I had somewhere else to go, but I did pop my head round the door of the pub an hour or so later. There were fifteen of the student rugby players left, including the women, and they were about to break into song. Nobody in the pub seemed to mind, and the rugby team were obviously regulars, so they can't ever have done anything *really* bad.

They were just getting ready for life, like I was when it was my turn. Back then, at the end of my three years of tended and sheltered ambition, I'd decided I was ready. There was no longer any need to play games, not even rugby. Rugby had done its job. I was fully prepared for whatever was out there waiting for me. And so off I went with only illusions for company, through many mistakes, all the way to the edge of the nation where I had no choice but to stop. Stop and think.

Quite obviously, looking back now, I wasn't as ready as I thought I was. I wasn't prepared. So it was only a matter of time before I went back to rugby, and resumed my classes in life.

Norwich RUFC, 1994–6

'I know that it is ridiculous, as I have done, to sacrifice all that time to a game that serious men find childish and brutal. But the way serious men spend their time is just as pointless, and not always as harmless.'

Adolphe Jaureguy

I arrived at UEA for Malcolm Bradbury's MA in Creative Writing in September 1994, just in time to miss pre-season training. By then, I'd been playing rugby with men for several years, and it was already a habit to search out the nearest club, looking for a game. In Norwich, the nearest club was Norwich.

Fresh back from Paris, this would be my first club rugby in England, and I was frankly worried about the buggers. By 1994, however, rugger was already being undermined by league rugby, and the lie that the points were all that mattered. In France, I'd been playing in the oldest rugby union championship in the world, dating from 1892. The RFU, after proper consideration and deliberation, took nearly a hundred years to agree that a league structure – why yes, just like the one those Froggies have who keep on beating us – might possibly improve our national standards of play.

In 1987, an RFU committee therefore wrote the name of every club in the land on a piece of paper, and decided more or less at random where each would start in the newly formed leagues, ranging from National Division One to South Lancs and Cheshire 3. This is still the world's largest integrated sporting pyramid.

Starting from nothing, the lottery of this abrupt beginning created a few isolated leagues of death. Norwich, I soon discovered, was in one of the most intractable of these, London 2. The only consolation was that teams escaping London 2 usually shot straight through London 1 and into the National Divisions. This would eventually happen with Norwich, but not quite yet.

First, we had to grapple with professionalism, which was officially introduced to the game in the summer between my two seasons at the club. The signs were already there when I arrived. We had the squad track-suits, sponsored by AirUK, whose logo was a fluttering Union Jack. Hanging the brand-new drill-suit on my graduate bedsit wall, squinting and a little drunk, it was possible to lie on my side on the floor and focus just on the blur of the flag, the nation's flag, and dream fondly of that first international cap my commitment so richly deserved.

In the amateur days, many players would represent one club all their lives, 500 games in the jersey. If anyone moved job or house, they'd join in when and where they could, usually the local fourth team, and it might take them months to understand the social and family networks blocking their way to the third team. And so on. The leagues instantly dispensed with all that, and for rugby nomads like me they were an unmixed blessing. It was now the best players who were usually selected, regardless of which family owned the chain-harrow, or knew the brewery chairman.

With the leagues, however, there also came a dark paranoia about player poaching, which meant a player moving to any new club had to serve a registration period of three months. It was like a quarantine during which new arrivals were free to play, but not in a match of any significance. I therefore spent the time until Christmas playing friendlies against feeble clubs from the league above, and floodlit matches on Wednesday nights against the RAF.

When I eventually made my league debut in English rugby in the new year, this wasn't the men's game as I remembered it from Paris. Points and pressure did something horrific to the English mind, and among other dumbfounded afternoons I recall in particular Norwich 0 Cambridge 0, the only no-score game I've ever played. Later in the season, the promotion decider finished Norwich 3 Staines 6, introducing me to the greatest strength and weakness of English rugby: we couldn't half convince ourselves that a game of rugby was important.

The French were different. They could fling the ball around with abandon because they didn't ultimately care as much.

As for the buggers, the fixture card initially made me nervous. It included league encounters with Old Verulamians and Guildford and Godalming. If rugger-buggers still existed, these sounded like their natural habitats, where at the end of their schooling boys never became men, but just older boys,

Old Boys. There was the clear implication of arrested development, and after my recent life of trial and error (effort and mistakes in Argyll and Paris), I wanted to have progressed from that.

It turned out not to be a problem. From Norwich we were country boys again, like in Argyll. We were the sheep-shaggers down from the north, and if necessary could keep our distance. Though in truth the Old Boys' clubs were as serious about their rugby as we were.

Besides, I soon learnt there was something compelling in a simply desperate 3–6 home defeat, an attritional 0–0 draw. It wasn't pointless in every sense, and I remember Greedy at Radley insisting that continuity wasn't the same as entertainment. He was right, and there was the added fascination of experiencing in close-up the stunted English psyche.

It's a national weakness; our capacity for choking isn't confined to rugby. The cricketers are unmatched at it, experts in all forms of capitulation and collapse, though my own favourite description of English sporting self-doubt comes from Gary Nelson's *Left Foot Forward*, about life as a footballer in the First Division. His team, Charlton, go one goal ahead. 'We can afford to relax. Only we can't afford to relax. Not if it's going to make us complacent. But we mustn't get uptight about not being able to relax, any more than we should get uptight about getting uptight. So let's just relax. Up to a point.'

Basically, the English think too much, and in 1994 when I arrived in Norwich intent on writing a breakthrough novel, thinking too much was my stated aim. It wasn't immediately clear to me where rugby fitted in, but while waiting at full-back for the next, inevitable high ball, I had no mind for Malcolm Bradbury even if he'd appeared on the touchline. I reassured myself with the old rugger standbys about becoming a better person; more importantly, I was loving it. I was often in the paper, *a rock in defence* or *impressive throughout*. I was even selected for the county, but I got the day wrong and wasn't asked again.

All the same, I was in Norwich to improve as a writer. Rugby was a distraction, an indulgence. Unlike cricket and football, it wasn't even a sport with a decent literary history, mostly due to the nature of the game itself. Sensitive writer types often object to a good shoeing at the base of a debatable ruck.

Back in Norwich in 2002 for the first time since UEA, I went to stay with the writers Andrew Cowan and Lynne Bryan. Although Andrew doesn't know this, and his life is therefore poorer as a result, he reminds me a little of the former All Black John Gallagher, whose career crashed spectacularly after the publication of a fate-tempting autobiography: *John Gallagher, The World's Best Rugby Player?* If Andrew was ten years younger, a few inches taller, still had his reddish hair and could run the 100 metres in under eleven seconds, well then he'd remind me a lot more of John Gallagher. And if he'd helped New Zealand win the 1987 World Cup instead of marching on Downing Street shouting Maggie, Maggie, Maggie (out, out, out).

Lynne doesn't remind me of any particular rugby player, and nor does their twelve-year-old daughter Rose. Though Jasper the brown Jack Russell has something about him of the early Christian Cullen.

Andrew Cowan has several England caps, including the *Sunday Times* Young Writer of the Year. His latest novel *Crustaceans* is a masterpiece, so minutely precise that it's almost abstract, like a micro close-up of a realist painting. Inexplicably, in recent times he's been overlooked by the selectors. It happens in all competitive sports, but perhaps most unforgivably in the top-level, no-rules, fight-to-the-death contest of contemporary literary fiction.

Not that either of us is in any way troubled by this. We're still going round the track, doing what writers do, writing, worrying, going to the pub to watch Manchester United. As a soccer man, and while standing at the bar as United go about their business, Andrew gradually confesses to a horror of rugby. It's the intimacy, the hugging, the hands between other men's legs. I try to describe the absolute pleasure of throwing another man to the ground. The tight shorts, he says, the songs.

I take no responsibility for the songs. In fact, I've only ever known the words to two, 'Dinah Dinah Show Us Your Leg' and 'The Ball of Kerrymuir'. These are the very old kind of rugger song with smutty rhymes and endless verses, and both of them I'd learnt at school from other boys. Which suddenly had me worried. I'd never thought about it before, but now I had a vision of a paunchy Radley father home from a hard day's maths at Merrill Lynch (*so you're thinking of a career in financial services?*). He loosens his tie, pours himself a drink, and plumps down on the sofa beside his son. His only son, that is, who he sends away to sleep in schools for thirty-seven weeks of the year, and the dad with a Scotch slopping in his hand teaches his son a smutty rugger song, which they sing lustily and in unison while mum's out of the house on the horse. Or worse, even worse, they do this on blustery seashores or drab public footpaths on the one weekend in two they get to see each other. And then the boy goes back to boarding school and teaches the song to me. He's very proud of knowing all sixteen verses.

It's a vision too horrific to contemplate, so I turn back to my fifth pint and assure Andrew that it's all true, all the intimacy and the hugging and the tangled limbs. But the rude songs are gone for ever. And so are the tight shorts.

Andrew's negative perception of rugby is not uncommon among literary people. Rugby is a code of football largely undeciphered; it simply doesn't have the same presence in the writerly consciousness as certain other sports. Despite that, I don't believe I'm alone. The enormous evocativeness of the British football sports has attracted the largest massed audiences in the history of mankind. The world also has very many writers, and they can't *all* like soccer. And of course they don't.

In France (where else?), rugby is part of the literary scene. It was the Nobel prize-winning author Claude Simon who used to procure Five Nations tickets for Samuel Beckett. It's worth stopping to picture this. Two separate Nobel laureates of different nationalities meet discreetly in a café in Paris. Tickets are waved in the air, slapped on the table, grabbed and pocketed with a laugh. Yes, with a laugh of triumph and expectation, even Beckett. And these tickets are not for ground-breaking theatre or experimental opera, but for France against Ireland at Colombes or the Parc des Princes. No other sport, to my knowledge, has Nobel support of this literary distinction.

Beckett loved his rugby. Although cricketers claim him as the only Nobel laureate in *Wisden*, he was also a tenacious scrum-half. Even near the end, on a cold February afternoon every other year, he'd step into the street outside his Paris flat for the distant green roar from the Parc. He'd then hurry back inside to catch the game on the radio, oblivious to the outside world, to every other type of nothing.

James Joyce makes frequent references to Irish rugby in *Finnegans Wake*, not that anybody would ever know, and the Anglo-Irish poet Louis MacNeice was a regular in the stands at Twickenham. England v. Ireland, of course, and in *The Strings Are False* he remembers the Irish three-quarter George Morgan 'loping through the English with arrogant indolence', but alas, as ever, the final whistle comes too soon. MacNeice's afternoons at Twickenham are heightened experiences with hangovers of pure poetic melancholy – 'it is not every day you can watch a rugger international. And you cannot read James Joyce all the time.'

In Norwich, concentrating on the writing, I too would have liked to read James Joyce every day and all the time. As it was, I was a student and writer during the 1995 World Cup, which meant I could watch every one of the tournament's seventy hours of live rugby live on the television. It felt like all the time. One day I watched six straight hours, which might even have satisfied MacNeice.

P.G. Wodehouse was an avid supporter of his school team Dulwich, and watched them whenever he could. The novelist J.G. Farrell played centre for Brasenose before the polio got to him, and Robert Graves as a full-back was surely as combative as any of today's professionals:

In Rugby football I have killed more men,
Playing full-back and tackling with ill-will,
Killed them, I mean, in murderous intention,
Than ever I killed at Loos or Passchendaele.

The scrupulous R.S. Thomas had more love for the game than talent. At Holyhead, Bangor and Llandaff, he recognised his 'fate all along to be chosen and then dropped, getting to play more often in away matches, because of a willingness to pay for a train ticket'. He grits his teeth and admits, with a poet's loyalty to the truth, that he 'had no guts, no stomach'. Say it with a Welsh accent. It bites and hurts.

More recently, the Scottish poet Gavin Ewart has demonstrated that no subject is beyond the reach of poetry, literally none, not even that great prosaic lummox of a lock-forward, Billy Beaumont. In 'The Retirement from Rugby Football of Bill Beaumont', the poet eulogises that 'wonderful winsome match-winning walrus' (walrus! Perfect!) 'so solid, lumbering, rollerlike, steaming, wholesome, well-loved and home-grown!' Ewart also writes poetry about Botham's Ashes, from those faraway days of our youth.

This is not a long list of literary greats, I realise that, and it's tempting to add flash-in-the-pan popular outbursts. There was an inter-war fashion for the late Victorian public school stories of Talbot Baines Reed, many of which celebrated the essential rugger spirit – 'Well played indeed, Spotiswoode!' Or failing that, I could fall back on rugby's always reliable stronghold, New Zealand.

In New Zealand, though predictably nowhere else, many plays and novels are set in rugby clubs. At random, I picked out *A Wreath for the Springboks*, by Jason Calder. Calder is a New Zealander and his novel begins (and novels should begin with a bang): 'Charles Kennedy walked up the drab flight of stairs to the offices of the New Zealand Rugby Association.'

On the second page, a parcel arrives in the post containing a book. It is a history of famous All Black matches, and Kennedy's heart beats faster at the memories. He reaches for the book, touches it reverently, opens it. It explodes in his face, killing him instantly. There then follows a tangled plot to assassinate the entire touring Springbok XV. It is therefore not so much a thriller as a classic wish-fulfilment novel, a New Zealand national dreamscape.

This is perhaps unfair. Rugby is important in New Zealand as nowhere else, and there are more considered fictional works which explore this society against a background of timeless rugby themes such as struggle, defeat, and hope springing eternal. There's Maurice Gee's novel *The Big Season*, and Junior All Black Greg McGee's hit play of 1981, a classic set in a rugby changing room with the keening title *Foreskin's Lament*.

When I first arrived in Norwich, I was primarily interested for self-justifying reasons in writers who played and wrote at the same time. Or if that wasn't possible, writers so fascinated by rugby that they attempted to reconcile such two seemingly incompatible activities. In his brilliant novel *This Sporting Life*, David Storey invents rugby league tyro Arthur Machin. Storey once played professional rugby for Leeds, and later said in an interview that he transferred a belligerence from his rugby to his writing, from one world to the other, even if his writing only truly blossomed when he gave up the game for good. This wasn't the kind of news I wanted.

I also preferred to disbelieve the conclusion drawn of a whole nation by the Welsh novelist Gwyn Thomas: 'This game, with its magnets of remembrance, has drained off much of the ardour which might have gone into a more sedulous cultivation of the arts.' If that could be true for the nation of Wales, I hated to think of the ardour which might have been drained from me personally, when my pursuit at this time was exactly the cultivation so mourned by Thomas.

All these years later, I'm still not convinced that art can flourish alongside rugby. I therefore decided to solicit an opinion from Malcolm Bradbury's successor at UEA. The current Professor of Creative Writing, Andrew Motion, is the nation's Poet Laureate and a former rugby player. I know this because during my visit to Radley College I noticed that the new library had been opened by Poet Laureate and Old Boy Andrew Motion, whose name they'd proudly engraved on the glass of the door. Motion would have been a boy at the school during the days of compulsory rugger. Even if he'd been sly enough *not* to play, he can't have been to that particular rugby-mad school and have no opinion about rugby.

I suggested we meet. All I wanted was ten minutes of his time to compare his opinion of rugby with his views on writing. Ask some questions and see what comes up. It was speculative, I admit, but it didn't seem uninteresting, at least to me. He declined my request, rejected my approach.

In a reverse image of this setback, I once made an equally speculative request to World-Cup-winning Australian rugby captain Nick Farr-Jones. I asked him to read my first novel, *X 20: A Novel of Not Smoking*. If he liked it, I'd appreciate very much a positive quote for the back.

'No worries, mate,' he said. 'Send it over.'

With all due respect, Mr Farr-Jones is a considerably greater man in his particular field than Mr Motion is in his, and I wondered if there was a lesson to be learnt from this.

I think there is.

Does poetry or rugby make the better man? If goodness can be defined by offers of help to strangers, a fairly consensual place to start, then I don't think I need to labour the point.

In the end, I never did send the novel to Nick Farr-Jones. I didn't dare, because I knew that his opinion would carry far too much weight. What if he didn't like it? I was also disappointed by the lack of enthusiasm and general ignorance shown by the publishers, as if they'd never heard of the infallible Farr-Jones/Lynagh axis. They politely suggested that rugby was of little relevance to contemporary experimental fiction, and that Farr-Jones wasn't a name which would encourage any ordinary book-buyer to take a look at my book.

They were wrong, not unusually. Thomas Keneally would have looked at it. For sure.

Thomas Keneally is a Nobel contender and he's made the Booker Prize shortlist as often as anyone. He's probably best known via Steven Spielberg for his novel *Schindler's Ark*, but among his many other books there are titles which give away what most of the time he really thinks about. *The Playmaker*. Or *Season in Purgatory*. He turns out to be exactly the writer I'm looking for. He's a great writer. He's also a rugby man through and through, and he knows how to close the circle.

The first time I suspected this I was reading his auto-biographical *Homebush Boy*. Keneally has just been remembering his adolescent love of poetry, and his 'hunger for grandeur'. He then confesses: 'I dreamed of the poet-athlete. I would have admired Gerard Manley Hopkins more – not less – if as well as writing his sprung rhythm English verse he had represented England in Rugby.'

He describes, as a schoolboy in Sydney's tough Catholic schools, a rugby league match in which he scores 'a weaving try from a long way out'. It is one of those moments in sport, he tells the reader, he tells me personally, when you perform beyond your known limits, when a divinity runs in you.

I know. When I first read that, I thought: this man *understands*. He knows what it's like to break through into the empty spaces behind the first line of defence, and then to stand up the full-back with a step off either foot (though Keneally, I feel, preferred the right). The game was 'our map of heroism and the universe', where 'will was not enough and grace was everything'.

Goodonyer, I thought, wishing I too was an Australian, goodonyermate, and decided to get in touch. No worries. Keneally is the athlete-poet of his early imagination, who immediately and without question offers to help a stranger.

The day before I spoke to him, he'd been to an evening Tri-Nations match in Sydney where Australia beat the All Blacks. And he'd spent some of the afternoon before that match in the dressing room of the Sydney Sea Eagles, who'd just

171

walloped Parramatta. Keneally is the Sea Eagles' 'number one ticket holder', and he'd had a fabulous rugby weekend.

I'd been hoping to discuss writing as well as rugby, but Keneally is unstoppable on rugby. He loves it. When he was invited to teach in the States, he kept his days interesting by coaching the University of California back line. He has a huge appetite for both the history of the game and the technicalities, and I can hardly believe that I'm talking to Thomas Keneally about the attacking alignment of outside-backs.

In his enthusiasm, he skits from one part of the game to another, taking in the sponsored streakers at yesterday's Tri-Nations game, rugby league in Papua New Guinea, and the working-class origins of the league game in Sydney.

'But I love it all,' he says, 'especially since professionalism. Now you get the same Sydney yobbos in union you always had in league.'

I piece together a patchwork history in which Keneally's father was a rugby league-playing legend for New South Wales Country, though with too keen a liking for the rough stuff. Keneally himself was a centre or wing who'd always enjoyed the 'smashed nose and crunched goolies' aspect of rugby, the 'traditional form of warriorhood'. Like everyone who loves the game, he has his reservations about recent developments, in particular the commercialisation and the sponsors' names on the shirts, 'corporate gangsters defiling the sacred colours'. He also thinks professionalism has drained some of the good stuff from the amateur game, but the gladiatorial spectacle remains, as does rugby as a way of working out regional and national conflicts.

He confides in me, dropping his voice, that a rugby player needs a 'kind of innocence to play well'. I like this idea, and feel myself responding to it even before I'm sure I know what he means. 'You have to be imaginative, and suspend belief that this is just a game.'

Which seems a relevant moment to return to the first of all rugby books, *Tom Brown's Schooldays* by Thomas Hughes. Rugby is not just a game, it's 'the meaning of life – that it was no fool's or sluggard's paradise into which we had wandered by chance, but a battlefield ordained from of old, where there are no spectators, but the youngest must take his side, and the stakes are life and death.'

This may seem far-fetched as a lesson to be learnt from rugby, but a certain amount of mythologising will always feature in a sport founded on a story-book. In 1857, the year of its publication, *Tom Brown's Schooldays* went through five editions and was enormously influential in creating a surge of interest in rugby. Hughes's imaginative account of the game set the tone: ' "I knew I'd sooner win two school-house matches running than get the Balliol Scholarship any day" – (frantic cheers).'

There's a romantic bravado at the heart of rugby. Despite its brutality, it's a sport for dreamers, for writers, and Keneally and I do eventually get on to rugby in relation to writing.

'Literary people have been tolerant,' he says tactfully, making it clear the loss is entirely theirs. 'But I've also sensed, this is a while ago, that people were saying – "He's interested in rugby, he can't really be serious about his work." '

Yes, I know that feeling. I ask him if he's aware of any

other contemporary writers with even the faintest idea. He has a think, but none immediately comes to mind. 'You don't meet too many.'

Keneally organises his reading tours of Britain to coincide with big rugby matches, or tours by the Australians. There's such a longing in his voice that I ask him, if it wasn't for the writing, if he'd have liked to play for Australia.

'No,' he says, 'couldn't have done it. That was the priesthood's fault.' At a formative age, Keneally considered entering the Catholic Church (he dreamt of Hopkins as athlete-poet, but of himself as the first rugby-playing Australian Pope). It put him off his game. 'And also,' he adds, as if this is the only other possible reason he never wore the precious green and gold, 'I was a premature baby.'

Keneally inspires me. I too want to be a poet-athlete, and that's what I've *always* wanted. When I first went down to London from UEA to meet agents and publishers, in my head I was re-running SCUF's play-off game in Alsace. You just remember, I kept telling myself (occasionally clapping my hands together like I do on leaving the changing room – *Come on!*), it's not enough just to be there. And on the way up in the lift to all those steely offices, all those fixtures, I always had an instinct to reach for my gum-shield. Still do, actually.

Back in Norwich, I used to reserve Sunday afternoons to read the writing of my fellow MA students. On a weekly basis I had the future of English literature in my hands, or so its authors frequently told me, and reading it through with a cut eye or a split lip I had to concentrate that little bit harder to work out exactly why it was bad. The MA itself taught me that I was rubbish at confrontation, at least the indoors kind in seminar rooms where I was introduced to a new verb, 'to workshop'. It means 'to savage incautiously'. I preferred my conflict codified, stylised, up on the plain of Norwich's Beeston Hynd, with ice in the air and a chill wind in from the Fens.

Come Saturday and the first catch of the ball and I was away, elsewhere, belief suspended, imaginative, innocent. I was playing like a man possessed, and with a robustness I'd never known before. It would make me lie awake in the night after the game, goading myself with my own success: 'What makes *you* so hard?' But by Monday morning up at the campus I'd know the answer: the softness of my sur-roundings. The other students couldn't understand what I saw in it, because rugby players were all animals, weren't they? I may even have liked to hint that yes, actually we were.

At Norwich, like every other rugby club, we had the full animal kingdom. There were gorillas and gazelles and hyenas; we had sleek panthers and at least one weasel and a flat-headed viper of Gabon. I gathered my kit, then as now, and made my way up to the club. If I had no better justification, rugby clubs were at least famous for their language.

By 2002, I knew things would have changed. In the summer of 1995, the IRB announced that finally, from top to bottom, rugby union could turn professional. For some years this had seemed inevitable. Twickenham was nearly always full, and the RFU could negotiate lucrative TV deals, yet as recently as the 1987 World Cup the players themselves were allowed just

£12 a day and a phone-call home. The disparity was untenable.

The RFU, never known to rush (soccer had made this decision in 1885), also stipulated a one-year moratorium during which the domestic leagues would remain unchanged. This would give clubs throughout the land ample time to scuffle for position, break the moratorium, wonder what the hell was going on, and finally for rumours really to fly.

It was particularly bad at Norwich's intermediate level. Professionalism was a no-brainer up in National One, because Bath and Leicester had been setting professional standards for years. And it wouldn't make much difference in Dorset and Wilts 3, either, where paying the players was unthinkable. But ambitious clubs like Norwich were stuck in the middle. They had no idea what to do next, partly because they couldn't be sure how much money their rivals already had in the bank. How much was club loyalty worth? More importantly, how much were the *other* clubs offering? Most importantly of all to Norwich, how much was *North Walsham* offering?

Norfolk is not a big rugby county, and ever since North Walsham was founded as a breakaway from Norwich in the sixties, these have been the two pre-eminent clubs. In 1995, North Walsham was in the National Leagues, and the club's still there now. Norwich was in London 2, but famously rich, and here was an enticing opportunity not only to catch the local rivals, but to move on past them.

At that time, there were endless fun rumours about who'd been offered how much to go where. There were also suggestions that the two clubs should merge, ignoring thirty years of unresolved rivalry. This possibility was so maddening to the second-team captain that he threatened to have the Norwich badge tattooed on his chest. So the merger was never going to happen. Instead a director of rugby was appointed (actually the old coach with a new title), and there was feverish talk of the arrival of Simon Hodgkinson, England's grand slam full-back from 1991. He never appeared, and we started the 1995/6 season without a single new player.

At first, nothing much seemed to have changed, except we now had a fluorescent electronic scoreboard, a clear sign that the club meant business. We also had a choice of physio-therapists, and a stated aim to reach the National Leagues. There was also a reduction in player-power. In an amateur game, no one is forced to play in a certain way. In 1995, when the coach told me that every ball I received inside the Norwich half had to be kicked, I felt for the first time an obligation to obey. The dynamic of the game was beginning to change. Pro players *must* obey. Their livelihoods depend on it.

Professional rugby brought with it other unfamiliar dilemmas. Replacements were now essential, even though at that time substitutions were only permitted for injury. E.H.D. Sewell had a typically forthright opinion on this even in 1944: 'Our Man's Game has no truck with such effeminate weaknesses as playing a substitute for a man hurt.'

In 1995, being a sub was an unwelcome experience which seemed to mean missing Saturday's game for no very good reason. Feeling my age, and the shortening vista of active Saturday afternoons, I refused to sub. And was accused of not buying into the new process of team-building. The language of business had already started to permeate, and we had prep meetings and video debriefings and man-management issues. Personally, I thought the man management at this time was fairly poor, but then the man I was thinking of was me. I'm temperamentally a first-team player, and therefore in any decent, well-run club, to my mind it follows I ought to be selected in the first team. But I kept getting dropped for a goal-kicker. Or at least that's the reason they always used, and I always used.

We liked to bitch about the first ever player contracts, which were always about to be offered. It was said that these were going to present a straight challenge to amateur assumptions. We'd be asked to sign away our right to miss matches for the weddings of friends, for example, while committing ourselves in writing to attendance at training or risk being excluded from the team. The players muttered darkly. At a club the size of Norwich, no matter how ambitious, the players knew very well who in the team the coach could and couldn't afford to drop, even if they never came to training, and had a wedding every other week.

I left before the contracts materialised, but since then Norwich have achieved their ambition and been promoted to the National Leagues. Before being relegated and sent back down again. As I made my way up to the ground on a hired bicycle on a cold Tuesday night in October 2002, I was interested to see how these issues had worked themselves out. What kind of contracts were offered now? How many new recruits had been needed to reach the National Leagues, with what effect on the soul of the club? The game had changed so radically, perhaps at this level more than any other, and I'd heard stories. More than stories. I'd looked up the club on the Internet and found it wasn't called Norwich Rugby Union Football Club any more. It had re-branded, and was currently known as Lion Rugby. Now what on earth was that all about?

North Walsham called themselves the Vikings. That's what it was all about. It was a marketing strategy, sure it was, but also one more scuffle in the little local tragedy of Norwich RUFC's resentment of their smaller, more northerly, more successful rivals. If this rivalry had sparked the club's ambition when the game went professional, then it was also to blame for Norwich's recent alarming slump.

Any city club will always have a relatively high turnover of players, as doctors and lawyers and their like routinely come and go. I was still surprised, though, not to recognise one face at Tuesday night's training session. Not one person. Even more shocking was the wreckage I found: only eight players up there in total, and one of those buggered off halfway through because he didn't like the cold. The coach gently offered the possibility of a little contact-work. The seven remaining players turned him down. There was then a lot of talking, with the youngest players who'd only ever known semi-pro rugby asking the coach formula questions such as 'What's your input here?' Strewth.

I looked round more closely. These were young, well-to-do chaps, and at least one of them had been to private school. I knew this because he had a Cash's embroidered name-tape on his turned-over socks. Damn good player though, and poached from Walsham, but that hardly made up for the difference between then and now.

When I joined only eight years ago the club had six teams. It now has three. Or at least, it has a second team and a third team, but they never play on the same day. It's tempting to blame this not on professionalism itself but on a misjudged reaction to what those changes actually required. On the stainless-steel table in the clubhouse kitchen, there's the gormless face of Lion Rugby's furry full-sized mascot, a lion. It's just back from the cleaners, crushed under polythene in a compressed square on the table like a scrapped car. Outside on the training pitch there are eight players, seven players, minus me six players, going down the tubes and counting. The lion is called Leo.

As it happened, I did know someone, but he turned up late. It was Elliot, former third XV captain and back-row forward, and I arranged to meet him at his work at lunch time the next day. I wanted to be fair, and to hear every side of the story.

I started immediately after training with the coach, Dave Everitt, and utility back and current director of rugby, Haydon Cocker. The problem soon becomes clear: the club has lived every horror of professionalism, no mistake unmade, as predicted by amateur pessimists everywhere. They've had the gutless mercenary players, the unreliable sponsor, the disaffected lower teams, the whole catastrophe.

At the end of last season Norwich had a full-time coach and director of rugby (£28,000 pa). They now have Haydon Cocker (£0 pa), a former player who's back to help out for one year only. After the first month of the season the playing results read Played 4 Lost 3.

'It's one season only,' Haydon insists, as we drink mugs of sweet tea in the club office, 'definitely.'

Haydon Cocker has the cheeky, apple-eating face of a mischievous boy. The last time I saw him, he was in his early thirties and giving up rugby to go and catch rats in London. He now specialises in pigeons, but gets back to Norwich often enough to be saving the rugby club, though at thirty-seven it feels late in the day still to be turning out on the wing.

He looks tired, but Haydon is typical of the kind of person, the only kind of person, who can rescue a club like this from its own mistakes. He's currently working forty hours a week for Norwich, unpaid. At last I've found a back paying back, but then Haydon's always been here, ever since he was released from Norwich Boys soccer as a fourteen-year-old. As a convert from soccer, and therefore a true believer, he remembers the eye-widening shift from the spitting and segregation at Carrow Road to sharing beer and sandwiches with the Welsh at Twickenham.

'It used to be a laugh and a beer,' he says, testing the swivel of his office chair, 'now the club's in danger of folding.'

I ask him about the lower teams, but he sits forward and says that realistically there's no point in having a fifth or sixth team, not these days, because they'd have no one to play against. Until this year's introduction of a merit table, they couldn't even guarantee fixtures for a second team.

'It's easy to blame professionalism and the television,' Haydon says philosophically. He's very calm: there's nothing a club like Norwich can do about it, at least not tonight. 'For a while, when the commercial razzmatazz started, it made players into spectators, even in Norfolk where there's no Premiership team. People drifted away from actually playing. There again, the TV also generates interest among children.'

At Norwich, the Sunday mini and junior section is thriving. Even better, Haydon tells me, it thrives with youngsters who aren't from the local private schools. This means they're more likely to stick around as young men rather than disappear to university or London.

'The club won't fold,' Haydon says, shifting in his seat. 'It's just a question of holding out until the youngsters arrive.'

The coach Dave Everitt then brings me up to date with all Norwich's woe. He's yet another ex-prop, heavily built, and from his bristling crew-cut his grey-bearded face gradually widens on the way to his massive neck. He speaks leaning back in his chair, his folded arms resting on the shelf of his belly. It's partly the game's fault. In the National Leagues they had to take twenty-two players to every match, including five front-row specialists. This had a knock-on effect which decimated the lower teams, because there just aren't that many competitive, short, fat, strong, violent people to be had. Not even in Norfolk.

But mostly it's the club's fault, for rushing in. It all started so well. The club recruited the best seven or eight players from outlying areas (including North Walsham), and were offered £100,000 over three years from Bull Computers, which had just acquired one of the city's leading home-grown IT companies. The club agreed to match this figure from its own funds. There were smaller sponsors, too, but if this still sounds like small change compared to soccer, think of Mid-

Argyll struggling three hours down the coast (Lochgair, Furnace War Memorial, Dunoon) for £380.

It seems that despite all our grumbling and the exaggerated rumours at the time, there were never any written contracts, although there was once a photo in the *Eastern Daily Press* of four new players sitting at a table signing for Norwich. Their pens were poised over blank pieces of paper. Norwich and other clubs at this level had discovered the legal insanity of trying to impose binding conditions on grown men for £50 a week.

So this is how they did it.

No match fees, of course, but travel expenses and all sorts of track-suits and training-tops to keep everyone sweet. The players were then given £20 after training on a Tuesday, £20 after training on a Thursday, and £10 after the match on Saturday. And maybe a car. I push it a little, and Dave admits that the goal-kicker might have had £100, but the principle of cash for training remained. Meanwhile, the lower sides were still paying subs and match fees.

The Norwich first team were promoted to the National Leagues; the lower teams buggered off, some to Diss, some to Lakenham, others to Wymondham. The club then had to recruit again to stay national, and these were players with new experience of their own worth, so now it was £50 on a Saturday. Those from London seldom came to training. After only two seasons in National 3, Norwich were relegated. The mercenaries moved on, but the club no longer had the lower teams to provide decent and committed replacements. It was the full circle of amateur well-being to professional distress.

When in doubt, club rugby players traditionally blame the club committee, so the next evening I was back at the clubhouse for a chat with Roy Bishop. He's one of the few remaining administrators from Norwich's high-speed boom and bust. He's a tall, fit-looking man in the rude flush of early retirement, looking tanned and healthy in a button-down denim shirt and chinos, and trendy lightweight specs. He's been on the committee for twelve years, the full ride, and defiantly regrets nothing. The game went professional. Norwich had a go. They failed. In the good old amateur spirit (some irony here, surely), at least they gave it a go.

He's another ex-forward, a former second-team second-rower, and in 1995/6 he fully supported the bold ambition of the club. Which was to stuff North Walsham. And then, if possible, move up the leagues. With the money from Bull, this at last began to seem feasible, and apart from the electronic scoreboard nearly all the money went on players. (I quickly make the calculation in my head: £50 × 22 squad players, every week for a nine-month season, equals about £44,000. Blimey. And that's before cars and kit and travel.)

'All you needed was money,' Roy says. 'And at Norwich, we'd always been rich.'

The club was in thrall to the meritocracy of league professionalism, dazzled by the bright chance of a gambler's longshot at the big time. With a glint in his eye that may possibly be the seed of a very small tear, Roy admits that there were once thoughts of regular fixtures against Leicester, Saracens, Northampton. (We used to play all their second teams, though hard-headed professionalism soon put a stop to that.)

'They might look down on us now,' he says, remembering the confident mood of the time, 'but if we'd got up there, they'd have *had* to play us, and that debut year in the National Leagues was a joy. We finished fourth, you know. A real joy. I think reality only hit home in the first match of the second year. We were away at Penzance.'

This meant leaving at four o'clock on Friday afternoon and not getting back until after lunch on Sunday. Then Bull pulled out of Norwich, and within one year of the twenty-first century, after 120 years of cautious accounting, the club found itself deeply in debt.

Roy is unrepentant. The committee had a vision. They went for broke, and that's what they got.

He says the debt is bad. People think it's bad, but it's worse than they think. Roy sighs. He takes me up onto the inside balcony of the clubhouse, so we can look out at the best hope for the future, the equity in the wholly owned pitches. A little further on, orange street-lights glow among the new estates creeping out from the edge of the city. Those lights and the local land values allow for a certain smugness, although ideally Roy would prefer a wealthy benefactor. He fancies another go.

'What about the soul of the club?'

'What do you mean?'

'The lower teams.'

The club needs playing members. They provide income, and can put their hands in their pockets in times of crisis, like now. As it is, the consensus among former members seems to be that the committee made this mess, and it's up to them to sort it out.

'The damaged soul of the club,' Roy says, 'was inevitable. It was the leagues as much as professionalism, although to be truthful, the committee was always aware that top professional outfits have no social side, no lower teams.'

Norwich didn't make it. They're not a top professional outfit, and Roy says he now sees the need for a serious *and* a social side, though he doubts that's possible. 'The fourth and fifth teams, the coarse players who want a game and a beer and a singalong in the bath, that's all gone. There's no demand any more for friendlies and getting pissed.'

Or in other words, it's the end of rugger as we know it. Perhaps. What Roy Bishop doesn't tell me is that Norwich RUFC lives in midnight fear of the Apache.

Across the front of Norwich town hall, overlooking the striped tarpaulins of the covered market, is an enormous banner. It announces the council's bid to be nominated as 2008 European City of Culture. I hope Norwich wins. If not, it could easily get a consolation nod as European City of Chips and Beer. That's how the city smells, of fresh chips and hand-pulled beer, and there's a reason for this: a seemingly unsustainable number of chip-shops and pubs.

It's therefore true to the law of local averages that my friend Elliot should run a pub, and I meet him at lunchtime the next day on Kings Street in the Bar Rio, his latest Norwich venture. He's behind the bar, working alone, and he's about forty-two years old, always was and always will be. When I was last here he was a 42-year-old 26-year-old, and as captain of the thirds he used to address his teams at half-time as 'Jennelmen'. As a newcomer, I therefore knew he was pubs or police.

Elliot is now forty-two in his early thirties, and witnessed the changes in the club from the perspective of the third team. As he pulls me a lunchtime pint, he thoughtfully shapes a neat publican's platitude, that rugby isn't a flower. Oh no. To gauge its health you shouldn't bother with the petals, but look instead at the roots. When it dies, it'll die from the bottom upwards.

'You need to speak to Woody,' Elliot says, neatly placing the beer on the counter between us.

'I'd love to speak to him.'

'You know what he'd say?'

The lower teams resented the first team's kit, the cars, the money, especially while they were still paying match fees. Not only that, if they wanted to watch Norwich play they had to pay four pounds to get into their own ground, their own club. On match-days the thirds had no oranges, no referees, and they were running out in rags. The shirt numbers were falling off, or they were all 6s and 7s. They once even had to wear Norwich Ladies shirts.

'Imagine that, Rich. The shame. Woody'll tell you. Woody even got us a new set of shirts, a donation from a rugby league club, up north.'

This, remember, is the same Norwich owning five pitches and paying out more than £40,000 a season on players alone. In five years the club went from six teams to two, which meant that at each AGM there were fewer players to vote against large numbers of ambitious non-playing members. The catalyst for the final breakaway was the appointment of a new club captain from Rotherham, when the local candidate was voted down. The older mentor-type players, the characters, drifted away. Or so it seemed. In fact, they were meeting secretly at the Murderers, Norwich's oldest and most sinister pub, where they hatched a plan of resistance.

'You need to talk to Woody,' Elliot says, 'you really do.'

In the meantime, for the rest of the afternoon, we put the rugby world to rights. People along the bar join in, an ex-navy man and a personal trainer. I concede that for team spirit and togetherness, even rugby must bow to the Devonport Field-Gun, but otherwise we mostly agree. Elliot identifies a missing generation between the ages of about twenty and twenty-six, many of whom are spending the afternoon in his bar. There are also fewer rugby players because of indoor lifestyles, and McDonald's, and gyms offering a supermarket type of fitness which is easy to consume. As a personal trainer, Jan from Bristol should know.

I'd already seen it for myself, up at Norwich's new Sportspark, a dividend of the Lottery and the millennium. The gym there was packed. You can stand outside on the pavement and through the plate-glass wall watch all that rowing, stairmastering, treadmilling. All that exercise taken and suffering endured and self-worth tested, but among all those people striving and sweating, not one of them was playing. It wasn't a game.

I wanted to take a closer look, but didn't have the correct magnetic card. Kindly, the staff let me wander around anyway, and in one of the quieter carpeted corridors I paid twenty pence for some hi-tech Speak-Your-Weight. Only the machine didn't speak, it offered me an eagerly flapping print-out.

Welcome to Sportspark, Norwich.
Your Weight is 78.6 kg.
This is approximately 12 stones 5 pounds.
The approximate ideal weight for a male of 5 feet 10 INS.
With medium bodyframe is
71.2 kg OR 11 stones 3 pounds.
PLEASE REMEMBER TO ALLOW FOR YOUR
CLOTHES.

My clothes weigh one stone and two pounds. Well I never. If they didn't, I'd probably have to consider some time in the gym, at no risk to my self-esteem. Anyone can use a stairmaster.

'They don't know what they're missing,' Elliot says, thoughtfully drying a pint-pot with a cloth. 'They take their recreation too seriously.'

He offers me another drink, or perhaps more than just one, and before long (by now it's four in the afternoon, mind) we have one of Elliot's bar-stools down on the carpet and we're demonstrating the virtues and dangers of different bridging positions in the modern game.

Cracking.

Later still, because unlike David Storey I still haven't resolved my conflicting double life, I go out on the town with Andrew Cowan the famous capped writer. I get drunk, lose my voice. Or lose my voice, get drunk – can't remember. Anyway, I already had an impressive head-start from Elliot's Bar Rio, which might explain why at some stage even later I became detached from Andrew and found myself watching performance poetry in an upstairs room over a vodka bar, which in all its branded iconography was intent on selling Lenin.

The next night at training we were eighteen. All from the first-team squad, so as Jean Hospital might have said, it was training for a team and not a club. We ran through drills in preparation for Saturday's eight a.m. start for Winchester. In the absence of the regular number 13, I even got to be the stand-in centre, but not by asking: my voice was still absent, and I was feeling dreadful.

The cold which had been stalking me since Radley now finally attacked, and battling against it I was struggling to keep up to speed. At thirty-five, I now remembered, not even Sean Fitzpatrick the invincible All Black captain had made it. He missed the '99 World Cup, too battered to lift himself one more time, the indestructible destroyed. I doubt he took the same measures as I did. Earlier that afternoon, I'd gone to the city centre in search of a nasal spray containing performance-enhancing drugs. Unfortunately, none were available, not on the high street, except of course in Olympic years to competing British athletes.

As I huffed and puffed through the session, I was reminded of Norwich the last time round, when at the age of twenty-eight I'd first suspected I wouldn't live for ever. Rugby is a simple game for the young and confident, but for me eternal youth came to an end in 1995. Size became an issue, as did speed, and my knees sometimes ached horribly for no obvious reason.

At least the breakthrough novel had been going well, better than I could have imagined, because whenever I felt lacklustre in training I'd look for refuge in a godly, Lottery-type voice from the sky. It would order from on high with daunting authority that everyone take their turn on the tackle-bags. Except me, because I was the greatest prose-stylist of my generation. I went on the tackle-bags anyway, of course I did, because that was the type of man that rugby had made of me.

Just as it had prepared me for stitches without anaesthetic in a changing room at Cheshunt. Norwich's captain at the time was a doctor, and it seemed easier than going to casualty. My knee had split open, and as he approached it with the needle, I gritted my teeth and thought of Geoffrey Household. In his essential novel *Rogue Male*, the main character is prepared for a life of inter-war espionage by a sturdy British education, including games. He's captured, has his fingernails extracted, his eyeball burnt, and the skin flayed from the backs of his thighs. He's then pushed off a cliff, but still manages to escape from Fascist bloodhounds by crawling through forests and streams on his belly. It's quite a complicated story, but as the needle went in and out of my skin, I knew that rugby had prepared me to endure the pain. A year earlier, it might have escaped my attention that rugby had also caused it.

Match-days gradually became more directly a test of willpower and manhood, and I have to admit that I was occasionally unmanned. My hormones were somehow less pugnacious, and this frailty seemed infectious. We'd have a run of good games, and just when we'd cracked it, a rival club in the league would turn up with a new coach who happened to be an ex-All Black. We kept the results going, but there was a new set of pressures I hadn't felt before, and the pressure is equally great at a lower level. The stakes may be smaller, but so is the ability.

I clenched my teeth (after upgrading my gum-shield), and didn't think of giving up. Even though my first novel was about to be published, rugby still provided some kind of structure, especially in an unstructured life like mine. In fact, I'd recommend rugby to anyone attempting a life of the mind, especially male writers, sedentary people with a pitiable urge to prove their virility.

They may even learn something from it. MacNeice wrote that the rugby tradition makes two virtues supreme – 'individual endurance and the open game'. Not bad watchwords for the novelist, either, and if the writer can play a bit he'll catch a winning mood. Jack Kerouac did. He was a college gridiron player, which gave him the righteous arrogance to keep on working at *On the Road*. Or in his own words, 'starting quarterbacks don't sell Coke'.

Contact sports have more to offer than contact, so it's hardly surprising I should still be at it. At the end of Thursday training, despite my cold and the night before's alcohol binge, I begged a game for the thirds. Saturday afternoon, they told me, three o'clock, home against Lakenham.

'Apache,' Woody said, 'not *the* Apache.'

I spent my Friday evening back in Elliot's bar with Woody, chief of the Norfolk tribe. Mike Woodhouse is the froth on the beer, the bubbles in the tonic, he's everyone's firmest friend. He has a shaved head, a beaming square face, burning gas-blue eyes, and a flat nose that descends directly from his eyebrows. He's also the former second-team captain who threatened to have the Norwich badge tattooed on his chest.

Woody has a passionate memory for the dissent in the club when Norwich started paying their players. In many cases, he tells me, they didn't necessarily want paying in the first place. They'd have stayed anyway and played for the badge, just as they'd always done. The committee pushed ahead regardless, and it wasn't long before the soul of the club started to flex and fatigue in a new culture of 'he's having it, why not me?'

The club shifted, first in spirit and then officially, from a co-operative organisation to a commercial enterprise.

The Norwich third and fourth teams used to consider the third and fourth teams the heart of the club. And not unreasonably. It's here that younger players on the way up are introduced to everything rugger has to offer, gradually turning into better and tougher performers while being shown the time of their lives by old sweats on the way back down. More pragmatically, Woody also points out that today's geeky second-rower in the third team is tomorrow's major shareholder in Bernard Matthews.

In the summer of '99, Woody had the idea for Apache. He would split from Norwich and start a nomadic club in the tradition of Barbarians rugby. They would play friendlies at any club in Norfolk who'd have them, and he reasoned that most clubs would give Apache a fixture – regular matches for the lower teams were increasingly hard to find.

'But why bother, Woody? Why not just leave it?'

'It's in my blood, Rich.'

Woody is now convinced that if he hadn't started Apache, all those players would have left the game for ever. He charged his members a one-off annual fee of £20, which included socks and a tie.

In the first two seasons, the nomadic Apache played twenty fixtures, and 204 people ran out in the shirt. Woody's on a roll now, but I think it only fair to mention that I've heard him called a parasite, that Apache does 'more harm than good to local clubs'. The argument runs like this: Woody can manage Apache without overheads, but he still depends on established clubs with grounds and clubhouses to provide a pitch and showers and a bar. And rugby. There's also the feeling that Apache leaches players who would otherwise join established clubs.

Woody jumps off his stool.

'I'm *generating* players,' he insists, up in arms. 'I've *never* picked anyone from a regular team. I just get talking to strangers in pubs and they run out the next day for their first ever game of rugby. Some of them like it so much, they join a club. Isn't that great?'

Yes, I say, I think it is. He sits back down again, and crosses his arms.

Apache is on temporary hold while Woody plays a season at Diss, for a last chance at some serious rugby, but Apache isn't dead. It has a lot going for it, and because the matches are only once every three or four weeks, it's always a big event.

'Hire a coach,' Woody says, his enthusiasm once more coming to the bubble, 'bring the girlfriend, clear the evening. It's like a mini-tour every single time, and the clubs love us.'

He points out that Apache are likely to arrive with forty-five people, twenty-five of them players, and an Indian visit can leave as much as £700 behind a clubhouse bar. They've nowhere of their own to go back home to, so they stick around with their girlfriends and supporters, with no plans to hurry on. At least, not quite yet.

It all suggests, contrary to what I've been told elsewhere, that there *is* a demand for beer and singing in the bath, for friendlies and getting pissed. For rugger. There are rugby people in Norfolk who say Apache damages lower teams and steals away the characters. But the clubs should ask themselves (if they can find the time between naming mascots and designing the first XV's training jackets) why these characters wanted to leave in the first place.

Woody never did have that tattoo. He's got more sense. It's the game that's important, he says, not the club.

'We shouldn't be so geographical about it.'

He has a vision which runs in parallel with the increasing popularity of the elite game. It's of a future in which every county has its own nomadic tribe. At the end of the season, some time in the golden sunshine or the slanting rain of May, all the tribes will gather for a chaotic and riotous weekend, probably somewhere in Derbyshire.

'Why Derbyshire, Woody?'

'It's the middle of the country, isn't it?'

I'd love to see that first congress of the tribes, the Norfolk Apache, the Devon Cheyenne, the Yorkshire Crow and all the others, all rolling up in battered economy coaches behind chiefs like Woody and spilling out, whooping and tom-tomming, onto an unsuspecting club in the lucky Derbyshire Dales. It'd be the time of their lives. Like rugby always used to be.

Rugby needs at least two Woodys. At the top, Clive Woodward, ex-England and British Lions, to keep England winning as a challenge to the attention deficits of children and television executives. And at the bottom, in conjunction with established clubs, as an outlet for all that interest from bored men in pubs, Mike Woodhouse of Norfolk, chief of the peaceable Apache.

'We have to spread the news,' Woody says, eyes wide and grabbing me by the sleeve, 'and I know how to do it. Hire some pretty girls and put them in rugby kit, get them to hand out flyers in Castle Mall. Roadshows. More flyers in pubs. I sit and think about these things all the time. And I can't be the only one thinking like this. I can't, can I?' He stares right through my head, at all the rugby people I've ever met and ever known. 'Come on, Rich, tell me. Can I?'

Whatever else changes, Saturday is still match-day, even with rain falling solidly. In the earlyish morning I go out from Andrew and Lynne's to the shop, and along with a Saturday *Guardian* (it's a writerly household), and the milk, I buy some high-energy cereal, an ideal breakfast for anyone considering an afternoon of top-level sporting achievement.

Which this morning I am again considering, as I have every other winter Saturday for most of my adult life. Perhaps today is the day, at last, that I shall do something truly remarkable.

Up at the club it's grey, with a kind of blank drizzle you can only see by looking beyond it. I look through and beyond it at the electronic scoreboard, which doesn't work any more. It had to be moved from the site of the proposed grandstand,

and was never properly reconnected. The grandstand, meanwhile, is two long mounds of raised earth – and a large dose of imagination for the glory that never came.

Today's third XV fixture is complicated by the fact that the Lakenham third XV is the old Norwich fifth XV. Which is the former Norwich second XV of several years earlier, and I'm about to find out how it feels to represent a club disliked by all the others. It must feel a bit like this to play for England.

It's time. In the corridor outside the home changing room, daubed in maroon paint on the overhead beams, bearing down on us as we head for the pitch, are one-word reminders: COMMITMENT, CONTROL, PRIDE. These last-minute flight-checks are slightly diffused in Norwich's case because the changing rooms are upstairs. After Commitment Control Pride, there's the rest of the corridor; you then have to open a door, go down a set of stairs, open another door, down some steps, and then remembering what it was you had to remember, accelerate through the gate to the pitch.

It's altogether a feistier occasion than I'd been expecting, with three sin-bins and a Norwich player sent off for mentioning that sin-binning was the only mercy in any contest which that particular idiot was reffing.

For me, the miracle of the game loses nothing by repetition. I'm not obsessive about rugby, and could never have made it as a professional because cheerfulness or some other interest would have kept on breaking in. But during the eighty minutes in which the game is actually happening, I'm totally absorbed. It's the nothingness, the forgetting, the Tibetan sneeze. In that sense, as the Welshman Gwyn Thomas was suggesting, rugby has probably held me back as a novelist. It makes me insensitive to the slights and injustices and obscurity, and has never allowed me a long enough run at truly creative misery.

Back on the park, I'm again frustrated by my inability to have a decisive influence on the game. We're leading 17–12, but it should be more, and when our 10 is binned I step up from 15, taking responsibility for running down the clock. I'm also gearing up for a spectacular long-range individual try. As it is, I have a clearing kick charged down in the last minute. This allows Lakenham to score under the posts, and win the game by two clear points.

Sorry, lads. It was my fault. But thanks anyway for the game.

In the bar afterwards, while apologising to everyone individually, and promising never to come back as long as I live, the shame fades only slowly. As we talk over the match, as you do, in the echoing clubhouse with its high walls stacked with photos of previous teams, I have a beer or two. Fairly soon I'm forgetting the details, especially the ending, and instead I'm looking forward to the moment when I can sincerely think that Norwich is a grand club, a truly great club, perhaps the finest band of men on the planet. But by six o'clock the bar staff are already stacking the chairs and sweeping the floor, and without making it my only aim I was never going to get misty-eyed in one of the great clubs of the nation before six in the evening.

I therefore cycle back into the city and pick up an Indian takeaway and some cans of Abbott and go back to Andrew and Lynne's. And it isn't very long at all before I start to think that Andrew Cowan and Lynne Bryan, as people, as writers, in their front room as a snug substitute for the cavern of Norwich rugby club, are grand, truly great, and that the three of us are possibly the finest band of writers assembled in the same living room anywhere on the planet.

In this or any other moment of euphoria, I usually start toying with the illusion that I could have played for England, if only at an early age I hadn't been overlooked. It used to happen all the time, because the amateur game had no fool-proof system for identifying promising youngsters. Players of great talent would sup on local glory, and happily end up with 500 spirited appearances for Bridgwater (after being ill on their one selection for the county, thereby missing the match which might have led to England; or simply getting the day wrong).

Unfortunately, Andrew is a realist, even a micro-realist – a new genre I've invented just for him. Truth is all, and he wants me to know about the scouting model for football, which is now so evolved and intrusive that absolutely nobody with any talent ever gets missed, ever. No one. In that sense, it's harder for an average soccer player to nurture dreams, and his life can be ruined at a much more sensible age.

Andrew mentions that he was a pretty decent footballer himself, the second-best midfielder at the Beanfield Comprehensive in Corby. He then tells me about the *best* player, and at Beanfield this particular boy was the best player *by far*. He didn't get missed by the scouts. At school he was a genius, the next Billy Bremner, and he was picked out from thousands of hopefuls for a professional career.

He played for Northampton Town. *Northampton Town.*

Not Manchester United, not England, and this boy was the best. Andrew nods sagely, point effectively made.

I'd rather not know this, I think. I'd rather be hopeful that I was overlooked like so many others in an era when rugby provided a welcome home for incurable sporting illusionists.

To keep Andrew happy (realists tend to get grumpy more rapidly than normal people), and to reassure him that he's not alone in his horror of intimacy and tight shorts, I remember one of Gavin Ewart's rugby specials, 'On the Ambivalence of Male Contact Sports'. This'll cheer him up.

> Among men who play Rugger
> you seldom find a bugger –
> nobody strokes a bum
> in the scrum.
> Nevertheless . . .

Sporting Club Geneva, 1996–8

'In order to understand and appreciate it fully, one must have played it . . . this beautiful sport.'

Baron Pierre de Coubertin

I arrived in Geneva in pursuit of my one true love. And because she wasn't English, I could also register at the nearest rugby club, which qualified as an intriguing hobby and not an immediate cause for separation. The nearest club was Sporting Club de Genève, and although they usually finished in the top three of the Swiss First Division, the rugby itself offered a timely drop in standard. At training, the Sporting used to share one floodlit pitch with the Geneva Seahawks gridiron team, in full armour, who were often being filmed for television. This meant there were always people everywhere, doing everything, and it was like running about in a sporting *Where's Wally*.

It came as something of a shock, in my first competitive game, to discover that the Sporting didn't seem overly bothered about losing. Yet before very long I was fully endorsing this cavalier approach. I was working on my second novel, and operating as far outside the comfort zone in writing as I was everywhere else (money, relationships, the usual). The comfort zone in sport was therefore a very welcome comfort.

In those days, the Swiss championship was dominated by RFC Hermance, who selected a mixture of Scots ex-pats and Swiss internationals. RFC Nyon were led by clever Welshmen who during the week accelerated invisible particles at Geneva's Centre for Nuclear Research. Zurich RUFC was packed with the worst type of banker and Englishman, chinless buffoons in their weekend business shirts, disasters waiting to prat-fall half-dressed off shaky trestle-tables.

And at Sporting, we were mostly French. I was therefore back in the land of the cool. On match-days, we needed drugs. Unfortunately, many of the games were in France, including the home ground of our closest rivals Hermance. This created complex problems for health insurance, which the Swiss Rugby Federation had well in hand. But there were also secondary consequences for smuggling drugs across international borders. The long-haired rugby players in dark glasses and camper vans would put a rugby ball on the dash and float unmolested across the frontier into France, waving cheerily at the cigarette-smoking police.

'Thanks, man. *Allez les Bleus.*'

But on the way back, after a devastating loss or an epic victory, I forget which, we'd always stop several miles before the border crossing in a secluded French lay-by. The lads would carefully hide the ball and the glasses, tie back their hair, and rigorously check the correct operation of all exterior parking lights.

*

As a consequence of professionalism, rugby now feels the commercial imperative to grow the business. Expand or die. Vernon Pugh, the former chairman of the International Rugby Board, expressed it more grandly: 'Capitalising on the upsurge in interest generated by the Rugby World Cup is the duty of the IRB, whose aim is to foster, promote and extend the game of Rugby Union – the very words that define its role. Ultimately, development is the essential factor in the long-term prosperity of rugby.'

It's true that sports can die. In England, rugby league is dying, shrinking itself to fit on that dusty shelf beside Derbyshire Football and Knappan and Winchester Rules. Rugby union is expanding across the globe.

Since my days with the Sporting in Geneva, Italy have entered the Six Nations, and in the year 2000 the Swiss set out to qualify for the 2003 Rugby World Cup with a satisfying victory over Bulgaria. This qualifying tournament involves all ninety-four member nations of the IRB, from Guam to Kazakhstan. It takes more than two years to complete, and Switzerland is in the European section of the IRB's attempt to validate the notion of a truly World Cup.

It may work. Rugby may conquer the planet, but it's worth remembering that the game has stuttered at the global level before now. In Germany, a rugby coaching book was first published as long ago as 1910. It was written by C.W. Hotz, and called *Rugby Fussball* (nothing as frivolous as rugger for the Germans). After witnessing from close quarters the idiocy of the British in the First World War, the game never caught on. In Russia it was a Scot, Mr Hopper, who attempted to launch the game, but in 1886 rugby was officially suppressed by the police. It was considered a 'brutal game conducive to manifestations and rioting'.

Despite or because of its talent for subversion (and the Russians should know), the game is now on the way back, as demonstrated by the scope of the qualifying competition for the 2003 World Cup. It used to be a foregone conclusion that the biggest fish among the European minnows, the nation most likely to earn the right to enter the genuine World Cup, would be Spain. The Spanish rugby team is packed with rock-hard Basques who jog daily over the Pyrenees to play in France. But suddenly the Polish and the Russians are very large, and impervious to pain. The Georgians are man-mountains with hearts like bears, and this time round the Basques have been out-willed and out-fought, which is not something I'll be shouting aloud in the streets of Bilbao. Though I might in Tbilisi, where the World Cup qualification play-off between Georgia and Russia attracted 65,000 fanatical supporters. There was snow in the air, and flares in the crowd, and at times like this it really does seem as if rugby, for all its virtues, could indeed go global.

There are outside factors, of course, as there were during the game's first great expansion in the days of Queen Victoria. Then, the mid-century Factory Acts democratised sport by giving industrial workers their Saturday afternoons off. Now, equally unstoppably, the expanding global media companies are greedy for televised sport as a lever for developing markets. Rugby has been a beneficiary at the elite level, but this only partly explains why the big-hearted citizens of Uruguay or Korea have grabbed a ball and run and tackle for the joy of it.

There are sports which can't expand whatever efforts they make, whatever the social conditions. In a grim lesson for rugby league, generations of Cornishmen attempted to popularise the regional game of hurling by staging exhibition matches in London. The first of these was in 1654, the last in 1820, but by 1879 the game had contracted to a home-and-away ding-dong between two Cornish parishes. Hurling didn't have what it takes.

In *Endless Winter*, the first of his epic surveys of the rugby world, Stephen Jones writes: 'Whatever strengths, inner goodness, whatever special culture, whatever appeal, whatever chemistry you need to reach people, the facts say that union has them.'

By luck, by a coincidence of timing, there seems to be a convergence between what the game has to offer and what people want, an arena which provides a sense of traditional masculinity in increasingly unstable societies. In supplying this demand, rugby appears to have a gift for adapting to different cultures. This is because it has at its core not local or regional or even British values, but universal masculine ones. We are not alone. Men all over the world would like to be tough, resilient, courageous, reliable, self-reliant, stoical, multi-skilled, and accepted as belonging to an admirably like-minded band of men. It's not just me.

Look at Japan, where the game was introduced by sailors into the port cities of Yokohama and Kobe in the mid-nineteenth century. Rugby now prospers as the collective sport best able to express and sustain the masculine samurai ideology of *seishin*. This is a way of living which involves the inner being, where spiritual fortitude and self-discipline are developed through particular physical training. All the virtues of *seishin ryoku* (spiritual power) can be found in rugby. There's *ganburu* (do your absolute best), *isshokenmei* (give everything), *konjo* (bottle) and *gaman* (endurance and perseverance).

It's still rugby, even if the Japanese approach it in a slightly different manner. Their training, for example, can resemble a form of monastic discipline: the endless repetition of simple, monotonous but physically demanding tasks. Basically, they run up and down the pitch passing the ball at full speed until they drop. This represents a quasi-religious struggle for control of the body, a version of manliness which favours toughness, a combination of *mushin* (no mind) and the famous *konjo* (fighting spirit).

Personally, I'd never thought about rugby in quite this way before, but I realise now that what I like about rugby is partly what the Japanese like. And they like it very much, so much so that at one time there was a long-running TV series about an inspirational high-school rugby coach, Mr Yamaguchi of Fushimi Tech.

The spirit of the game, finding a new vocabulary in each different nation, travels well. Rugby seems to express resonant myths which echo from Siberia to the Ivory Coast, from Chile to China. And in China – watch out New Zealand – they're even threatening to take it seriously.

Perhaps they've noticed how the international game is thriving at its source. The new or renovated stadiums at Twickenham, Cardiff and Murrayfield can take 75,000 spectators each, and in 1999 the knockout stages of the Rugby World Cup had a higher average attendance than the

equivalent stages in soccer. Twickenham, or as my old friend
E.H.D. Sewell liked to think of it, G.H.Q. Rugger, is as full as
an egg whenever England play, and the cheapest seats for
2003 are £40. The enduring popularity of the elite game
generates enormous revenue for rugby's premier nations.

Unfortunately, these funds are jealously protected. From
time to time media-friendly gestures accompany the IRB's
posturing about the global expansion of the game, but there's
always also Romania. The biggest scandal in rugby continues, and it mocks the IRB's pretensions to spread the good
rugby news. In 1957, 93,000 Romanian rugby supporters
gathered in Bucharest for the visit of the French, a match
which the home team narrowly lost. In 1991, this defeat was
avenged in Perpignan, where the Romanians beat France for
the first ever time.

We are now eight years into the brave new world of
professionalism, and in 2003 Romania is a rugby nation to
which junior British clubs send aid parcels of used boots and
faded training-tops. The IRB, despite all its resources, stands
behind this commendable private initiative as if it's the best
and only way to help. There is also the issue of New
Zealand's plunder of athletes from the Pacific Islands, and the
Tri-Nations' self-serving exclusion of the Islanders and
Argentina from both the Super 12 and the Tri-Nations itself.
This greed and blindness is no doubt 'the real, unforgiving
world' that rugby's professional managers were always
anticipating. And it's the world they've helped to create.

If the IRB do one day show a genuine interest in sharing
rugby's resources, in dynamically growing the sport, it's still
unlikely that Switzerland will ever contend for major

honours. In 2003, for the fifth World Cup in succession, they've failed to make the finals. They had their chance. All they had to do was win three qualifying pools of increasing difficulty to earn the right to take on a loser from the European Nations Cup, the tournament one below the Six Nations. This would have meant defeating the Netherlands (as if), so that they could then afford to lose to Ireland and Georgia. However, after beating Spain in a repêchage, a win over Tunisia in a second repêchage would have bagged the coveted prize of an autumn in Brisbane and Woolongong, there to get mashed by Scotland and big-boy neighbours France. *Hop Suisse!*

What actually happened was this: in the first group phase Switzerland had strutting victories over Bulgaria, Andorra, and Hungary. Easy. In round two, they beat Belgium but were narrowly defeated by Croatia. The guillotine finally came down in an epic and brutal match with the untamed giants of the Czech Republic, in which six Swiss players were stretchered from the field. Before half-time.

Despite this bruising defeat, the Swiss were rightly proud of their World Cup qualifying campaign, which now sees them confirmed in FIRA Division 2 Pool B, with a world ranking of 33. And for a country which has a thousand senior players and twenty clubs, that can't be a bad achievement. I decided to go and see the President of the Fédération Suisse de Rugby. I wanted to find out what the future held for the game in an outpost as unlikely as Switzerland.

Monsieur Luc Bataard is a secret banker.

So secret, in fact, that I didn't realise what he was until later in the week, when one of the lads at the Sporting took me aside and whispered the secret in my ear. Ah, I thought, that would explain the extreme beauty of the girls at his place of work, and the hugeness of Mr Bataard's desk.

Mr Bataard's office is on the fourth floor of an anonymous block in the Cours de Rive, at the more exclusive end of one of Geneva's busiest, tramlined avenues. There is no plaque at street level mentioning a bank. Instead, in the slot beside the entrance buzzer for the fourth floor, there is a narrow brass plate with a mysterious inscription: SWISS BARBARIANS.

I'm buzzed in. I climb the stairs. It is a very quiet building.

At first sight, the President of the Swiss Federation of Rugby is not a man over-acquainted with joy. A short, solid prop-forward whose propping days are over, Mr Bataard takes over from one of several stunning young women in reception, and leads me to his office while mentioning in an offhand way his former clubs. Before RFC Hermance in Switzerland, he played for Harlequins in London, and in Paris for the Racing Club de France. I look at him closely as I settle into the leather chair on the junior side of the vast desk. Even though my padded chair is slightly lower than his, I lean forward and frown and stare him out with my steeliest eyes.

'Well,' he says, looking away and coughing into his hand, then quickly doing something with a computer to one side which sets a printer buzzing, 'not the first team.'

It's possible that this little misunderstanding sets us off on the wrong foot, but his ears will always betray him. He has the unmarked ears of an office man.

He still loves his rugby, I think. It's hard to tell. He unscrews a black fountain pen as thick as a cigar and draws me, very slowly, detailed little charts and diagrams of the administrative structure of Swiss rugby. I now formally declare this quarter-hour my personal entry in the category Demonstrations, World's Most Boring.

If nothing else, I do at least manage to work out how much of the wealth of G.H.Q. Rugger is currently redirected to Switzerland. The Federation has a debt of 100,000 Swiss francs, which is about one eightieth of the gate receipts from a Six Nations match at Twickenham. FIRA (the subsidiary of the IRB for the smaller nations) pays 75% of the Swiss team's travel costs, and allocates the Federation £25,000 a year. Or to put it another way, about £475,000 short of the amount needed to open a personal account with Mr Bataard. He points out gloomily that for after-match banquets £25,000 goes a whole lot further in the Ukraine than it does in Geneva. I'm not sure I have enough compassion in my soul to feel pity, exactly, about this. However, it does make me hope that before I die I'll get invited to a rugby banquet in Kharkov.

Mr Bataard's most recent contribution to Swiss rugby has been to scour the French championship for Swiss-qualified players, so that now there are only five or six international caps who actually play in Switzerland. The problem, he tells me, is that of the six clubs in National Division One, three are utterly rubbish. As he talks about possible regional structures, and very slowly draws me yet another diagram, I can feel his pain. The national team must be such a burden.

Remembering the plate by the door, I change the subject to the Swiss Barbarians. In 1996 in Lausanne, on probably the best ever day of my rugby life, I played in the curtain-raiser to the final of the Swiss Cup, a match between the Swiss Barbarians and a scratch team of ex-internationals. Genuine all-time hero-internationals, and not from the countries in the qualifying competition. The line of my rugby life had never been the shortest distance between two points, but here at last I was about to take the field with the stars.

Our opponents were like a representative side from a retirement home for rugby legends, and on that specific sun-drenched afternoon in May, I'd rather have been nowhere else on earth. Led out by skipper Nick Farr-Jones, here they come: John Gallagher, Peter Winterbottom, Brian Moore, Hicka Reid. There was even a celebrity referee, Derek Bevan.

Quite unbelievably there are many people, including most of the Swiss population, to whom these names mean nothing.

Mr Bataard perks up immediately. He even screws the top back on his fat black pen. 'It's all my own work,' he beams. 'In the last four years I've personally sponsored the Barbarians.' His little eyes light up as he names some of the players he's invited: Philippe Saint-André, Olivier Roumat, Gavin Hastings. 'It's an independent and occult group,' he confides gleefully, 'independent of all federations everywhere. No one knows how the Barbarians works.'

The attraction of the Barbarians model to Mr Bataard suddenly becomes clear: it's secretive, and exclusive, and open only to the invited. But I was still a bit confused, because my own Barbarians match was longer ago than this, five or six years ago, apparently before Mr Bataard had even invented the team.

'No,' he says, picking up and putting down his pen. 'There was no game then.'

'I played in it.'

He points to a display-case on the wall containing a folded rugby shirt. 'Did you play in the blue-and-white quarters?'

'The shirts were green, with yellow hoops on the sleeves.'

'Maybe,' he says, dismissively inspecting his lower lip, 'I know nothing about that match. Maybe it was for some anniversary. I wouldn't remember.'

He waves away the subject with his pudgy hand. Mr Bataard is the President of the Federation. The Barbarians wear blue and white, not green and yellow. I start to doubt myself, as if the best ever day of my rugby life might never have taken place. Instead, it's a rather sad myth of my own making, a dream, but so real in its intensity that I always feel privileged to recall being picked up bodily by Peter Winterbottom and then upended, still clutching the ball, onto my head.

'Thanks, Peter, that was great.'

'I'm sorry. I just had to.'

'Not a problem. I feel a bit dazed.'

After a bang to the head like that, it was quite possible that one day I'd doubt whether any of it had ever actually happened.

Thomas Keneally had taught me that imagination was vital in rugby. Maybe I'd imagined an entire game. While assessing this possibility, I spend the next few minutes agreeing fervently with Mr Bataard that the best Swiss club teams (let alone the national team) could hold their own in the French Second Division (! sorry, Luc, but no way, not even close). He leans over to the computer and takes the print-out he set going earlier. It is his three-year plan for the development of Swiss rugby, and it runs to several pages. He carefully squares the edges, then stands up and holds it out to me over the vast desk.

'This is confidential,' he says gravely. 'You may read it. But after you've read it, you must please destroy it.'

I look closely into his eyes for the sanity of humour. Nothing. I stand up and solemnly accept the three-year plan. As for the future of Swiss rugby, I apologise but this is information I'm not at liberty to divulge. It's a secret, and world domination may or may not be the aim.

Whether or not the Swiss Federation succeeds, it did occur to me that at the start of all great institutions, like for example the French Imperial Guard, there was a short, humourless, highly competent individual such as Mr Bataard. However, I still don't know what to make of my discovery that the immense fortunes of some of the world's most discreet charlatans are managed by a banker in Geneva who frames rugby shirts and mounts them on his office wall. And fantasises about once having propped for Harlequins.

It wouldn't wash in James Bond.

Then I remembered Switzerland's World Cup opponents, Bulgaria and Croatia and the Czech Republic. Then I thought of the huge sums of money being pumped into professional rugby across the world, in which more cash goes in than ever comes out again. And I began to imagine, dimly at first, but then ever more vividly, Mr Bataard and the Swiss Rugby Federation as an essential though secret cog in the charade of professional rugby union – itself nothing other than the largest ever money-laundering operation in the history of organised crime.

If only I could make public what I know from that document. But I'm a rugby player and man of my word. I ate it.

At six o'clock on Tuesday, still an hour before the start of training, it's a mild evening and the municipal green pitch is flooded with late autumn sunshine. I see strange cloud formations in the distance, which when I focus become the peaks of distant Alps. Closer by, there's the looming presence of the Salève cliff-face where Frankenstein's monster, the most famous of composite men, escaped his earthbound pursuers.

It was here on the green open spaces at Vessy in Geneva that the Swiss were mangled by the Czechs. This is an international municipal ground, and the Sporting Club de Genève's junior section are already out on the grass.

Thirty youngsters, both boys and girls, are separated into five groups according to age, each with its own coach, and they're all careering about in the red, yellow and black of the Sporting. Even in Switzerland there are slow fat children and small quick children who love to run, to pass and tackle, to roll and slide and make solid contact with the good Swiss earth.

The Sporting Club de Genève is the oldest club in Switzerland, and although much of its history is obscured by myth and folklore, it started out as Geneva Servette. Nobody knows when. There are no written records, and since then the club has had to change its name several times. Only last year it officially changed again to the Rugby Club de Genève, but for the moment everyone still calls it the Sporting, a treasured legacy of the club's merger in the seventies with a pub team, which briefly brought Genevan rugby under the influence of the mysterious Heinz von Arx, a shady Swiss German with an Irish accent.

It may have been during the same era that an image of the Geneva water-jet was adopted as the club badge. At the Geneva end of Lac Léman there's a 145-metre water-geyser, which in a rare example of Swiss competitive instinct rivals a similar jet in Canberra. Someone from world sport should have warned them. At 147 metres, the Australians win again.

In the warm Geneva evening, an American mom has brought her son along to the rugby. It's their first time. Ron is a big ten-year-old and has played gridiron in the States. He's introduced to Fabrizio, the Sporting's chief of junior operations, but bursts into tears when Fabrizio says hello in French. Fabrizio calls over one of the trainers who speaks some English, and a little later I wander over to see how Ron is settling in. He's playing British Bulldog, and laughing his head off. Rugby is already good for Ron, I think, and in any case he could do with losing a few pounds.

As I'm leaving to get changed for senior training, I overhear Ron's mother chatting with an Anglo-mum from Scotland. She says she hadn't expected so much full-on contact. Not straight away. 'Doesn't it worry you?'

'Yes.'

'What about the kids?'

'They love it.'

In the States, Ron was so big for his age he wasn't allowed to touch the ball.

The senior Sporting training session was brilliant, inspired. The club has sixty adult licence-holders, and at least half of them were out training in the fading light, led by Frenchman Pascal Racaud, a storm, a force of nature.

Les gars, vous êtes pas en forme! Au bulot!

In Paris, the SCUF's limited practice strategy of running round and round had bored me to distraction. Here I was enthused. Everything was the same, teaching all the same basics, but everything was different. We ran two against one, but sprinting up a ridiculous hill. Instead of piling into the heavy bags, Pascal had the defender pick up the bag and use it to attack the runner. I don't know what this was supposed to achieve, but it was very funny.

Pascal has the kind of washed-out blue eyes which suggest that as a player, at full-back for French Students and later Begles-Bordeaux, he was a bit of a nutcase. But he loves his rugby, and he's the fastest talker I've ever heard, even from the speedy south-west. His ambition is to train the Swiss national team, and he's only thirty-four – a coach who's younger than I am. I don't care. He's the best.

There are more English speakers at the Geneva club than there used to be, four or five, including a Finn and a German-Australian, with all the defects of character such a horrific mixture suggests. The view of the English-speaking players is that there are too few drills. They don't like the way Pascal actually makes them play in training. They're also uncomfortable with the dope culture, and perhaps worse, the Swiss

216

tendency to visit a restaurant halfway through a Saturday evening. Sometimes, heaven help us, the Swiss even stop drinking before they're drunk. And the language can be a problem. Why do they have to speak in French all the time?

The most integrated of the English, John Evans, has a rugby nose which starts off in one direction, the sensible one, but soon takes a diversion. He doesn't speak any French, and in the final match of last season he broke his broken nose and was rushed to the nearest hospital. Within an hour, this being Switzerland, he was being treated by an anaesthetist and a plastic surgeon, and for a week afterwards he wore a mask of bandages. As each day passed, he could hardly wait to see his straightened nose. Whenever he passed a mirror, he'd wink at his reflection between the bandages (you handsome devil, you). Unfortunately, because John couldn't speak French, the surgeon hadn't been able to ask him what he wanted. The doctor and nurses had therefore looked in John's wallet while the anaesthetic took effect, and rebuilt his nose from the photo on his residency permit. When John eventually peeled off the bandages, his nose was as perfectly ugly as before.

I like this story so much I even hope it's true.

The Sporting is sponsored by the Auberge de Coutance, a classy restaurant specialising in the hearty gastronomy of south-west France, and training inevitably finishes back in town at the Auberge. There's a weekly deal. We can have any main course we want for ten quid, including wine and coffee and a chamberpot full of Swiss chocolates. Nobody can explain the chamberpot, but this is a bargain (about a third of the normal price), and you can tell the Auberge is authentic to the French south-west because leather rugby balls hang by their laces from the ceiling, and the waiters share Eric Cantona's dad.

I talk about my Barbarians match with Laurent, a regular in the Swiss team who also played on that special day in 1996. He's a scrum-half or a full-back, and a Swiss Belmondo: all the looks and none of the hurry. He can't remember what the opposition was called, or why the match took place, and I'm beginning to worry about the ingenuity of my memory. I ask Laurent about the Swiss team now, and he tells me that since the arrival of Mr Bataard they no longer have to pay if they swap their shirts with the opposition. He then reminisces about the good old days, and a particular trip to Spain when the Swiss held the grizzled Basques for thirty minutes, at least. As for the French imports, they were all right, but they made no effort to speak to the Swiss Germans, and that wasn't very polite, was it?

The conversation bounds up and down the table, gestured back and forth with bread dipped in wine and the *plat du jour*, but everyone seems agreed that not even the wealth of the RFU would make much odds in Switzerland. Switzerland has everything, and it works impeccably, like an enormous public school but with immigrants and women and a fair justice system. Every sport is open to everybody, yet the nation excels in nothing.

As well as rugby, to sort the men from the boys in Switzerland there's ice hockey and ski-jumping and the Vaudois game of *hornussen*, in which the aim is to intercept the *hornuss* with the *schindel*. It's all too much, too prosperous, and when I was last here there was a national depression because the Swiss couldn't even win at skiing. In their fetching Calvinist way, they hated themselves for being so adult and well adjusted that nobody in the country could be found mad and bad enough to excel at international sport.

George Orwell once famously wrote that 'sport has nothing to do with fair play. It is bound up with hatred, jealousy, boastfulness, disregard of all rules and sadistic pleasure in witnessing violence; in other words it is war without shooting.' Equally famously, Switzerland doesn't do war, and perhaps sport means something different in a neutral country. Here, unlike in Paris, the advance of material comforts *had* made men soft, and it was hardly surprising the men of the nation were battered by the Czech Republic.

There's a justice to international rugby which appeals to me. It's a game which rewards the muscular capital peasants and industrial workers build up over generations of hard manual labour. In exchange for one hundred years of English exploitation of coal in the valleys, the Welsh had the Pontypool front row. This may not seem like a great swap, but ask anyone when the Welsh were routinely humiliating the English at Cardiff Arms Park, and it was definitely worth something. Now the Poles and the Ukrainians, their backs massive from shifting communist steel, are crushing the indolent Swiss and Belgians, and I like the justice in that.

Of course, the Swiss could always *train*, but a good example of their distance from sporting success is offered by the annual Twenty-four Hours of Rugby. This was in its second year in 1996, and *Vingt-Quatre Heures de Rugby* was true to the promise on the car stickers: twenty-four hours of rugby, raising money for charity, to which the clubs sent all the volunteers they could muster, an outing for the rugby-playing nuts of the nation. The day started at noon with some mini-rugby games in the eighty-degree heat. The Swiss season takes a winter break, to avoid the worst of the snow, with the consequence that the season continues well into early summer.

The afternoon of *Vingt-Quatre Heures de Rugby* is taken up by the two semi-finals of the Swiss Cup. This is a model of Swiss efficiency – the semi-finals take place on a neutral ground with many spectators and take care of at least three and a half hours of the twenty-four. On this occasion, the Sporting are narrowly beaten by RFC Hermance, which is actually a great blessing because it makes us available on the day of the final for the Barbarians. Immediately after our semi-final, which marks the end of the season, the president of the club Olivier Rouby leads us proudly to a small marquee in which there is nothing but a long row of blue-and-white cool-boxes. We have just played eighty minutes of rugby in full sunshine and heat. We're still in our kit, socks rolled down and jerseys over our shoulders. But with an irrepressible urge to be loved, the president gleefully flips off the lids of the cool-boxes, and for his players, for his brave *gars*, he has provided twenty-four bottles of champagne and one hundred and forty-four oysters.

After that, there are seventeen hours of pick-up matches, although as the floodlights come on and the night stretches ahead and people lose their boots, the game resembles less and less the modern sport of rugby. It's fun, and nobody cares who wins, and no one's playing for the points. The Swiss do fabulous public parties. They have a talent for tents and trestle-tables and flag-waving and griddled sausages and the unmissable feel-good of the oompah band. But it will be some time, I suspect, before they triumph in pre-qualifying for the Rugby World Cup.

Sadly, Laurent tells me that the Twenty-four Hours of Rugby is no more. There was a third edition after those first two at Avusy, at Meyrin, but the event faded and hasn't happened since. I help myself to a chocolate from the chamberpot and ask why. A dark look settles on Laurent's face.

'They started serving paella instead of sausage.'

Quite reasonably, I think, for an ordinary Tuesday training night, I'm back home in bed by 12.41 a.m. The next morning I take things easy, and in the bath I find myself thinking of Laurent's nostalgia for the more innocent rugby in the days before Bataard. He means rugger, of course, Norwich's six XVs and the Mid-Argyll seconds drinking their petrol money on the long journey home from Newton Stewart. Even for those of us who were there, it's not always easy to remember if the amateur days were better, worse, or just different. Incidents can be isolated, like my own fantasy game for the Swiss Barbarians, and a match like that would never happen today. The international players wouldn't be released, wouldn't be insured, wouldn't be free. But then isolating another professional consequence, Brian Liebenburg wouldn't want it any other way.

I suddenly remember that in my rucksack there's a video of the original Barbarians, which I've been carrying about since Lochgilphead. In playing terms, the 1973 Barbarian–All Blacks is generally considered a peak of the amateur era. I have a free morning, and a video machine in the front room of the flat where I'm staying. If it really was better in the old days, I think, maybe I'll be able to *see* it.

I pop in the video, and it's a misty January twenty-seventh at Cardiff Arms Park in 1973. Cliff Morgan is commentating, and I'm straight in the mood. For the All Blacks it's the end of a long tour, and to a man they need a haircut. They assemble their semi-circle for the haka . . . and don't seem to know what they're doing. The actions and words seem unfamiliar to them, unlike the modern All Blacks who perform the haka in perfect aggressive unison. (Of course, I think, these days they must practise. Surely they must. As professionals exploiting every small advantage they'll want to make the haka as intimidating as they possibly can, and I imagine them rehearsing, in mauve leggings, with a choreographer. It's suddenly a lot less intimidating.)

In another change which had never registered with me, the 1973 All Blacks do the haka to the crowd, not in the faces of the opposition. Not scary; obliging, almost nice. But there's something else, as they do that final jump in the air in their unrehearsed dribs and drabs – whisper it, but they look (shh!) weedy. I can't see the muscles in their legs, arms, necks. These days, even *I've* got visible muscles.

As the match kicks off, I catch myself looking for weaknesses in the old amateur game, for the failings of pace and dynamism that are claimed as the great professional improvements. And it's true that the kicking of the leather ball is noticeably less tonic than the kicking of the plastic ball is today. There's a softness to it, a boomlessness. There's also less athleticism among the forwards, and to start with there's an uncapped Cambridge Blue called Wilkinson who's having a shocker. Both teams drop the ball a lot, to which the crowd don't particularly react, and before the game finds its shape it feels like watching keen and promising children who deserve parental support.

Then, out of nowhere, there's the famous try. From one end of the pitch to the other, starting with Bennett and finishing with Edwards, with the best of British rugby in between (meaning, at that time, mostly the Welsh). It's a marvellous try, truly, even now. And then the match begins to take over, the match itself, and the soul of rugby then as now is not in the marketing package or the advertising (*Cossack*, *Rael Brook Shirts*) but in the variety and commitment of the game itself. It's fantastically exciting. I can't really explain it, but it's stirring, and it gets even better when despite the famous try I realise I don't actually know the result.

Dawes is the man, with all the modern skills. And Edwards. And Phil Bennett, of course. And JPR. But *apart* from that? There's always David Duckham.

The forwards suffer more by comparison, but there's no lack of ferocity. As well as the unstinting All Black resolve to garotte JPR, there's some gratuitously nasty rucking and some speculative punching (who's weedy now?). And at half-time I'm breathless and need a cup of tea, but it's really captivating to see the players still on the field redoing their hair, looking worried, looking exhausted. That, too, is entertainment.

There's a great moment in the second half involving the All Black wing Grant Batty. He's already been booed by the Cardiff crowd for aiming a haymaker at the untouchable

Gareth Edwards. He then makes a break, kicks ahead, and scores a stunning individual try. He dives on the ball, stands up, and in the silence around the ground he demonstrates no 'passion' whatsoever, no shouting or screaming or telegenic tub-thumping. And yet I know, and everyone else knows, as he walks pigeon-chested and deliberately expressionless back to the halfway line, precisely what he's thinking.

Up yours, you stuck-up pommy bastards.

And when JPR scores, I jump off the sofa. I really do. Thirty years after JPR swayed and stepped, I could still be made to jump from my seat. Now that's a good game of rugby. And I'm not going to spoil it for anyone else by saying what happens at the end.

It did beg the question, if the game could be quite so good, why we needed to change it. I was asking much the same question that afternoon in the Olympic Museum, not just of rugby, but of all our sports and games.

In the lakeside city of Lausanne, a short train ride from Geneva, the Olympic Museum is the personal project and fiefdom of Juan Antonio Samaranch, ex-president of the International Olympic Committee. In certain lights, it's a horrid little place, with a sinister décor of Nazi-revival pillars and moving athletic body-parts. But on the afternoon I went, the light was sunshine in sparks off the glittering lake, and it made me want to be generous.

In 1892 Baron Pierre de Coubertin, the founder of the Olympic movement, refereed the first final of the French rugby championship. It was a cracker between the Racing Club and Stade Français at Bagatelle Park. De Coubertin then made the mistake of attributing the ideal qualities he observed in rugby to all other sports, and so the Olympics were born.

The Olympic Museum is a testament to what happens to sport with the idealism removed, rugby with no trace remaining of rugger. It's a pompous, self-important, humourless, puffed-up, essentially empty enterprise: a defeat for the human spirit. Even in nice weather, and however much I wish it wasn't.

First of all I go to the basement, ignoring the bright arrows to the upstairs exhibition and instinctively following the signs to LIBRARY (it takes all sorts). I want to know if there's a rugby section, and there is, and astonishingly, I find on the shelves a large glossy hardback I've never seen before. It's called *World in Union, A Celebration of Rugby and Its People*.

Inside the front cover, I'm excited to find an inscription, handwritten in special-occasion ink:

> To President Juan Antonio
>> from Vernon Pugh, with
>>> very best wishes.
>>>> Vernon Pugh
>>>>> September 2000

No, Vernon, no. You've done it all wrong.

Vernon Pugh, former chairman of the IRB, is guilty of too much rugby chumminess. Too much assumption that all men are equal. And Juan Antonio is having none of that. Vernon obviously didn't know that for at least ten years Samaranch has preferred to be addressed as *Marques*, although in conversation or court proceedings he's sometimes prepared to settle for *Your Excellency*. He's a lesson to all mankind in the human characteristics best avoided (pride, self-importance, vanity, to name but three of his anti-rugby vices), yet this book was 'Copy number 1 of 12 for the IOC', an exclusive and specially created grovel to the Olympic Committee from the IRB.

All that effort, all that money. Such a handsome book full of fine colour photographs and 'rugby's Olympic aspirations' in three languages, English, French and Spanish. Sorry, chaps, and I'm only the messenger, but Samaranch valued his personally inscribed gift so highly that he disposed of it on the open-access shelves of a library in the basement of his museum.

Mind you, a bit of proofreading wouldn't have hurt. I particularly liked, in this grandiose and glossy production, the Fijians with their 'unbridled joy and daft handling skills'. Pugh concludes the limited edition by sycophantically repeating 'the Game's so far unfulfilled ambition, to rejoin the Olympics as a competitive sport'. As if this was all our sport ever wanted or needed to make itself worthwhile.

Well, I never knew that. But I can't think of any good reason for licking the Olympic feet. We've been in the Olympics before, and look what happened then. In the 1900 Paris Olympics, the rugby gold medal was won by France, 27–17 against Germany. Unfortunately, only three teams entered, and the third was Moseley Wanderers. There was no rugby in St Louis in 1904, but in London in 1908 Australia beat Britain to the gold by 32–3. This time Britain was represented by Cornwall. In 1920, the USA beat France 8–0, but the trouble started in the re-match four years later back in Paris. USA were the underdogs, but they came through 18–3 in a final which was 'marred by violence on and off the field'. The US flag was torn up, and the Welsh referee forcefully insulted, both of which I'd like to have seen.

And I did. In a nice touch, the entrance ticket to the museum entitles each visitor to watch two three-minute clips from the Olympic video archive. Not expecting it to be there, I typed in the bad-tempered 1924 rugby final. Amazingly, they had it, and I settled back in my booth for some gratifying on-screen violence. I wasn't disappointed, even in the allocated three minutes. In front of a rowdy crowd at Colombes (recently sold by the SCUF), and in black-and-white film-stock which accelerated the action, it was immensely satisfying to see an American in a tight woollen jersey (visible muscles) kick a Frenchman in the head well after he'd dived over to score. In return, there was superb half-time footage of an American having his head stitched, right in the middle of the pitch.

It was just as pleasing to recognise other familiar aspects of the game. The French crowd booed their own team, and according to the voiceover the Americans would later discover that their wallets had been stolen from the changing room. There was no visible evidence of the crowd violence cited as a reason for discontinuing rugby as an Olympic sport. But it was true that the fearsome tackling and total emotional commitment of both teams had none of the preferred Olympic allure of, say, beach volleyball.

I then watched Ovett beat Coe in Moscow.

We shouldn't forget that in the old days rugger wasn't always honest. But then Switzerland isn't actually all that clean. What did I expect? As for the Olympics, it's hard to understand why we'd want to get involved. Some years ago, it was argued that Olympic recognition would persuade the countries of the communist bloc to take rugby seriously. Now this argument has been transferred to countries with large Olympic budgets, like Spain. But look at the price: the Olympic Museum is now a shrine to sport as commodified entertainment. I just can't understand why we'd want to hitch up to that.

The museum constantly prompts questions we're now beginning to ask about rugby. Is sport for the athletes, or the sponsors? In the museum the answer is clear, and uncomfortable. The corporate sponsors ('partners', please) hijack the event, and dictate its terms and meaning. The museum wants it known that 'the partners provide 30% of Olympic marketing revenue', before helpfully pointing out that these days the Olympics couldn't be staged without sponsorship. That's the take-over, the end result. Not *now* they can't be, because ever since Samaranch's Los Angeles in 1984 the Olympics have been redesigned to fit corporate requirements. The Games didn't have to develop like this, and nor does rugby.

I propose allowing the USA the title of Olympic rugby champions in perpetuity, and with it the distinction of a rare occasion when America quit while still ahead. The rest of us will just have to learn to live another hundred years with our game on the dishonourable list of interrupted Olympic sports, along with cricket, speed-boating, and tug-of-war.

De Coubertin was a decent chap, unlike some of his IOC successors, but he got it wrong. Moral claims can't safely be made for all sports (we *know* what happens to pro footballers), though it was an easier mistake to make in previous centuries, when all the sports were new. The virtues of rugby inspired de Coubertin to found the Olympic Games. Since then, the Olympic ideal has been extinguished, while a sense of the moral value of rugby survives. Is this because, for rugby, it may actually be true?

After the grub under my fingernails from the Olympic Museum, I was glad to get back to rugby. I was looking forward to another of Pascal Racaud's fizzy training sessions, and he didn't disappoint. After an hour and a half of rugby, much of it high-speed and full-contact, he ran us all off to a nearby sports hall. Boots off in the doorway, socks off on the lined basketball floor.

'This is Roger Zucherro,' Pascal said, introducing us to a small thin man in judo pyjamas who was standing patiently by the far wall with his legs apart and arms crossed. 'Do not cross him, for he is deadly.'

When we were ready, Roger Zucherro beckoned us forward, and we lined up in rows for an hour of Daruma Taiso. This is a complex martial art which involves, among other things, learning to clutch like an eagle and walk like a duck. Nobody knew this was coming, and we all stood in lines in our shorts and bare white feet, inhaling and stretching and exhaling 'Hah!' It was quite wonderful, but it revealed to me in my lack of suppleness the wreck I actually am.

After the first ten minutes of stretching and breathing and

meditation, some of the English-speaking twits walked out, to go and eat burgers at the restaurant Quick (*c'est l'epoch qui veut Quick*). Meanwhile, our new Japanese-speaking master-san Roger Zucherro invited us to surrender our prejudiced selves to the basic principles of Daruma Taiso. There were many advantages. We'd learn how to concentrate for longer periods, maximise the strength in our muscles, and eventually to suffocate a man using only the tip of the thumb.

'How long will that take?' asked someone.

'Months. Many, many months.'

'It's just that the match is on Saturday.'

The Auberge de Coutance is generous to the club, but it can't afford two subsidised meals a week. On the Thursday we therefore went for kebabs in the Vittoria pub in Carouge. By then, I'd managed to pin down Pilou, once and still the beating heart of the Sporting. As we settle down in a corner, the first thing he tells me is that coach Pascal Racaud is mad, and not for a moment to be trusted. They know each other from their days at the Second Division Jex club in France, where Pascal was a head-case of a back-row forward.

'Not a full-back then?'

Pilou looks at me curiously, and I decide not to press him about Pascal's glory days with French Students and Begles-Bordeaux.

Pilou is a genuine rugbyman, about my age, and therefore retired. Six years ago he was a joy to play with, a truly gifted player, a running outside-half or centre who was big and strong and skilful. Maybe not in Trevor Wright's class, but close, and who knows? If he'd been born ten miles to the west, over the border in France, and had gone on to play at the top level (which he surely could have done), he might even have learnt to tackle.

He made his debut for the Swiss national team at the age of seventeen, but credits the '87 World Cup for providing Switzerland with its first serious matches. That year, aged twenty and playing fly-half in the famous 19–6 qualification victory over Israel, Pilou scored fifteen points. His last match in the white shirt and red shorts of Switzerland was as a replacement earlier this year in the bloodbath against the Czechs. After countless matches for Switzerland (he genuinely has no idea how many) he retired after an international career spanning seventeen years and two selections as captain.

I ask him if he has any regrets.

'God yes, if only I was seventeen again.'

'You could have been a pro.'

'Not for the rugby, don't be crazy. For all the other stuff.'

Whichever way he looks at it, Pilou can't see professional rugby ever catching on in Switzerland. In his opinion, the Swiss have no great record in professional sport for one simple reason. It's because their education system and their labour market actually work. If you put in the time and get the exams you'll find a comfortable and well-paid job. Why take the gamble of a risky career in sport?

When Pilou was starting out, it was the choice between a bank in Geneva or a job in a post office in Narbonne, with some extra beer-money in the boot. And even if he'd been a Narbonnais star, it doesn't mean much back home on Lake Léman that you've just played a blinder against Dax. Even now the wages of a First Division pro in France (Liebenburg's

£500 a week) don't approach those of an apprentice banker in Switzerland (where the average monthly pay is the equivalent of £2,700).

'It's all economics,' Pilou says. 'We have national pride, sure we do, but it doesn't bring anything in.'

Pilou is a rarity in Switzerland, a scruffy banker. He has a habit of widening his pale-blue eyes when he wants to be persuasive, and not blinking at all when he's just made a joke. He flings his hands about as he talks, as he tells me he doubts the game in Switzerland is ever likely to develop. There are still fewer registered players than there are clubs in France. He shrugs. And along with the rugby, Pilou could have shrugged for Switzerland, all the way to the World Championship Shrugging finals, inevitably against the favourites France, where he'd shrug a deciding five-set play-off against the SCUF's Monsieur le Président, Bruno Martin-Neuville. Who wins? *Bof*. They both shrug. Who cares?

I ask Pilou about the Swiss Barbarians, and he's played three or four times at the invitation of Mr Bataard, with Hastings and Bernat-Salles and Bertie Aherne (which seems unlikely). But I want to talk about my 1996 match, our match.

'Ah yes,' Pilou says, at last confirming what I've always suspected. 'Out of all the matches, that was the best.'

He then reels off the memorable names, with particular fondness for Brian Moore ('*zee peetbool*'). As for how the match came about, he has a story I haven't heard before. There is money involved, but not in a nasty way, because according to Pilou that one-off match between the Swiss Barbarians and all our heroes was the whim and folly of a

Welsh millionaire. An expatriate living with his fortune in Lausanne, his name is Davies, or Evans, or perhaps Jones. And on that sunny afternoon at Stade Lausanne, after organising the Swiss and the ex-internationals and Bevan the referee, Evans or Jones or Davies changes into crisp new kit and takes the field with his team of superstars. He is past fifty and overweight and white-haired, but still he plays the first three minutes of the match at prop. Ever after, as he modestly leaves the field to much applause, he can honestly list these legends among those with whom he'd played the game. In the good old days.

It's getting late, and Pilou gives me his card. I don't think I've ever known his real name. I look at the card, and my heart misses a beat when I see that he's not just a banker, but that he too works in one of Geneva's private banks. In fact, he's the man who checks out the credentials of investors. So if anyone has a minimum of one million Swiss francs, from fiscal evasion or a minor military coup, and if whoever you are you value your privacy, then I can unreservedly recommend the services of my good friend Pilou, scruffy secret banker and attacking outside-half.

I can't, however, tell you his real name. Only the bank and his parents are allowed to know.

I get home at 1.23 a.m., so on Thursday we must have trained forty-two minutes harder than we did on Tuesday.

Earlier in the summer, when I was still thinking this might be a book about rugby, I went to London to interview Brian Moore. My thinking went like this: if the joy of rugby is partly a question of spirit or soul, then I ought to pay homage to those in whom this spirit or soul most strongly resides.

This doesn't necessarily mean those with the most ability. In my own personal rugby hall of fame, the likes of Graham Mourie and Stuart Barnes and Daniel Herrero would have to wait their turn behind Rhys Kelly and Frédéric Butez, Ashley Johnson and Ian Wilmshurst, Mike Woodhouse and the great Swiss playmaker Christian Meyer, more commonly known as Pilou. However, Brian Moore would definitely be in there somewhere.

And he could also tell me his version of the Swiss Barbarians game.

Moore is an iconic figure for anyone about my age. Until Brian Moore, English rugby union had been stumbling through a seemingly endless twilight of underachievement. Think of the cricket, and that's how bad it was, so bad that Eddie Waring, a rugby league commentator on the BBC, was a national figure, impersonated on television by prime-time comics. People often forget Eddie Waring. But in those days, unlike England v. Wales at Twickenham, Leeds against St Helens on *Grandstand* was both a contest and so much easier on the emotions. The English always won.

Rugby union in England needed saving, and even though by 1987 I was twenty years old and waiting for the call, they turned to Brian Moore.

Brian Moore obliged.

England suddenly had an intensity and ferocity we'd been missing for decades, and which foolishly we'd hoped Eddie Waring might find for us in the corridor between Bradford and Hull. After 1987, we didn't need rugby league. We had

Brian Moore instead. He even looked like a league player, with his shirt-collar tucked under to make a collarless V, and he was so inarguably hard he could even look league in a Harlequins shirt.

Of course, he didn't save English union all on his own. Between 1988 and 1994, he was one of fifteen who gave us back our self-respect. But the loudest, squattest, angriest, chippiest, fiercest, most vociferous one of fifteen. He was also on a mission to surprise: the terrifying pitbull on a Saturday was during the week a steady partner in a law firm.

This didn't stop me being nervous when I went to meet him. I'd read in his autobiography that for motivation and top performance 'you have to have doubts'. This was good, because on the train to London I was full of doubt (Brian Moore. Brian Moore!). In his book he also wrote, echoing the thoughts of so many of the older rugby men, that 'if people know you're involved in the game they tend to assume you're a certain type of person, one to be trusted and helped'.

This kind of thing always sounds like so much baloney, but it's amazing how often it applies. Moore himself was already proving it, because I'd contacted him without any warning and without any friends in common. We'd once played a game of rugby together, five or six years ago, and now one lunchtime towards the end of summer I was waiting in the reception of his London law office. I was a little late, and therefore full of dread.

Then bam, he's out of the boardroom and into reception and we're in the lift while still shaking hands (I think I'm taller than him). He's wearing an open-necked shirt, white of course, but with the collar in its proper place. I'm in a lift with pitbull Brian Moore, who's shaved his head, and then I'm out of the building and down the street with Brian Moore, who walks from his massive shoulders, surging them side to side, head forward, making swathes through pedestrian traffic.

He knows a Thai restaurant in the angle of a quiet arcade, and they sit us down at a table outside. The owner nods and hurries over with menus. To demonstrate I'm no pushover, easily impressed by a retired sportsman who just happens to have saved my favourite sport, I say: 'I'll have what you're having, Brian.'

I'm in awe of his head. It's newly shaved, and shiny except where old stitch-wounds are matt. He has scars on his forehead and between his eyes and along his eyebrows. His ears are lumpy and moulded by rugby, and I think of his face clattered so many times, imagine the shocks, the bangs, the indelicate scrapes. And then the coming back, with Brian always the coming back. It's a folklore face, a big face, and yet . . .

Brian Moore is a very handsome man.

At this stage, I still hadn't met Hayley Moore of Cambridge University Women's Rugby Club. If I had, I'd have asked Brian if they weren't related. He has similar brown eyes, and there's something inscrutable about him, possessed and oriental. As he speaks, I try to count his teeth, but he's too fast and too articulate, and I have to listen closely.

Moore can't remember the name of the team he played in against the Swiss Barbarians, or even if it had a name. Or who organised it. Someone rang up, he says. But he does remember the game itself, and he smiles, as if there's other stuff to remember which wasn't the game itself.

'We all stayed in someone's flat.'

'Whose?'

'I don't know.'

'All of you?'

'I think so.'

It's worth remembering that this includes the winning Australian captain of the World Cup, two England internationals, two All Blacks, and probably several Welshmen with thirty caps or more who everyone now forgets.

'Actually I do remember something,' Moore suddenly says, pausing with his chopsticks raised and looking into the air above my shoulder. 'I remember sitting in the dressing room before the match. I looked at Peter Winterbottom and thought how fat he was, and whether that's how it had to end.'

I imagine Winterbottom and Moore half-naked in a sudden Beckett-like silence in a Swiss changing room, staring at each other's bellies. After all those years, all those battles, everything had already been said. But as in every changing room everywhere, still they went on speaking. 'God, Winters, you're fat.'

I'm chuffed when Moore agrees that Lausanne was a great weekend, a good laugh, though he confirms that the same kind of game simply couldn't happen today. In every professional contract there'd be a solemn clause forbidding 'freelance' games. And anyway, the insurance costs would be astronomical.

Since his retirement, Moore has played rugby twice. In the first game, he broke someone's nose, in the next he was sin-binned. He decided to call it a day, again, and replaced rugby with skiing, kick-boxing, and just briefly some Sunday-morning over-35s soccer. Only he was quickly fed up with all the effing and blinding. He finally packed it in when an opposition centre-half refused to have a drink with him after the game. Playing centre-forward, Moore had kicked him.

'I fouled him, but it wasn't a bad foul, and I said sorry.'

Which was more than Vincent Moscato ever got at the Parc des Princes, but the footballer still wouldn't stop swearing. 'He was boring me. He was boring everyone. I offered him round the back of the hut.'

They didn't actually fight, of course. It was soccer. Brian Moore in a mood is also a frightening prospect, which is why players in the basements of English rugby have been imitating him for years. Front-rowers all round the country still tuck their collars under, in the certain knowledge that Moore used to do it for devious, technical, dark-arts-of-the-front-row reasons.

'I thought it was cool,' Brian confesses. 'People started talking about it, so I kept on doing it.'

Then Wade Dooley did it, and even Will Carling did it, and I have the evidence in the video *England: The Glory Years*, which I sometimes watch late at night in secret. But mostly it was hookers all round the country who did it, and even today if you ask them why they'll wink and tap their nose and suggest the impenetrable mysteries of the hidden front row.

And besides, Brian Moore used to do it.

As well as his career in the law (I *am* the law), Moore is a trustee of the Professional Rugby Players Association and commentates on rugby for the BBC. He claims to have no interest in helping to manage rugby's continuing transformation, which is just as well because on rugby's important subjects his views are clear and intelligent.

'The challenge facing the game is for different levels to offer players the experience they want. We should allow for diversity in clubs, as in people. We shouldn't all try to be Premier League.'

Absolutely. I picture him on the board of the RFU, or the IRB, but he says he isn't interested. I don't believe him for a moment. In my lifetime, I predict that Brian Moore will be Lord Chief High Justice of all rugby administrators everywhere. And possibly Emperor of the Universe.

Then I walk with him back to his office, his broad shoulders surging, his head bobbing forward, just to check that I am that little bit taller. I am, you know.

That Saturday, I turned out for the Sporting Club de Genève. I was looking forward to it. It was a league match against one of the three weaker teams of the six in the top division, Neuchâtel, and I was replacement but promised a half. Replacements are still a rugger/rugby issue yet to be resolved. As well as crippling intermediate clubs like Norwich, replacements diminish some of the gladiatorial element of man against man. There's no doubt, for example, that during the 1973 Barbarians–All Blacks the fatigue of the players at the end of the game helped make the spectacle, allowing the fittest and strongest to break through and play.

On this occasion, however, I was glad for replacements, and even managed to grab my favourite number 20. As we warmed up, passing and catching and running, the standard jolts and warnings bustled through my mind. *Practice doesn't make perfect, perfect practice makes perfect. Set yourself standards. Don't let yourself down. Commitment, Control, Pride.* But I'd heard so many versions of these, so often, that they didn't really work any more. I was too old and analytical.

If not you, who?

Well, them, presumably.

If not now, when?

Um. Later?

And anyway, I could still remember how rugby in Switzerland has a tendency to level out the variable quality of players. Why take on the only decent player on the other side, someone who used to play for Stirling County and knows how to tackle? Much better to wait a little until you're up against the Swiss guy who's quick but only started playing a year ago, and then only because his sister was playing at college in England. Only somehow that was the guy you'd never quite come up against.

Even the fighting in Switzerland has its own national characteristic. Two people start a fight, and the other twenty-eight immediately intervene as mediators.

Though as it happened, on this particular day, none of this was relevant. The other team simply didn't turn up. They'd been thrashed so soundly the Saturday before by RFC Hermance that it seemed unreasonable only a week later to come back to Geneva for more. They were therefore being very sensible and Swiss, opting instead for a neutral no-show.

Unfortunately, this left all twenty of us in Geneva at a bit of a loose end. Not even Pascal, with all his inventive enthusiasm, could really come to the rescue. We played a game of soccer, then had a desultory practice session before Pascal called it off and set up a kicking contest between forwards and backs. We had to do *something*, because rugby was a valuable weekly parenthesis during which we could safely express our masculinity. More importantly, Pascal had organised beer and *pastis* for afterwards, and huge platters of salami and gherkins.

Smelling sweetly then, it was some time later when a solid core of the Sporting (basically me and the French and Swiss lads) suggested expending some unused manly energy on ice hockey. Watching, not playing. That evening it was the local derby between Geneva and Lausanne, and since the Patinoire des Vernets (the ice-hockey stadium) was within walking distance of the Vittoria pub, it wasn't a difficult decision.

We drive to the pub and walk to the stadium.

I've never been to ice hockey before, but it's very noisy, and at each end there are rocking, chanting fans, like at the soccer in the Parc, but less intent on killing each other. If you watch them stoned, which some people are known to do, they tend to make meaningful patterns in waves.

The Swiss love their ice hockey, and in a space the size of a decent swimming-pool there are 6,700 spectators, more than for Sale or Neath's opening home game in the Heineken European Cup. For a novice supporter like me, the skaters are difficult to follow. Of twenty-two in an ice-hockey squad (the same as rugby) only five are on the rink at any one time. If the same proportions were applied to rugby union, there'd be eighty-five players on a very long bench, running on and off and on. This should be a warning to us, as all the chopping and changing makes it difficult to warm to the game's various personalities. To help identification, the best player on a Swiss hockey team wears a yellow helmet. This ensures that opposition hard men make no mistake when smashing him into the barrier-boards.

Geneva won 5–3, just as PSG had comfortably thumped Strasbourg when I was among the support. Must be lucky. By the time the reserves jumped over the barriers to celebrate the end of the game, I was fairly convinced that ice hockey could also teach manliness and the moral virtues. Just like rugby, it presented emotional and physical challenges, and therefore developed character. It encouraged a non-precious attitude, a team ethic, and the players had to work hard to achieve results.

However, it also occurred to me how complicated we were as human beings, to have invented a game like ice hockey with its carbon-fibre sticks and arcane zonal rules, and yet the main pleasure for the crowd is still in seeing our guy smash their guy as hard as possible against the trembling plexiglass walls.

I'm having an exciting evening, but there's always something unsatisfactory about spectating, desperately wanting to be a part of something, over-acting, failing to be a part of it, wanting it more. And so on.

We the Sporting still have an unsatisfied urge to participate in something, because that's why we turned up in the first place, and by one of those miracles which makes for the best of evenings, the Vittoria pub has karaoke. I watch as my French and Swiss team-mates participate with a little more energy than is probably required, or even strictly allowed. Commitment, Control, Pride, up at the mike they've got it all.

Karaoke turns out to be an excellent vehicle for community singing, because nobody needs to know the words. They're up there on the screen, and anyone can join in heartily with all sorts of strange Euro anthems (*Bambino, Bambino, ne pleure pas, Bambino*). As late becomes later, and the rest of the bar joins in, I suddenly find I'm all in favour of European union, not necessarily across the board but definitely with European shop-girls. All is well, I feel, and all will always be well, and the Sporting Club of Geneva is a grand club, a truly great club, surely the finest band of pacifist Europeans on the planet.

The remnants of the team are now providing chorus and backing tracks for anyone who asks, and they're called upon again and again, especially by fat people, who sing so much better than thin people. I don't know why this should be, but it's all so good and joyful that I have a welling, swelling feeling of harmony and love and European fraternity, and almost believe it's karaoke which presents emotional and physical challenges, and therefore develops character. It encourages a non-precious attitude, a team ethic, sacrifice, stoicism. Does it?

My judgement is by now so severely impaired that it won't be long before the terrible moment when every song is deep and profound of meaning. No poetry ever written could possibly compare to Celine Dion's 'My Heart Will Go On'. Really, just listen to it, listen to the majesty of the words.

And that, surely, is time for home.

Midsomer Norton RUFC, 1998–2003

'It is indeed very very good to feel that one has the honour
to belong to a race which invented and which, to the crack
of doom, will play the man's game, Rugby Football.'

E.H.D. Sewell

The former mining-town of Midsomer Norton is as close
as it's possible to get to the centre of English rugby's
heartland. It is the heart. Standing indomitable and Asterix-
like against the imperial forces of soccer, England has a
swathe of green pitches and H-posts stretching from
Worcester and the lower Midlands down the Severn estuary
and on into Somerset and Devon. The south-west of England,
like the south-west of France, is a rugby stronghold
characterised by social inclusiveness and anti-urbanism, and
in the early years of the century thousands would travel to see
Weston, Tavistock, Bath and Bridgwater compete for the
Somerset Cup. Fighting among players and spectators was
not uncommon.

While I'd been away, Midsomer Norton had been winning
handsomely. Each week I'd checked on the Internet their

progress in the cup and their unbeaten run in the league. These weekly victories were the worst news I could possibly have had. At this rate, I'd never get back in the team. Or I'd get back in the team, and that was the week we'd lose. Even at the time, I could appreciate that these were not the positive thoughts of a champion, whose destiny and right it is to play at the highest level. Fortunately, the lads lost badly the week I was singing karaoke in Geneva.

There were injuries, too, and a problem at number 10: I was back in the team. We started winning again. We lost. We won some and lost some. By Christmas it was a season like any other, and the games had begun to merge. I'd enjoyed my tour into the rugby past, but there was nothing like playing at home in the present, wherever that happened to be. And for Midsomer Norton on any winter Saturday, I'll usually have been excited since well before lunchtime on Thursday.

There's always the chance that this next game will be the one, finally, when I do something truly marvellous on the field of play.

If I'm lucky, I'll get a lift up to the club with Ty, and not have to worry about driving. In the passenger seat I'll talk nonsense and sharpen my appetite for the shared ritual of Saturdays, for the battle and a brutal match against the good men of Gordano or Tor, in which the blood inevitably rises. I'm in my number ones, my button-down blue shirt with the club crest on the pocket, and a striped club tie. It's a Pavlovian trigger which starts the adrenaline; a shirt and tie must mean it's Saturday.

As we pull up in the gravel and puddled car-park, it may

not look like much, but Midsomer Norton is the best-run club in the area. This can partly be judged by the thriving junior section and the four senior sides, the three pitches and the free-standing if modest clubhouse. But mostly I define the quality of a club by whether I get picked in the first team. This would explain the current weakness of other clubs in the region, like Bristol and Bath. They're so badly run they wouldn't select me. Which, now I come to think of it, is another reason I've never played for England. What a shambles, what an absolute shower.

I've played at Midsomer Norton longer than anywhere else, more than twice as long. Years ago, when the map of my life resembled a series of evasive actions, I needed rugby as a stabilising influence. Here, it's different. For a while now I've been living near Midsomer Norton like an unrolling stone, hoping to gather some moss. The rugby is moss, but I've also needed excitement, and rugby has been generous enough to oblige with that, too.

As I swing open the doors to the clubhouse, I know by now what to expect. At Norton, the physical diversity of rugby is alive and well. The conformity of gym-built freaks who come as standard with the professional game is yet to seep down the leagues (though we see it occasionally in the cup, and mighty impressive it is too). Instead of muscles, we have the lock Matthew Plummer, famous in the *Somerset Guardian* as 'probably the tallest sportsman in the county'. At six foot nine, he's more than a foot taller than scrum-half Robin Browning, who in turn is about seven stones lighter than lock Wayne Cole, though still heavier than the leaf of a winger Tom Lovell. Wayne is actually carrying most of a Tom whenever we run out to play, and to be honest, it looks like it. But as well as some heroic guts, some glorious stomachs, we also have flankers who build housing estates with their bare hands, and a hip-hop winger who's a skin-and-bones skateboarder.

We also have a fair share of idiots, but they're *our* idiots. They'll greet me fondly, and probably call me a cunt. Ah, the banter.

I like being among grown men who have no fear of making fools of themselves. I'm not even the oldest, though getting closer every year. And despite the different shapes and sizes and ages (this year we have Ross Miller, aged eighteen), this is a team of players with a genuine and deep affection for their club. They *are* the club, and no one comes from much further than nearby Peasedown St John. This is not very far. There's a bracing parochialism about Midsomer Norton, and a genuine feeling that rugby anywhere else in the country is soft (though particularly so in Frome).

All the same, the lads are smart enough to mock themselves (before someone else does it for them). There's a well-worn joke that some of the older players are in fact widely travelled. They haven't just stayed in Norton all their lives, oh no. We even have veteran campaigners from vicious upcountry skirmishes in the Nam.

That's right. Chippenham.

We have the gratifying rugby mix of people, some of them ugly, some less so, and a boy you can tell has an exceptionally pretty mother.

On this particular day of days, in which a season's fixtures merge into one, England are playing at Twickenham. On one of the two TV screens in the clubhouse the build-up on Sky has already begun. Most of the players ignore it, and chat to people they haven't seen since at least Thursday. There's the subject of today's tricky match, and shouted farewells to the seconds and fourths travelling away, and some updates on the valley-jack rafters in the new Barratt executive homes. What? Been to university and don't even know what a valley-jack rafter is?

At Cambridge, Dick Tilley identified a conflict of interest which is wrenching at the game. Those entrusted with marketing rugby want people to watch. The rest of us want to play, and we want other people to come and join us. We know what the game has to offer – turn off the television and try it. Don't go to Bath and sit down. Come here, and run. While it's always consoling to know that Stadium Australia can bring together 110,000 people to watch an international in Sydney, it doesn't seem to mean so much if there aren't youngsters with a ball at Norton Down.

I think the old amateurs knew they had something valuable, but weren't quite sure what it was. As society became increasingly commodified, they held fast to their rugby. It fulfilled a longing for adventure and comradeship, but it was also a distinctive island of unmediated experience. The old boys in their blazers sensed the value of that, and in their clumsy way they tried to protect it. They didn't *want* their game to be popular, despite its brilliant and far-reaching appeal.

They were wrong, and rugger without rugby wouldn't now be up on Sky at lunchtime on a Saturday. It would have ended up a closed world, a bizarre outdated ghetto. For the moment we have both: rugger with the added vim of rugby, rugby with the virtues of rugger. The divide may be widening, but amateur rugby isn't yet like amateur dramatics, a hobby more than a genuine pursuit, eccentric and faintly amusing. We want to play. The rugby futurists want us to watch. The second-team winger decides it. He's only young, but he flicks the TV over to *World Wrestling Federation – Slamdown.* Now that's a sport for spectators.

We hoist our bags and head for the changing room, and this one like all the others is not for the faint of heart. Every time anyone opens themselves to ridicule, they are ridiculed. That's the only rule.

It's all part of the training, not for an imaginary future in a sticky Empire, but for life now that's happening around us every day, in Business Forms Express and Rookery Farm and GM Engineering and the Avon and Somerset police. We sit there in the narrow rectangular room like Brian Moore and Peter Winterbottom, eighteen of us week after week after week. Everything has already been said, many times, but still we go on talking.

This Saturday, some of the youngsters are curious about the sin of Onan, which I mentioned last week and may have made up, they're not quite sure. Others have encouraging words for the number 7 who has his court appearance on Tuesday and may miss next week's match. From the sound of it, you'd think he wouldn't be missed. And Bula Hawkins is off on an inspired riff about the Vindictaphone, a hand-held tape-recorder exclusively for spiteful jibes.

There are so many stories to tell, and to select one or two would be pointless. It's in the nature of rugby that everyone has a better story, or probably a very similar story but in a much funnier version: their own. Like rugby-club dinners, all the clubs and stories are different and all the same, and to confirm this I did once go to the Midsomer Norton end-of-season dinner. I expected the worst, and I was right.

Midsomer Norton is not a joke team, a decent fixture for the Bagford Vipers. Judged by league hierarchies this may not seem like serious rugby, but I can tell you it is. The players are committed, they make sacrifices, and our skills make us the same standard as any team in New Zealand, of the same standard. We do the training, we put in the time, and the Commitment Control Pride doesn't have to be daubed on the walls. We each know what the others expect of us.

From midday every Saturday, we all share the intention of playing in the greatest ever game of rugby. And it's rugby we have in mind, not rugger. Winning and losing matter. Losing will make us think the worst of ourselves and each other, that we're losers, incompetent and ineffective, not manly in the heat of battle. In the right frame of mind, about now on a Saturday afternoon, this isn't a game. It's about achievement and determination and self-worth.

Afterwards, we might drink some beer and lark about, I shouldn't wonder. For now, though, that's almost forgotten and we're desperate for promotion to the league above. We have to be canny, competitive. We're the only team in the Somerset Premier League without printed track-suits, and we have to make that work for us. For some unspoken reason we're secretly proud of it, and can use it to our advantage. Outside it's cold, it usually is in the Mendip winds, and we pull on hats and hoods and all sorts of mismatching tops.

We look like a club from Romania after a Home Counties charity drop.

Before running out, I sit in my corner and close my eyes and summon the vision of retired sportsmen on tractor-mowers, wishing they'd let the occasion, any occasion, get to them. I let it get to me a little each week, with the weather brewing over the hills and blowing in from the west. I remember former glories in my various team strips where I did one thing or another memorably well. I try and remember when I last went out into that kind of rain.

I'm glad to be here. I'm grateful that I've had the chance to observe my body growing older, carefully, in ways I may not have noticed had I never played. I've learnt that at thirty-six I bruise more easily, and age makes me scrawny, but after all these years of blows and recovery I know myself in detail, my knees, shoulders, ankles, elbows. It's a more helpful map than the back of the hand.

Of course, I still have no perspective. If I did, I wouldn't be here. As I lace my boots and tape my socks, clap my hands twice together (*Come on!*), and plug in my gum-shield, I don't wonder how many times I've done this, and how many times I'll do it again. I think: this game is the most important game ever, and I want to win it. It's still not too late to play for England, either. I feel I could do a job, even if I've started to notice that the international players are not only bigger and stronger than me, but faster and with a wider range of skills. It all adds up, and I am Northampton Town, at best. But as Gavin Ewart wrote, and in poetry too:

'*Nevertheless . . .*'

We jog out for the warm-up, and depending on the time of

year it's too hot or too cold, too wet or too windy. The field is hard and harsh, or soft but treacherous. We're out when the grass is slick and forgiving, and out when the grass is gone. Under clear skies and when clouds skid and shift and when there's nothing but wraparound grey.

There's mud, more often than not, on our boots and shucked up our socks. This is our land, our earth, and we run about and laugh and it feels good. We simmer down, run through our warm-up drills, swear a little, play at rugby.

At Midsomer Norton, I can safely say that as yet we're untainted by professionalism, although Gurt Kev was once offered fish and chips and £50 to sit as a replacement on the Clifton bench. Not because he's a good player, which he is, and a good man, or because they wanted to have a drink and a gentle hur-hur-hur with him after the game. But because at that time the regulations of the National Leagues required Clifton to select at least two front-row replacements, and there simply aren't enough props to go round. Quite rightly, Kev refused. Even when they offered to double the chips.

All the same, money is important, just to keep the club on its feet. Like many junior clubs we have a mobile-phone transmitter in a corner of the playing-fields. It pays for some armoured suits, and other necessities, though the parents of the minis sometimes joke uneasily that the radio waves are breeding mutant champions for the future. It doesn't seem to put anyone off. Rugby is still a great game to play, and many young boys and girls take instinctively to the mud and the rough and tumble. I did, and the junior section at Midsomer Norton has over 200 subscribed players.

*

Before the match itself, after running through the backs' moves, it's worth stopping a moment to stretch pet muscles (hamstrings, neck) and consider the next generation. They're the future of the game, after all, kids raised in rugby the living pulse of any club, the warm welcome of years to come, the ongoing health of the organism. Wherever I've travelled in the last six weeks, I've seen youngsters who love the game. Admittedly, it helps if they possess the rugby prerequisites. They have to like being outside (where they can remember what's important, like the weather). They should enjoy physical confrontation, though controlled and codified. And they have to be committed when they put their mind to something (they can't just turn up, like they can for five-a-side soccer).

In Paris, the SCUF's Ecole de Rugby attracts 120 children every Sunday morning, both boys and girls, though there's so much paperwork for French mini-rugby that the coaches man a desk on the field. Bring the balls, bring the cones, bring a desk and chair. Once the disclaimers have all been signed, the laughing humming mass of mini-*SCUFistes* in black and white is co-ordinated by Peter MacNaughton, a Paris-based Scot with his own communications business. He's fluent in French and has an M.Phil. in Contemporary Theatre Space, the ideal qualification for coaching French rugby. MacNaughton's face is full of the character of ten years in tough SCUF packs, four of those in the Second Division, and I stand back in admiration of his expert management of ambitious dads ('my young 'un's tough as they come') and anxiously fretting mums ('excuse me, but his knee is *bleeding*').

In a rare free moment, he tells me not to be surprised at the numbers. Rugby has specific advantages in the crowded market-place for kids' attention. The physical contact, for example, which most children enjoy.

'But let's not over-complicate this,' MacNaughton says, before offering me an insight which is pure Theatre Space. 'In rugby the concept of scoring is easy. The target is thirty yards wide, look at it. It's enormous! It's not a tiny basket or a goal. Thirty yards. And when you get there all you have to do is fall over. There's not a child in the class who doesn't think he can make it.'

At Norwich rugby club on an October Sunday morning there were minis and juniors everywhere, children from seven to seventeen all over the five pitches, and the place was jumping with the excitement of a series of matches against Diss. The boys and girls loved it, and a fifteen-year-old sub was shouting 'Come on, Lion!' as he hurtled with his cage of water-bottles up and down the touchline.

There was even a sponsor there, Alan Macalister of URL. URL sell after-the-event insurance policies, and as an insurance professional Macalister says the compensation culture will soon be influencing a club near you. To control claims for injury made against them, all sporting clubs will need contingency funds, and this is a growing problem. If he's right, then the outlook is bleakest for rugby, a game of accident in a changing world which doesn't allow for accidents.

While we've been talking, the mini and junior matches have been keeping the man from St John Ambulance busy. At any given time on one of Norwich's five pitches, there's usually a boy bleeding or in tears. I'm reminded that it's a hard game, however big you are.

On that one Sunday morning I happened to be there, I saw a broken arm and a concussion, and heard touchline parents making friends by comparing waiting-times in casualty at the Norfolk and Norwich. And then, without any warning, after a messy series of tackles and rucks, a sixteen-year-old from Diss collapses on the Norwich try-line. The referee urgently clears him a space, and sends a player to find St John's. The St John's man runs over, feet heavy on the hard ground, his medikit rattling. He kneels down, takes one look at the boy, and calls over his shoulder for a doctor.

The match is abandoned, and the boy is now in the recovery position, covered in a mound of coats and all-weather warm-up jackets. His legs are shaking, his feet still in football boots jumping in spasms off the ground. He's hyper-ventilating, I can hear the desperate grunt on each fast intake of breath.

On the other pitches, the games go on. The boy wets himself. An ambulance arrives, but one of the Norwich under-16s has already lost interest. Perhaps he's seen this before, but he's in his own world, collecting the padded flags from the edges of the pitch. At the far end, when he thinks no one's looking, he hurls them one at a time like javelins, like spears.

The paramedics brace the injured boy where he lies, back, neck, strap him to the plastic stretcher and load him up and drive him off. Out on the Walsham road, the siren starts and all this, I think, for a game. Just a game. But I knew the risks, didn't I? Don't we all know them, every time we run out? One of the thrills of rugby is braving fate, and living the delicate balance between risk and reward. At first, it might not seem balanced at all, but everyone who plays and plays again is proof that the rewards like the dangers must also be great.

Between risk and reward, there is fear. Emotionally, this can make rugby compelling to watch, though not necessarily when played by the best. International players have a fear of failure, I'm sure they do, but I don't believe they have fear in its purest state, physical fear. Thomas Castaignède, one of France's most brilliant buccaneers, once said, 'Look at me. I am very small. But I am afraid of nothing.' I believe him. He's had to prove it so many times on the way to playing for his country, and I don't think with all those trials and all those team-mates and all those stats and cameras you can fake it.

At Castaignède's level, there's video surveillance and strategy and planning. At our level, it's mostly a straight dogfight. Rugby and rugger. In rugby, new laws supposedly diminish the brutality of the forward confrontation. This news hasn't yet spread to the forwards at Midsomer Norton, and the idea of diminished confrontation makes me laugh. In top-level modern rugby, the loonies have all but disappeared, except perhaps in South Africa. Hardly surprisingly, they haven't vanished off the face of the earth. I can assure people that the rugby loonies are alive and mentally unwell, and they're playing in the Somerset and Gloucester leagues.

This is all part of Saturday's excitement – you never know what you're going to get. We occasionally have teams pass through our division with an outside-half who once played for Bristol and an Australian student on the flank. We let them go, not without a fight, but even playing with pride and fire a community team like Norton will get beaten by a semi-pro team playing with an imported Maori, and a daft Fijian on the wing.

All the same there's an edge, an unpredictability to every match, especially as we frequently come across players who are big enough, strong enough, occasionally even good enough for first-class rugby. Only they're the rejects, too barmy, too nasty, too free-spirited, too erratic for the professional game. They have some tragic flaw, from dodgy hands to sporadic cowardice to an uncontrollable temper. Usually, it's the temper. My own tragic flaw is that I'm not Thomas Castaignède. *Look at me. I am very small. Of course I'm bloody frightened.*

Muscles loosened, bodies steaming, we pile back into the changing room and peel off to the Norton red and black. We hang on to each other and bounce up and down, making rhythmic tribal noises with our studs while practising our counting to five. Onetwothreefourfive. Quicker. Louder. Come on!

I often think, at about this moment, *What the fuck are you doing?* At the top level, the first time you have this feeling you must know you're close to the end. For us, it's always there, week after week, and doubt is just one more of the game's many challenges. You fold it away and sprint out all the same, simplifying the whole one-hundred-year jumble of rules and laws to their simplest basic essence.

Tackle hard. Run fast. Score tries.

Right, off we go then. The whistle blows, and as soon as the ball slaps into my hands, the anxiety vanishes. I'm playing for fun, and the beauty of the thing, and playing to win. I'm playing because the only weakness incompatible with rugby is fear, and I am not afraid, not really. Once it starts I can barely remember what there was to be frightened about.

For the first few minutes of every game the play is cramped and cute, the big tackles going in early and some random marginal play as a marker of masculinity. This means vigorous rucking and a punch or two, just to get things moving. Inevitably, the opposition escape unpunished for scandalous assaults, while we're always caught in the act. 0–3. Probably 0–6, if Hairsy's playing. We're against the wind and up the slope, and now the graft begins, the defence of our territory, the edging out, the doggedness.

Every Saturday at Norton Down I realise I spent four years at school learning how to play, and seventeen years in clubs learning how to cheat. But if both teams agree to cheat, it's hardly cheating, is it? Let the ref decide on his own inter-pretations, like the rest of us, making it up as we go along. We're creative artists, we're all Thomas Keneallys on the lookout for a special moment touched by grace, a sense of the sporting divinity which lives in us all and can make us perform beyond fixed limits. Not that our forwards are aware of this, at least not all the time, but it's true.

Into the cold wind, against the driving rain, Parf cinches the line-out and the ball is swept outside to the centres and Ian Tiley. He cuts inside on our own ten-metre line, dragging two men with him, and from a supporting position I scream up on *his* inside, and break through the first line of defence. All of Somerset is opened up to me and I claim it yard by yard, breathing deeply the heady air of conquered terrain. I beat the last man off my left foot and arc outside the covering winger, straightening to dive and slide just inside the corner-flag. 7–6 to Nor. Now that's what it's all about.

We're playing at home, and nobody much is watching, but all the rugby virtues are exaggerated when no one's watching. Without spectators, the game is a more authentic test, more true to life. Internationals who play splendidly and with courage in front of a crowd of 75,000 are like people good in a crisis. Useful in their way, but hardly that surprising. Far more admirable are the kind of people good in no crisis at all, when it doesn't seem to matter, when no one's actually watching.

It's not fair to say that *no one's* watching. We have a core support of about fifty, among them former ITN chief correspondent and best-selling author Gerald Seymour.

Gerald Seymour alternates Saturdays at Norton Down with his season ticket for the Recreation Ground in Bath. I really don't know what he sees in Bath, especially these days.

At the club, we joke about how rich Gerald must be, after twenty years as a best-selling novelist whose thrillers are televised starring ex-*EastEnders*. In fact, stung by my own meagre royalty statements, I may be the one to bring this up, and it may not be a joke. Go on, I probe, you've seen Gerald's house, how much would *you* say a successful writer earns? Of course, I have no idea how rich Gerald actually is, except he's among the richest men alive. He must be, because he has two debenture seats at Twickenham.

At his hideaway stately home not far from Midsomer Norton, we sat in his office one foggy weekday morning and talked about rugby. The office was tucked away on the ground floor, between the ballroom and the swimming-pool, and lined with shelves of Gerald Seymour books in many languages, and videos of film adaptations dubbed into Italian. Not that I was *counting*, but there were hundreds. There were also posters for *Harry's Game* on the wall, and photos of Gerald as a younger man on ITN assignments in Cyprus and Aden, and in shorts and a T-shirt alongside the England World Cup squad which failed in Mexico in 1970. Jack Charlton is doing something wacky with a hat.

Luckily for me, Gerald is no Tony Money, a secret soccer man, though it's interesting to compare his earliest memories of Britain's two major football sports. Gerald is a romantic and an enthusiast, and his sportsmen are knights in shining armour. With soccer, he sensed this heroism for the first time while listening on the radio to the 1952 FA Cup final. Jorge Robledo put Newcastle one up, and the Arsenal of Joe Mercer staged an epic but ultimately futile attempt to recover.

As for rugby, the same sense of grandeur is in a memory of Kelly College second XV away at West Buckland School, in the hailstones and mud of a Devon winter. The boys on that day of legend were Greek gods. They even overcame the elements, and Gerald was among the best of them. He was not in the Arsenal team which contested the 1952 cup final.

It's as if soccer appeals to the voyeur, rugby to the active participant. As a boy, Gerald was big and fast and wanted to play on the wing. He was big, and English, so he played in the second row. This may explain why despite that heroic experience at West Buckland, unmatched by any other sport, Gerald's interest faltered. Besides, he was soon travelling the world, looking for televised trouble.

ITN called him home in the winter of 1969, to follow the touring Springboks. It was the sleepy British provinces in winter-time, but there was trouble enough for everyone: smoke-bombs in the Boks' hotel and tin-tacks on the pitches, police wielding truncheons and pacifist hippies in crash-hats. Even better, South Africa kept losing, and the story was always live.

Gerald covered all the tour's controversies from September through to January, with the bonus of two Bok games a week. Never mind the hippies and their sarcastic Nazi salutes, what's the score in the game? He began to understand what rugby was all about, learning from the lightning counter-attacks of H.O. de Villiers and the defensive steel of Tommy Bedford. He saw every match of the tour except the last, when the Biafrans inconsiderately chose just that moment to end their long-running war. Gerald Seymour was there for ITN, but his heart was with the Barbarians at Twickenham.

Only rugby can do this. Gerald also reported on three soccer World Cups, in Mexico and Germany and Argentina. He attended three consecutive Olympic Games.

'Funnily enough,' he says now, 'I never had the urge to buy a stopwatch and start hanging about at the Crystal Palace.'

His sons adored the game, and Gerald didn't discourage them. When he moved to Ireland, he went along to the Palmerston club, south of Dublin. There was nothing like it. Moss Keane and Ollie Campbell used to drop by to confirm in person the fellowship and democracy of rugger clubs the world over.

'I felt the positive power of the clan,' Gerald tells me, 'of the tribe.'

He's been devoted to the game ever since, and he was at the Parc des Princes among the English fortunate and faithful for that epic quarter-final against France. With no reinforced steel barriers to obstruct his view, and no flares or burning programmes to distract him, he could quite clearly see the lengthening face of President Mitterrand in the tribune across the pitch.

In 1984, after the runaway success of his early novels demanded a finer estate than any available in Ireland, his son played a season for Midsomer Norton. Gerald's been going ever since.

'It's a most extraordinary . . .' he begins, but immediately brings his hands together and changes direction, 'Not in a gushing way, but . . .' and as he looks away I suspect like me he's wary of the club's enormous appetite for ridicule, 'It's just a very nice place to be.'

I couldn't agree more.

'I'll tell you another thing,' and now he's looking straight at me with his sharp newsman's eyes. 'I had more pleasure watching Midsomer Norton win the Somerset Cup than I did from England's Grand Slam.'

Gerald regularly sees rugby at three levels – England, Bath, and Norton – and it's Bath which worries him most.

'It would be folly to believe that because Twickenham is full, everything is rosy, because it isn't.'

In particular, from the amateur days, he misses the loss of contact with the players. 'At Bath, and even England, they used to be part of our world. They were our doctors, our builders, our policemen.'

I know what he means. Now the players can seem distant,

kidnapped by a rather unimaginative cult at a tender age and returned to the field cyber-formed but empty-headed from some dim and religious full-time gym. And whatever a marketing department may like to imagine, no amount of Bath Rugby lunch-boxes or key-rings can replace the sense of community offered by Jerry Guscott in the bar with a pint and a fag.

'Norton's in a stronger position than Bath,' Gerald says. 'It's also more important. If the world of Midsomer Norton goes under, the whole thing packs up, I think.'

We're 7–6 in the lead, we're not going under, but I should have learnt by now the importance of staying concentrated. My mind elsewhere, I flash half-heartedly for a tackle, and a big centre whacks through my bicep with his knee. It's not all glory, it never is. Wincing and clutching my arm, it's time to prove I'm a hard campaigner, a reliable human being, out on the mud of the Down smashing brash wing-forwards back into the pack they came from.

I am tough, resilient, enduring, reliable, stoical, multi-skilled, and accepted under a welcoming canopy of masculinity by a like-minded band of brothers. Standing up to be counted, dropping my shoulder at speed into an obdurate crash-tackle, I bounce another man and bring him down. In the lively ruck that follows, I'm trapped on the wrong side, and get a good shoeing and a solid boot to the head.

This is what's supposed to flash before me: my English childhood, schooldays and college, the Duchess of Argyll, the flair of Paris, Norwich and the *Sunday Times* Young Writer of the Year, Geneva and neutrality and blankness. In fact, when I'm concussed, I get sums. That's it, free-floating sums, isolated figures and formulas white on black and black on white, definite rights and wrongs. Otherwise, I lose all context and there is no time. As I stand up and look around, I'm ready to believe I'm fourteen, or sixty, and why is everybody running around like that? Why isn't anyone wearing trousers? Concussion is like a black hole in the head; it can be very wonderful.

The last time this happened, after the sums, after the elation of mental free-fall, after mysteriously finding myself on the side of the pitch, I asked Nellie the coach if I was a success as a writer. He and the supporters and the replacements laughed uproariously. And because it was the rugby, or because I was concussed, it was many open-ended minutes before I knew if this meant yes or no.

In my composite game of all the Norton games, I recover quickly. I know which way I'm playing and the score is 7–6. No? It's now 7–13, and it's the second half. We're playing down the hill with the wind at our backs and there's not much time to go. I look around at the Norton boys, and it's impossible to be redder in the face, angrier, more full of blood, of guts, of stomach, of vitality. I find another gear, a fiercer thing which rugby has taught me I hold in reserve. All together, with all our heart and combined desire, we drive to the 22. We're there, in the scoring zone, and as a 36-year-old I score a try of such classic simplicity, with such a mastery of technique, that I remember I was once a truly classy player.

Snapping onto a Stuart Parker half-break from the back of a scrum, I hit his speculative flip-pass on a needle-straight line. I step off my left foot, heading for the corner with only the full-back to beat. I'm not pulling him far enough across. I step again off the same foot and now he has to move to cover me, and as soon as he does I drop my shoulder and come off the other foot, my right. It leaves him floundering, adrift, and I scuttle over between the posts, sliding over the line to score.

I'm pumped up by my own surprise brilliance, by the reality of doing something genuinely marvellous which week after week I never do. Not exactly. But now at last I have, and on the way back to Norton territory I pass the full-back still on the ground where I left him for dead. He's kneeling in the mud staring at his hands, and I'm so pumped up on my own evident superiority, I throw the ball at his head.

Obviously, very soon, I feel pretty bad about that. It's a silly thing to do. Not very courageous, nor virtuous. Not manly in the least. If there's a God, we therefore miss the conversion and lose 12–13. If there's a God, the conversion goes over and we win 14–13. I can't bear to look, and turn away.

And then it's the final whistle.

The game may be over but the rugby isn't, the rugger. We move through the showers quickly enough, because the treasurer has his eye on the cost of all that water. Still, it's worth recording that throughout Europe, in my experience, the toughest of men wear flip-flops in the shower.

The Midsomer Norton clubhouse is a large, rectangular space designed for drinking. It serves its purpose well, but nobody's in a hurry. We stand around at the bar, itemising the various technical and personal frailties of the referee, while drinking at least one orange juice and lemonade. If we've won the match, the observations about the ref can be skipped. If we've lost, the flawed officiating is entirely to blame for our missed promotion, again. Somehow, no one is inconsolable. And besides, the league above involves teams from the Gloucester outback, who are known to take no prisoners.

As in most amateur clubs, money is changing hands. Every Saturday we pay £3.50 to the captain as a match fee, demonstrating week after week that professionalism isn't the only model of organisation possible or even desirable in sport.

Midsomer Norton is run like a co-op, by the members for the members. Until recently, nearly all rugby clubs were organised this way, more of a social experiment than a reflection of society. We have a woman club secretary, Corinne Edwards, and every Saturday the vice-presidents put on their aprons and heat and serve the pasties and beans, so it's hardly a bastion of traditional male values. Those critics who are still fond of dismissing rugby union as a toff's sport for chauvinists are simply not looking in the right place.

The colonels of the RFU used to warn that vast swathes of players and administrators would leave the game when the top clubs went professional. It's amazing now, looking round the bustle of the clubhouse at Midsomer Norton, to think how little they understood the game they were supposed to be running.

The true heroes of rugby, alongside Rhys Kelly and Jean Hospital and Pilou and Elliot the publican, are still those officials who toil for nothing, not even glory. Our own unlikely chief hippy at the co-operative is the treasurer Jim

Dando, a former bank manager from the town who makes a huge and unpaid contribution. I say: peace, Jim, peace man. Nice commune.

Up on the two TV screens, England are bashing seven bells out of somebody or other. These days, it could be anybody, but in general we're not that bothered about England. We wouldn't change our own kick-off time to watch them, for example, though it's nice to see the highlights in the clubhouse afterwards. Sure, there are international matches I've enjoyed, but I never really remember them.

Our own game is far more important, as it should be, and with the rules always changing and the variable inter-pretations, we often fail to agree on what actually happened in the game we've just been playing. That's why afterwards in the bar we have to discuss, listen, debate, and endlessly josh and crow. And now while drinking beer, as if by happy accident.

Up on the TV in the after-match interviews, Johnson or Woodward is saying that playing in itself is never enough. The team has to win. I know this, even though the sound is turned down, because this is what they always say. Why should it be any different for us? Playing in itself is never enough. We don't necessarily need to win, but we do need to stand at the bar for many hours afterwards. We need peripheral benefits and compensations, like the reality that inside the clubhouse social class means nothing, this and other labels lost long ago in battle. We need the emotional refreshment of our affection for the game, and our confidence in rugby's welcome for all personalities and shapes and sizes. Week after week, Midsomer Norton the club and its people sustains rugby's warmth as a fact, as a bold and surviving reality.

On the screen, though, rugger has definitively been smothered by rugby. In front of those portable sponsored interview screens, modern rugby union is a business, a serious pursuit (as if one defined the other). Much of the good remains, but not all of it. Those with more knowledge and experience than me, the best of the rugby writers like Stephen Jones and Denis Lalanne, are in agreement with coaches like Greedy and Dick Tilley about recent flaws in the law-making. If they all agree, from their different countries and back-grounds, it suggests they must be right. In particular, they all instinctively oppose the assumption that continuity equals entertainment, except perhaps for floating consumers new to rugby. There's a short-term sell-out here: it's not cost-effective, easy, or quick to educate the public about rugby's intricacies. The marketing men therefore prefer to change the game.

Read Jones and Lalanne. Independently, lucidly, they both put the case against the number of allowable replacements, the excessive influence of coaches, initiatives to make the game more predictable (gloves, indoor stadiums), and Australia. They know their rugby, and have confidence in it, whereas the pro administrators seem as nervous of the game as their amateur predecessors. Their system of bonus points in Premier League matches, for example, suggests a lack of confidence in the simple battle.

I don't know what'll happen. Perhaps the mobile phone transmitters buzzing in the corners of so many local grounds like ours really will breed a new generation of mutant champions, and England will rule the rugby world for a generation. I'd quite like that. At any rate, the 2003 World Cup will place rugby in the public eye as never before, and I do think we ought to try and win it before it becomes a ridiculous dream that England should win at anything, and not just at cricket and football.

England's success is one of the dividends of rugby over rugger, but the transformation of sporting cultures can never be total. Traces of the old will always be incorporated in the new, and therefore there's bound to be some rugger in the rugby. As the evening wears on, former players will gibber in the corner, codgering on about the old days, using the privilege of their former glories to complain on a weekly basis that things ain't what they used to be. But then they never were, and the old bores are right, and that's what's so annoying. They always say the same thing, and they're always right. Things *aren't* what they used to be. So what?

The nostalgia most commonly heard for amateurism can seem limited and unconvincing. In the amateur days, in the good old days, the rain was warmer, the beer cheaper. Presumably the mud was also muddier, and the oafs oafier. But as A.A. Thomson wisely said as long ago as 1955, in the daringly titled *Rugger My Pleasure*, 'nothing is going to the dogs; at least not in a straight line, and certainly not all the time'.

Like Gerald Seymour, I know I can come to Midsomer Norton rugby club every Saturday with the certainty that it's . . . a very nice place to be. But not in a gushing way. For some reason, the wrestling's back on the telly and I have another pint. I feel great.

Actually, that's not strictly true. My eyes are marked and bruised on both sides, on the protruding upside of the sockets, where the ridges of bone take first contact in most blows to the face. My nose has been flattened, so I feel like a pug-dog, from the inside. My knees ache so I have to stay standing up, and I can't lift my arm which was injured when I fluffed that tackle. Come to think of it, I feel awful.

Maybe it's time to stop.

I'm thirty-six, and I've been lucky. I'm still in one piece, but still being in one piece is an excuse for not doing all sorts of things. On the rare occasions I've thought it through, I supposed it might be time to stop when I could play a better game in my head than my body was capable of. But that's always been true, and then it's just degrees of separation.

Even so, it's increasingly frustrating to be better than my opposite number, but not be able to show it because I'm too knackered. Or too old. Or actually, on reflection, as I offer him the outside and he effortlessly takes it, because I'm not quite as good as him. Now *that's* frustrating. Always was, and will be again next week.

Despite my age, I'm still aiming to stall my decline, even though I can already see a future in which I'm picked exclusively for the more distant away games (after a calamitous run of injuries). A few months after that, I'll drive home fast after training to share the good news with my family that I've been named among the replacements.

I can't deny there's a slowing down. Quite recently, I had a dream of playing for England A. I usually dream of the proper team. In Paris and Norwich I wanted to play well. In Geneva, well enough. Now I just want to play, even if it's badly, and perhaps I'll gradually work my way down the teams, my temperament changed for the better. I'll end up like Tim Moon, captain of the Midsomer Norton Optimists, who's been playing for ever and now gets to select his son. I shouldn't stop just because I'm not as good as I want to be. Don't be so humourless. If I applied that principle to everything in life, I'd never do anything at all, and especially not writing.

At least at Norton I'm confident the club will outlast me. When no one has the right or the will to scrum down in the fields of Somerset, that'll truly be the end. I won't miss the ache of Sunday mornings, and I'm looking forward to the consoling kindness of nostalgia, memory with the pain removed. Nor will I miss getting home on Saturday nights in time to squint at *Match of the Day* with a one-pound bag of frozen peas on my knee. Actually, I will miss that.

I'll miss the whole fiesta, because it's always been with me. From childhood the shapes of the game, in particular fearful tackles and breaking into space, have seemed the only convincing answers to the questions on my mind. Whatever those questions may have been.

As the codgers say, you're a long time retired. I therefore frequently remind myself that the good old days are now.

Mum used to say, and now my wife says, 'Stop playing games!'

I used to think that one day I'd agree with them. When I was twenty-four in Argyll, and still attempting an eventful childhood, it felt like I could replay my early life as often as I

271

liked until eventually I got it right. I never did get it entirely right, and my early life is over. Yet I still seem addicted to my epiphanies once a week on Saturdays during the winter months of the year.

I worry about stopping. What if the hypochondria comes back? I may have solved that problem by getting older and playing too much rugby and making the damage real. What if I miss the culture of risk? God, I hope not. It scares me to think I'll need to transfer all that energy into something equally risky, like chasing younger women. Making all those years of hard moral training effectively count for nothing.

Rugby has been an integral part of my adult life, and quietly, I hope it's fulfilled some of those early public-school promises. I want it to have made me more of a man. After twenty-seven years on the pitch, I know there are some people nothing can change, not even rugby. It won't make a wise man from a fool, for example, but what rugby will do is provide him with a superb opportunity to act the fool he is. In any language.

I asked Brian Moore if rugby made better men. When he was employing new staff for his law firm, for example, did leadership on the field demonstrate leadership qualities in general?

'It probably shows more potential than if you're an *idiot* on the field.'

It's still something of a disappointment that I've not become Eric Liddell, the kind of rugbyman morally ready for China and a saint to prisoners of war. I doubt I'd even qualify for the final of the Olympic 400 metres.

Actually, it's worse than that. Sometimes, even now, I can

be a rugger-bugger. Like Lawrence Dallaglio, however hard I try to hide it, it sometimes breaks out. I drink too much beer, and then some vodka and lemon I should think, probably through a straw. For the rest of the evening my body is used as a host by the restless spirit of a complete pillock.

There are times, then, when I fear that the rugby hasn't worked. I've been living an indulgence, a childish pleasure I could never discard, allowing rugby to fill gaps in my character or my life which should have been occupied by something else, something more significant.

Perhaps I just never grew out of a public-school philosophy which glorifies athleticism, a philosophy installed as deeply in my make-up as the sidestep, as Jesus at Easter. I had it all wrong. It was *stopping* rugby which would have made me a man, and the moving on to whatever it had best prepared me to do. As it is, Christmases go past, and each Christmas despite children of my own I'm still not an adult at the table. Not quite. Not yet.

If I have any great regret, after journeying back into my rugby past, it's always the same one. In Scotland, in Paris, in Geneva, in Norwich, I wish I could have stayed and played 500 games in the jersey, seen all the things I hadn't seen, lived all the stories I was later told among the friends I once made. My flitting about makes me lesser, and a lesser rugby man than I could otherwise have been.

I don't know if in the hard times, and the times of challenge, I draw strength from an army camp in Aldershot, or a February game in sleet and mud in front of the single wooden stand at Wiveliscombe. At the very least, I have a metaphor for life, a rugby code. I appreciate that this is not a universal language, but in the wording of that code I'm a born 10 who's played mostly at 12 and 15. Now I'm older, I'm back at 10, and that's where I intend to stay. Webb Ellis picked up the ball and ran with it. That's the natural urge. Not to kick or pass it. Run. Eat meat and potatoes. Run, man.